D0389662

JOYCE AND FEMINISM

JOYCE
AND
FEMINISM

Bonnie Kime Scott

INDIANA UNIVERSITY PRESS
Bloomington

THE HARVESTER PRESS
Sussex

This edition first published in the United States in 1984 by
INDIANA UNIVERSITY PRESS
Tenth and Morton Streets, Bloomington, Indiana
and in Great Britain by
THE HARVESTER PRESS LIMITED
Publisher: John Spiers
16 Ship Street, Brighton, Sussex

Manufactured in the United States of America

Library of Congress Cataloging in Publication Data

Scott, Bonnie Kime, 1944–
  Joyce and feminism.

  Includes index.
  1. Joyce, James, 1882–1941—Political and social
views. 2. Joyce, James, 1882–1941—Characters—Women.
3. Women in literature. 4. Feminism and literature.
I. Title.
PR6019.09Z79445 1983   823'.912   83-47678
ISBN 0-253-33159-5
1 2 3 4 5 87 86 85 84 83

British Library Cataloguing in Publication Data

Scott, Bonnie Kime
  Joyce and feminism.
  1. Joyce, James, 1882–1941—Criticism and interpretation
  I. Title
  823'.912   PR6019.09Z/
  ISBN 0-7108-0686-8

To my fathers
ROY MILFORD KIME (1907–1978)
and
THOMAS RUSSELL SCOTT (1915–1981)
And to my colleagues in women's studies

Contents

Illustrations

Acknowledgments

Thanks to interested colleagues and friends, writing this book has been a lively and engaging process. Many of what I consider to be the best ideas came from conversation, not previous scholarship. I am also grateful to those who read my early drafts and helped me with delicate problems of tone and interpretation. For useful conversations, suggestions, or leads, I thank especially Margaret MacCurtain, O.P.; Suzette Henke; Maureen Murphy; Noel Fitch; Richard Ellmann; Robert Boyle, S.J.; Fritz Senn; Mary Reynolds; Jane Lidderdale; Andrée Sheehy-Skeffington; and Dame Rebecca West. Barbara Gates and Lindsey Tucker read early drafts with patience and care. I thank Zack Bowen, my chairperson and most available Joycean, for believing in this project and encouraging it at all stages. Thomas R. Scott, Jr., my husband, merits a sentence apart for his all-around support and intelligent suggestions.

Several institutions, through their special collections, have put me in touch with Joyce's female contexts. Primary among these are the National Library of Ireland, the British Library, the Lockwood Memorial Library of SUNY at Buffalo, and the Princeton University Library. I am indebted to the Society of Authors in behalf of the Trustees of the James Joyce Estate for permission to quote from the previously unpublished letters of James and George Joyce; to Quentin Bell for permission to quote from Virginia Woolf's notebook, "Modern Novels," housed in the Henry W. and Albert A. Berg Collection, the New York Public Library, Astor, Lenox, and Tilden Foundations; to Andrée Sheehy-Skeffington for permission to quote from the unpublished papers of Hanna and Francis Sheehy-Skeffington; to Monro Pennefather & Co. for permission to quote from Harriet Shaw Weaver's unpublished letters; to Frederick Dennis for permission to quote from the unpublished letters of Sylvia Beach; and to Maria Jolas for permission to quote from her unpublished letters. Chapter 7: "Emma" was developed from my essay "Emma Clery in *Stephen Hero*: A Young Woman Walking Proudly through the Decayed City," published in *Women in Joyce,* and I thank the University of Illinois Press for permitting me to draw from that essay. I am very grateful to the Morris Library of the University of Delaware for acquiring microfilms vital to this project and for obtaining dozens of books through interlibrary loans. The University of Delaware Computing Services provided my instruction in and equipment for word-processing.

Finally, I should like to acknowledge the support of the University of Delaware's General Research Fund for two grants applied to this work and to thank the American Philosophical Society for a grant from its Penrose Fund.

Abbreviations

CW   Joyce, James. *The Critical Writings of James Joyce*, ed. Ellsworth Mason and Richard Ellmann. New York: Viking Press, 1959.

D   Joyce, James. *"Dubliners": Text, Criticism, and Notes*, ed. Robert Scholes and A. Walton Litz. New York: Viking Press, 1969.

FW   Joyce, James. *Finnegans Wake*. New York: Viking Press, 1939.

JJ   Ellmann, Richard. *James Joyce*, new and revised ed. New York: Oxford University Press, 1982.

JJQ   *James Joyce Quarterly*

L I,   Joyce, James. *Letters of James Joyce*. Vol. I, ed. Stuart Gilbert.
II,   New York: Viking Press, 1965. Vols. II and III, ed . Richard
III   Ellmann. New York: Viking Press, 1966.

MBK   Joyce, Stanislaus. *My Brother's Keeper: James Joyce's Early Years*. New York: Viking Press, 1958.

P   Joyce, James. *"A Portrait of the Artist as a Young Man": Text, Criticism, and Notes*, ed. Chester G. Anderson. New York: Viking Press, 1968.

SH   Joyce, James. *Stephen Hero*, ed. John J. Slocum and Herbert Cahoon. New York: New Directions, 1963.

SL   Joyce, James. *Selected Letters of James Joyce*, ed. Richard Ellmann. New York: Viking Press, 1975.

U   Joyce, James. *Ulysses*. New York: Random House, 1961.

JOYCE AND FEMINISM

Introduction
Feminist Frameworks for Joyce

──────────────────── 1 ────────────────────

☐ There are both attractions and challenges to writing about a major male author like James Joyce in feminist terms. Feminist literary criticism has presented problems of definition to its own practitioners, has been misrepresented by its detractors, and has been neglected by a large proportion of the scholarly community. One of the principal undertakings of this chapter is to offer a current, working definition of feminist criticism, demonstrating the application of its multiple aspects to Joyce. A related purpose is to open the possibilities of feminist approaches to individuals schooled in more traditional forms of criticism. Both the text and the notes of this book should provide a starting point in feminist criticism for the uninitiated. Sandra M. Gilbert offers a challenge, responded to in this work: "While it is obviously important for women of letters to talk with passion and conviction to and about each other, I think it is just as important for us to talk to—and be heard by—our male colleagues."[1] Feminist critics must also reach a large number of women of accomplishment who identify themselves with traditional, androcentric forms. Critics, old and new, male and female, feminist or not, can come together over the subject of Joyce, who was one of literature's great unifiers.

The consideration of a male author in feminist terms is also an affirmative return from separate studies of female subjects (necessary in themselves) that dominated feminist critics' work in the 1970s. In an attempt to reintegrate feminist criticism in the 1980s, Gilbert

1

acknowledges historical literary ties between men and women, noting that "just as female texts have so far been written mostly in patriarchal contexts, male texts have in some sense always been written about or for women."[2] This book attends especially to Joyce's female audience, past and present, and their critical reactions to his works. I expect its readership will include some who have little experience with Joyce but are interested in the female contributions to his literary and social climate—backgrounds that transcend Joyce in their significance. The book is also designed to carry them through many of Joyce's texts.

Feminist criticism cannot be given a simple or single definition. It tends to work beyond the borders of traditional disciplines. Over the years it has had different focuses and different critical allies, and its tone and its concerns have changed. It both builds upon its earliest forms and offers correctives to them. In "Some Notes on Defining a 'Feminist Literary Criticism,' " (a 1975 article that has become a landmark of feminist critical definition) Annette Kolodny presents several sets of activities conventionally labelled feminist criticism. These definitions invite comment, expansion, and application to the problems of studying James Joyce in feminist terms.

The first, amusingly broad definition is "any criticism written by a woman, no matter what the subject."[3] It naively assumes that, because a critic is female, she must be feminist. Since this disregards the particular woman's attitudes and subject and disqualifies males as feminist critics, the "female critic" definition is not sufficient in itself. But it suggests some positive and useful directions. It asserts the value of attending to women critics, who in general have been less plentiful and less deferred to by the scholarly establishment. Even women who would not identify themselves as feminists reward the feminist critic's efforts of collecting their work, analyzing their viewpoints, and assessing their reception by the scholarly community. Often there are affinities that support the existence of the "female world" theorized by sociologist Jessie Bernard or a muted female literary culture described by Elaine Showalter in *A Literature of Their Own* and her recent essay, "Feminist Criticism in the Wilderness."[4]

Applying this "female critics" definition to Joyce, we find that, from the start, women were James Joyce's publishers, financial supporters, and literary critics, and as such, many of them reacted to his writing. These female critics of Joyce have never been viewed as a group, and their writings have remained scattered and scantly considered. An effort to appreciate their own conceptions of their roles in Joyce's career and to view them seriously as his critics is undertaken in central chapters of this book. Chapter 5, "New Free Women in the Company of Joyce," considers Joyce's female patrons, publishers, and supportive colleagues. Chapter 6, "Feminist Critics on Joyce," assembles a group of Joyce's critics who can be defined as "feminist." Most of them are women.

A second definition of feminist criticism is more specific about subject matter, while still favoring a female critic: "any criticism written by a woman about a woman, about a woman's book or about female authors in general."[5] The female-centering of this endeavor represents the major effort of women's studies in the 1970s, and reflects that decade's degree of feminist separation. Kolodny sees it as a compensatory activity, "attempting to make up for all that has previously been omitted, lost, or ignored."[6] The underexplored subjects are many. Ones especially pertinent to this study are neglected women authors and their writings, the lives and work of average women in specific settings, extraordinary women who may have been neglected in history or trivialized in its usually androcentric perspective, and lost female-centered myths and religions. "Compensatory" criticism recovers not just lost figures, but also neglected alternatives to a male-centered world, visible only when female culture is taken seriously.

Purists within this feminist framework might argue that James Joyce is disqualified by his gender from being himself a feminist critic or that he has received far too much attention from the male establishment to require any compensatory effort from a feminist critic. But, in existing scholarship, Joyce has been related almost exclusively to male-centered contexts and institutions, and his male characters have received much more attention than the females, except for Molly Bloom. The realistic women characters in his early work have been especially neglected, in favor of more symbolic and archetypal forms of woman, favored by many male critics. Obviously, there is much scope for compensatory work. Chapter 2 of this book explores the female-centered mythical, cultural, and historical contexts for Joyce's life and works; chapter 3 considers Irish and Continental backgrounds to the political and literary feminisms of his era. Both chapters treat significant manifestations of these forces in Joyce's works. Chapter 4, "The Female Family of James Joyce," discusses

Joyce's mother, aunt, sisters, wife, and daughter. Each is considered in her own right as well as in her special relationship with Joyce.

It is profitable to compare Joyce and women authors, the favorite subjects of compensatory feminist literary criticism.[7] There was a particularly rich selection in his literary period. Dorothy Richardson and Virginia Woolf are established favorites for such comparison. Chapters 5 and 6 offer expressions of their affinities to Joyce made by the women themselves—Virginia Woolf, Rebecca West, and Djuna Barnes.

Joyce himself engaged in a form of compensatory feminist criticism. His works portray under-represented areas and perspectives of women's lives. He was interested in female Dubliners caught up in the familial, economic, and religious nets of their environment, as well as more exceptional women who sought education, the vote, an Irish Ireland, or a profession. He restored strong women to their central roles in mythic literature, searching little-known myths and reinterpreting the classic ones. These accomplishments are documented throughout the book, which concludes with three chapters on selected woman characters: Emma Clery, the young college woman and nationalist of *Stephen Hero* and *A Portrait*, Molly Bloom, the "indispensable countersign" (L I, 160) to the male world of *Ulysses*, and Issy, the most real, and most evasive, woman of *Finnegans Wake*.

A third category of feminist criticism features a "feminist perspective" or ideology. Basic to feminism is a belief in the virtue of male-female equality and a corresponding balance in culture. The ideological approach is more obviously political than most forms of criticism. Post-structuralists have taught the latest generation of critics to detect power and politics in all language, but resistance to this remains strong.[8] Feminist ideology creates a wariness that propaganda rather than critical insight may be offered, as feminists acknowledge.[9] Detractors of feminist criticism are apt to recognize no other form of feminist criticism than this one, pointing to its most radical expressions and labeling them as "shrill," "irrational," or "political." To practice ideological feminist criticism, one must break with a traditional belief still shared by many humanists. As Gilbert expresses it, "Most of us literary women . . . rather romantically believed, as we thought we had been taught (but were we?), that the literary mind is not only disembodied but genderless, a kind of spiritual neuter forever burning with the hard gemlike flame of disinterested inspiration."[10] As initiated in the late sixties, ideological

feminist criticism has an aspect of consciousness-raising, and sometimes takes a fault-finding, protesting approach that can be considered negative, threatening, and conducive to male-female antago-
nism and feminist separatism. Yet threatening intentions should not
be widely suspected by conventional critics.

Several lines of inquiry are pursued productively in "ideological"
feminist criticism. Roles played by men and women may be compared
for their relative importance and power. Marxist feminists are particularly concerned with woman's absolute and comparative productive and economic status. Perceptions of women as stereotypes
or male-projected symbols, archetypes and fantasies may be detected
and evaluated for their authenticity to women's self-perceptions, life
experiences, and lost histories.[11] Critics may detect and question
woman treated as "other" or "second sex" (Simone de Beauvoir's
term) instead of central perceiver or creator. Male projection colors
Freudian theory, and, indeed, psychology seems to have deepened
existing male bias in literature and criticism up to the 1970s. Modern
psychologists like Karen Horney and Clara Thompson have challenged Freud's emphasis on the phallus,[12] and feminist critics may
benefit from their reassessments to deal with colleagues' continued
assertions of such androcentric theory. Chapter 6 cites a number of
feminist critics who challenge James Joyce on ideological grounds.
An objective throughout the book is to demonstrate the ways in
which Joyce was and was not limited by the male-centered assumptions of previous literary and cultural traditions.

A more philosophical and utopian form of feminist criticism should
be added to the foregoing three types. "Reintegrated feminism" will
serve as a provisional term. This type probably indicates a new level
of assurance, built upon historical and realistic perspectives, and new
capacities for self-criticism and redirection among feminists. It allows
women to value a fuller range of female roles, including some conventional ones. This form of feminist criticism accuses less, and builds
upon the enhanced gender-consciousness of our era, much of that
consciousness residing in cooperative men. It remains ideological,
but seeks a transformed world more than women's equality, interpreted as equal opportunity in male-generated, bourgeois power
structures. Female inspired and perceived metaphors and aesthetics
are sought as contributing models for the new culture, which will
also require allied reforms in racial and class attitudes. Carolyn Heilbrun and Catharine Stimpson describe a feminist critic who is an

alternative to the "textual archaeologist," who practices the compensatory and ideological forms of feminist criticism, described above. This critic searches for a "new consciousness," to have "the grace to see what, until this moment, the masculinization of society has prevented us from seeing."[13] In *Reinventing Womanhood*, Heilbrun steers women on a course beyond the "crippling cult" of imposed motherhood, and even the successful woman's equally limiting membership in the establishment's "male club." She suggests that womanhood can be remade in a form that allows one to be simultaneously female (with a choice of styles) and autonomous (which was rare in a world of female dependency and submission).[14] Betty Friedan's recent *The Second Stage* is critical of a supposed "*feminist* mystique" and reasserts the importance of family life for feminists. Friedan probably neglects pre-existing feminist concern for family life. She overemphasizes the same radical feminism that has been exaggerated by feminism's detractors, risking a misunderstanding of her intentions, which are really similar to Heilbrun's and Gilbert's. Rather than sending women into a regrettable retreat from intellectual pursuits and worldly equality, she would bring about a reshifting of culture toward the family and personal relationships that have conventionally been woman's responsibility.[15] Whether Joyce attained a corresponding utopian vision of a world shifted toward female values, a kind of androgynous world balance, is one of the most profound and persistent questions asked in this book, and especially in its final chapters. It is also an important premise of this book that a new feminist consciousness will facilitate new discoveries on Joyce.

Feminist critics of Joyce inherit useful methodologies and categories from the androcentric critical establishment. These they enhance with newer critical tools and a full range of feminist approaches. Feminist critics can conduct interviews and search the archives for letters and memoirs,as did the fine biographers of Joyce before them. They have the advantage of previous scholars' bibliographical leads, and often their personal help. But feminist critics follow the female strands of Joyce's experience farther, ask different questions, and assemble patterns that are organized by female experience. Critics have been amused by traces of misogyny in Joyce's conversation and letters. To compensate, feminist critics must consider the corresponding attitudes of the usual male audience for such pronouncements. They must also focus upon Joyce's feminist statements, never carefully collected and attended to in previous criticism. They note allusions and traditions, but may look for and value ones that previous critics have slighted. That Joyce's disposition should be considered dominantly and almost exclusively Classical, for example, seems dubious, following feminist reassessments of romantic and mystic human capacities. Many close readings of Joyce have overemphasized fetishism or selected details of woman's triviality or her threatening potential for engulfment and betrayal. Feminist critics add close reading that focuses upon updated psychological theory and abundant evidence of Joyce's consideration of female problems and capacities. Feminist critics turn to newer work based on psychoanalytic-linguistic theories of Jacques Lacan. They are also attracted to post-structuralists like Jacques Derrida and Julia Kristeva who take woman as a central metaphor in their process of decoding language, and focus upon "desire" as a force in language.[16] As noted above, symbolic and archetypal assignments customarily applied to Joyce's women come into question in feminist analysis. The favored categories of "temptress," "virgin," and "whore," and even the *Gea Tellus,*" or earth mother, and the Muse are tainted by their sources in male projection.[17] Some feminists reject all female archetypes, urging instead a careful consideration of real women. This realistic focus is a rewarding one that has characterized much of the early feminist work on Joyce, and is demonstrated by many of the essays in *Women in Joyce,* the first female-centered volume on Joyce.[18] Some feminist critics seek female-founded archetypal images for women that go beyond the "*anima,*" "great mother," and "archetypal feminine" of Jung and Neumann or the "eternal feminine" of Goethe.[19] The androgynous individual was the most widely discussed model in feminist criticism of the mid-1970s, and discussions of the goddess, reconsidered in feminist terms, were being published late in the decade. The goddess moves powerfully among the discoveries of the last chapters of this book. Biographers and memoir-writers have noted Joyce's contacts with women, but they have paid more attention to what the women did for Joyce than to the women themselves and their intellectual powers. Joyce's interactions with Harriet Shaw Weaver, Sylvia Beach, Adrienne Monnier, Carola Giedion-Welcker, and with his sensitive, gifted daughter, Lucia Joyce, now claim enhanced attention from the feminist critic.

Specific feminist correctives of individual Joyce critics are reserved for the chapters that follow, though this is not the principal emphasis of the book. The reworking is most extensive where most required, in chapter 8, on Molly Bloom. That chapter begins with a survey of non-feminist criticism on Joyce's most-studied woman character, identifying conscious and unconscious male bias, and assessing the progress toward feminist awareness in male as well as female Joyce critics.

In her essay "Towards a Feminist Poetics," Elaine Showalter calls on feminist critics to "find a new language, a new way of reading that can integrate our intelligence and our experience, our reason and our suffering, our skepticism and our vision."[20] While this book cannot hope for this ideal fusion of tradition and new feminist language, it aims in that direction. It works with not one but many definitions of feminist criticism. It deliberately shifts from contexts to individuals to texts, in order to provide a re-vision of women and Joyce, in a fullness of diversity that seems appropriate to Joyce's own shifting vision.

Mythical, Historical, and Cultural Contexts for Women in Joyce

$$2$$

□ At first assessment, James Joyce's intellectual, social, and religious contexts would seem to have been overwhelmingly anti-feminist, and even anti-female. In the Celtic prehistory of Ireland, women enjoyed considerable power, but their status deteriorated in historical times, reaching rock-bottom in the nineteenth century, just before Joyce's birth. Prominent male thinkers from Aristotle to Freud imposed a vision of female limitation. To Aristotle, women possessed an abundance of the material aspects of the soul (the vegetative and sensitive) but only insignificant intellectual qualities.[1] Freud centered his theories on masculine development; he imagined that woman must envy the male's penis and, in the form of an engulfing mother, castrate her sons. The church imposed patriarchal control of women's lives and offered narrow images of her as virgin, temptress, or whore.

If, like Joyce, we delve into prehistory, we find women of heightened stature and power. In early hunter-gatherer societies, women probably gathered more food than their men hunted down; females were the primary inventors of agriculture and the stable family unit. Women in such cultures even today seem to enjoy better relative status than their sisters in modern technological societies. The goddesses of these earth-oriented, non-technical people represent not only the primary principle of fertility, but also the roles of "creator and lawmaker of the universe, prophetess, provider of human destinies, inventor, healer, and reliant leader in battle."[2] The goddess was powerful both as a beautiful woman and as a hag and frequently

9

changed from one into the other. In the rich hypotheses of *The White Goddess*, poet Robert Graves suggests that early people worshipped their goddesses in a magical language of poetic myth that the world has lost in the intervening centuries.[3]

Joyce's Irish context included strong female prehistory and myth. The great megalithic tombs and passage graves of Ireland seem to have been shrines where seasonal festivals were held and offerings were made to the goddess. The stones of sites like New Grange were aligned so as to mark the winter solstice, probably in conjunction with seasonal rites. Prehistoric stylized motifs in many parts of Europe, including Ireland, may also have been celebrations of a highly valued female principle. Though patriarchal forms prevailed in later, differently situated warrior societies, worship of the goddess survived in nucleated villages, as did traces of matriarchal patterns of social organization. There, women's laments and keening rituals that predate written literature were preserved. Place names, especially of pap-like mountains (The Paps of Anu), life-giving rivers (the Boyne, named for the goddess Boann), and wells (Brigid's Well) often bear the name of a goddess, a strong woman from myth, or perhaps a matrilineal ruling family.[4]

Ireland's basic Celtic group, the Milesians, worshipped as gods the Tuatha de Danaan, "the people of Dana," probably previous inhabitants who took their name from the Irish version of the Great Goddess, Dana. The names and myths of the Tuatha de Danaan resemble those of pre-Greek and pre-Hebrew civilizations, whose traditions may have come to Ireland *via* displaced Aegean people, according to Graves. Features of both mythologies include emphasis on mother-son rather than father-son relationships among the gods and the presence of strong goddesses as principal deities. The Tuatha de Danaan women of the Síde, who rode horses over the landscape of Ireland and lured mortals into their world, were minor Irish goddesses whose roles were comparable to the Amazons and to Artemis. Goddesses were often fertile mother figures—as were the fairly universal White Goddess, the Irish goddess Dana (who is occasionally identified as the White Goddess's mother), and Brigid. St. Brigid, founder of the seventh-century monastery of Kildare, who achieved status equal to that of a male bishop, often merges with the like-named goddess; traditions attribute to this saint a supernatural birth and magical powers very like those of a goddess, and wells named for her are still visited for their supposed curative effects.

In the introduction to his translation of the myth *The Táin*, Thomas Kinsella comments, "Probably the greatest achievement of the *Táin* and the Ulster Cycle is the series of women, some in full scale and some in miniature, on whose strong and diverse personalities the action continually turns: Medb, Derdriu, Macha, Nes, Aife. It may be as goddess-figures, ultimately, that these women have their power; it is certainly they, under all the violence, who remain most real in the memory."[5] In addition to the strong-willed Medb, *The Táin* offers three warrior goddesses (Nemain, Badb, and Morrígan), a poet prophetess (Fedelm), and a beautiful pawn (Medb's daughter, Finnabair, used repeatedly as a political enticement). In a "pillow-talk" with her husband, Medb exclaims, "I never had one man without another waiting in his shadow."[6] One interpretation is that, unlike Ireland's male rulers, she survives the ages. Equated with Ireland, the earth itself, she and other goddesses cast as queens grant success, a flourishing of the land, or withhold it. Unless considered worthy and ceremonially wedded to her type, the king lacks sovereignty and the bounty of the land. Remnants of a marriage rite to the goddess-queen survived into recorded Irish history.[7]

Female-derived sovereignty is also suggested in the historical example of Devorghilla, whose desertion of her husband for another chieftain became the occasion for the Norman incursion into Ireland. Devorghilla retired in 1170 to the convent outside the walls of the monastic settlement at Clonmacnoise. The Nun's Chapel, sometimes said to have been built in penance by her, still stands. Its savage animal carvings and the ornament of a tiny female erotic acrobat still suggest a measure of aesthetic power in that separate female community.[8]

Irish architecture offers another powerful early female image, the Sheela-na-gig, whose exact meaning we may never know, if indeed it ever had a simple explanation. Sheelas are grotesque, erotic stone carvings, often associated with medieval structures, but loose stones and relocated carvings suggest that some of the figures may be much older. A typical Sheela-na-gig is crouched with open crotch, pointing to or even fingering exaggerated genitals. Sheelas usually have large heads, forbidding facial expressions, and skeletal torsos with little or no breast development. A vast range of significances has been suggested for Sheelas: they may be charms to ward off the evil eye, another suggestion of magical power in the female; they may be fertility figures comparable to aspects of the goddess, especially in

Sheela-na-gig from a church at County Cavan.
Photograph by Yvette Sencer.
Stone figure in the National Museum of Ireland, Dublin.

her hag form; they may be loose women, displaying themselves; in folk custom, stone dust obtained by scratching the mark or the cross upon them is attributed with curative powers.[9] Their combination of highly accessible vagina and deathly face suggest the continuity of fertility and decay that is often associated with the goddess. But one also wonders if they are not misogynist warnings, the product perhaps of a medieval period when male celibacy was being strongly urged by the church, and woman scorned as a deadly temptress.[10] Whatever their meaning, they emanate power, even to the modern observer.

Women deities and mythical figures practiced crafts and the arts of healing and magic; they wrote poetry, satire and song; unlike male warriors, theywere not constrained by a multitude of taboos; they survived and mated, though kings came and went, and were lusty and sovereign. Perhaps in heightened form, they resembled the women of the cultures that imagined them.[11] The pages of *Finnegans Wake* are suffused with the goddess Dana, with "shee," which suggests "Síde" and "Sheela," and with Brigid and Bride, instances which we will probe in chapter 9.

Time brought chauvinistic reactions to the strong female figures of Irish myths and tradition, a tendency that Joyce recognizes in the remarks of the Cyclops figure, and in Mr. Deasy's comments on women in *Ulysses*. Among Deasy's villainesses is Devorghilla, not introduced by her name, but as "MacMurrough's wife":

> A woman brought sin into the world. For a woman who was no better than she should be, Helen, the runaway wife of Menelaus, ten years the Greeks made war on Troy. A faithless wife first brought the strangers to our shore here, MacMurrough's wife and her leman O'Rourke, prince of Breffni. A woman too brought Parnell low. (U, 34-35)

It is notable that the only woman granted her own name in Deasy's list is Helen. His modern example of female treachery is Kitty O'Shea, wife of a British officer, whose divorce scandal brought the downfall of her lover, Parnell, champion of Home Rule in Parliament, and James Joyce's childhood hero. Joyce makes Deasy's exposition on woman so bigoted as to become its own criticism, however.

Moving from myth and stone to later history, we find that Irish women retained significant rights to property and personal dignity that they had possessed under Celtic marital custom even through Norman times, but this was greatly diminished with the advent of

English law in the eighteenth century.[12] After centuries of English
plantations and the disaster of the famine in the mid-nineteenth century, the ideal of the Irish peasant woman became the Irish colleen,
a young beauty with submissive, downcast eyes, a humble shawl, and
a pale, starved cheek. In the cities, the rising Irish bourgeois middle
class followed Victorian English dictates of femininity. Young women
should be virginal and ignorant of sexuality. Marriage was their future vocation. Until they married, it was acceptable for them to do
menial, charitable, or clerical work, always grooming themselves to
be marketable brides. Once married, they should submit to their
husbands, procreate, and serve as pale, self-sacrificing "angels in the
house," a model of femininity offered in the verse of Coventry Pat-
more, and one that haunted even the great female novelist and critic,
Virginia Woolf.[13] Irish wives' lack of financial independence is evident in stories of the Joyce household, to be treated in chapter 4.
Margaret Cousins, an acquaintance and contemporary of James Joyce,
regrets the degrading position of her mother, who was forced to
plead for the money needed to run the household, humiliated even
though money was readily available to the patriarch.[14] Older women
could look forward to being idealized as the sorrowful, silver-haired
widow, but this was a pale image in contrast to the powerful hag,
whose curses inspired dread and respect in the hearts of the Irish.
Real women continued to work in agriculture and in cottage and
service industries, doubling their work loads with family responsi-
bilities in many cases. Brothels flourished, as *Ulysses* testifies, fur-
nishing outlets for men who could not satisfy themselves with angels
and income for single, ineligible women, who needed an independent wage for survival.

Some aspects of Catholicism were as unfavorable to woman's position as the English influence. In tracing the decline of women's
images in hagiography, Margaret MacCurtain notes that, from the
time of St. Brigid until well into the twelfth century, women ruled
men and women in Kildare, one of the primary monastic centers in
Ireland. The female image and role in ministry was gradually reduced, however. One work symptomatic of this trend, according to
MacCurtain, was Pseudo-Clement's *De Virginitate*, which encouraged fear of women and cast them into the popular, male-projected
role of Eve, the temptress.[15] It is notable that St. Brigid usually lacks
heroic stature in *Finnegans Wake*, which debases the great institution
at Kildare to the equivalent of a women's finishing school. Joyce can

be seen here as a chauvinist, unwilling to grant Brigid due respect. But his attitude to the church complicates this simple assessment. Brigid represents woman in the church to him—a combination that, as we shall see, he considered destructive. His treatment of Brigid also serves to satirize the church's own debasement of female roles, as represented by MacCurtain. The legends of St. Kevin, are also taken up in *Finnegans Wake*. St. Kevin offers the most famous examples of male rejection of alleged female temptation in favor of celibacy. Here, Joyce works with fairly obvious irony by assigning the role of St. Kevin to his establishment man, Shaun.

Mariology, the growing Irish reverence for the Virgin Mary, was especially strong in Joyce's era. MacCurtain associates it with the hardships and adversity following the Norman conquest. The legendary apparition of Mary at Knock, Co. Mayo, in the late nineteenth century strengthened the tradition. The mature Mary, Mother of Sorrows, became "the most appropriate model for a generation of women," many widowed in post-famine Ireland.[16] Joyce used it seriously as a primary image for women throughout *A Portrait* and with mixed intent and effect through the end of his canon. One may also suspect that the cult of the Sacred Heart, favored in Ireland, reinforced the pattern of family-centered, chaste, severe, and non-progressive roles for women. Stephen feels its conventional power in the emblem, displayed on a parlor wall in *Stephen Hero* (SH, 44).

Joyce's awareness and criticism of the limits imposed upon female roles and aspirations in early twentieth-century Ireland is readily established in the early, naturalistic works. In *Stephen Hero*, Stephen contrasts his own possibilities with the largely imposed limitations upon Isabel, his simple, pious, sickly sister, whose role is discussed in detail in chapter 7. In Dilly of *Ulysses*, Stephen is given a more intelligent, independent, and motivated sister. Seeking her own betterment, she purchases a French primer. Dilly's situation moves Stephen to remorse:

> My eyes say she has. Do others see me so? Quick, far and daring. Shadow of my mind.
> ....
> She is drowning. Agenbite. Save her. Agenbite. All against us. She will drown me with her, eyes and hair . . . (U, 243)

Help here might not have been so vain, Dilly's potential being greater. Stephen's selfishness wins out, as does his fear of relatedness. The actual case of Joyce's female family will be treated in chapter 4.

Throughout *Dubliners*, women are placed in self-sacrificing nursing, serving roles. In "Eveline," two generations of women dedicate themselves to family service. "The Sisters" serve their brother, the priest, even after death; Maria of "Clay" serves first the women of the laundry, and then returns to her role as nurse and peacemaker to her brothers. In many cases, Joyce allows us to see a parallel between the female protagonist and the Virgin Mary. Unlike some of the men of *Dubliners*, who detect the paralysis of their positions through an epiphany, often touched off by a woman, the women of *Dubliners* are denied such illumination.

Marriageable women are often deliberately juxtaposed with money, reminding us of the financial aspects of the institution of marriage. Thus in "Araby" the young, romantic boy goes to the bazaar to purchase a gift for Mangan's sister, who is unable to attend because she is engaged in the pious exercise of a retreat. Money is an obstacle to his reaching Araby, and his final disillusionment comes as he overhears a girl carrying on a vulgar flirtation, a dialog preceded by men "counting money on a salver" and followed by the narrator's allowing his "pennies to fall against the sixpence in [his] pocket" (D, 35). "Two Gallants" and "Counterparts" embroider the theme. The former story involves the reversed purchase of Corley's sexuality by a slavey; "Counterparts" registers Farrington's frustration that he lacks, among other things, the money to pursue a woman he meets in the Scotch House (D, 95). In *Stephen Hero*, Stephen tries to develop and communicate ideas about "simony" in male-female marital relationships, as opposed to free love—a series of exchanges we will pay considerable attention to in chapter 7. The notion is preserved in *A Portrait*, when in a dance Emma's "hand had lain in his an instant, a sort of merchandise" (P, 219), as if something to be sold instead of given.

Stephen's religious conditioning toward women is visible in the intense sermon section, a part of *A Portrait* whose very oppressiveness invites the reader's skepticism. Stephen is told that the devil "came to the woman, the weaker vessel, and poured the poison of his eloquence into her ear. . . . Eve yielded to the wiles of the archtempter. She ate the apple and gave it also to Adam who had not the moral courage to resist her" (P, 118). When he enters his monastic, pious phase, Stephen is comparable to St. Kevin, as he "shunned every encounter with the eyes of women" (P, 150). It is interesting that, despite his eventual rebellion from the church and its impact upon women like Isabel, Emma, and his mother, Stephen still projects the image of the Virgin Mary upon the women he fantasizes as his inspiration, Emma and the bird girl. Obviously, Stephen is a very complicated observer, who must be viewed as much more than a perceiver of women's limitations in his culture.

In the latter half of the nineteenth century, led by their Anglo-Irish sisters, Irish women began to win back power in public life, and also in the creative imagination. In the Ireland of Joyce's youth, woman's role in politics was persistent and frequently merged with the Irish Suffragist Movement.

Fanny Parnell had indirectly led Charles Stewart Parnell into nationalist activity. She composed patriotic poetry which he delivered to her Fenian editors, thus making their acquaintance. Fanny and her sister Anna founded the Ladies' Land League in 1881 to carry on the work of the Land League while its male leaders were imprisoned. As Hanna Sheehy-Skeffington records with some bitterness, "When women had done the work, they were set aside."[17] Parnell dissolved the organization for the sake of a political compromise with English Prime Minister Gladstone, dismissing what had been an asset to his own movement as unfortunate disorder under female administration. Still, the Ladies' Land League set the precedent for women's nationalist groups in the country. The role of women in politics was renewed in the new century by strong women like Maud Gonne, Constance Markievicz, and Hanna Sheehy-Skeffington—the last in this list an important acquaintance of James Joyce. Gonne and Markievicz live on in legend as well as deed, the legend written in large part by Joyce's elder literary rival, William Butler Yeats.

Constance Markievicz subordinated the accepted norms for women in Anglo-Irish country life to take up rebel activity, both preparing for and fighting in the 1916 Easter Rising. She joined Inghinidhe na hEireann (The Daughters of Ireland), a feminist as well as nationalist group that encouraged patriotism in Irish schoolchildren and conducted protest demonstrations against the British. She still chills us today, posed strikingly for the photographer, wearing her 1916 uniform, holding gun in hand. That Constance Markievicz has impressed modern feminists is obvious in the fact that The Feminist Press selected her biography by Jacqueline Van Voris for republication.[18] Markievicz has her detractors among the Irish male literary establishment. Sean O'Casey declares that Markievicz, like Gonne and

Constance Markievicz.
Photograph courtesy of the National Library of Ireland.

Hanna Sheehy-Skeffington, could not understand the people as well as a working-class man like himself.[19] Yeats regrets Markievicz's voice grown "shrill" in the poem "Easter 1916." Poems written about her imprisonment ("On a Political Prisoner" and "The Leaders of the Crowd") suggest an ungracious decline from greatness. To some extent, however, Markievicz had become the scapegoat for his beloved Maud Gonne. Both women fit the role of "hysterical women" cited in "Lapis Lazuli." Clearly, Yeats wished that Constance Markievicz had remained the ideal young woman of her youth, when she was "young and beautiful," riding under Ben Bulben.[20]

Maud Gonne's image still fascinates today's women, both in and beyond Ireland. Resembling in beauty and stature the Tuatha de Danaan women of the Síde, and cultivating this resemblance in her dramatic clothing and gestures, she rode off like an angered Medb to battle evictions. Through the Daughters of Ireland (which she founded), she orchestrated demonstrations against the visit of Queen Victoria. She tried to unite the Irish Party in the era following the downfall of Parnell. Gonne chose a single deity—a female personifying Ireland—and served her unswervingly. She used her writing to encourage others to do the same. Mother Ireland is the "Queen" referred to in the title of her autobiography, *The Servant of the Queen*. The call for sacrifice and loyalty to Ireland's sons is also articulated by the mother and daughter characters in her short play *Dawn* and in *Cathleen ni Hoolihan*, the drama that Yeats wrote in order that Maud might play the title role of her most admired figure.

Yeats's attempts to cope with this independent Irishwoman in life and poetry are widely known. He tried to interest her in marriage, wooing her in "the old high way of love,"[21] and hoped that she would further his literary projects. There was a definite overlapping of interests, but if anyone ended up the helpmate, it was Yeats. He joined in her search for early Celtic religions, wrote *Cathleen ni Hoolihan*, and involved himself in political activites that were alien to his aesthetics and his aristocratic nature. In his early poetry inspired by Maud, he placed her image on a pedestal befitting a goddess and exempted her from common standards of morality and conduct. In "The Rose of the World," Yeats describes a type of proud female "beauty"—be she Helen or Deirdre—who acts as a catalyst in the lives of "the laboring world." Though she "passes like a dream," she is ageless; indeed God "made the world to be a grassy road/ Before her wandering feet." In "No Second Troy," he excuses Maud's

Maud Gonne.
Photograph courtesy of the National Library of Ireland.

actions and treatment of him because he recognizes that she is one of this immortal type. It is not her fault that she did not live in Helen's era, when her genius might have been better satisfied. Yeats's description of the powerful female of this poem is extraordinary, partaking of none of the stereotypical feminine attributes of paleness and submission, but "high and solitary and most stern." Her beauty, compared to a "tightened bow" suggests potential power and even aggressiveness, along with lovely form. Elsewhere, the body of Yeats's ideal is compared to haughty, vigorous animals, including the eagle and the horse. There are some ambiguities in this and other early poems inspired by Gonne which invite a more critical, limiting interpretation of the female figure. Like Aristotle, Yeats seems to question woman's intellectual function. How complex and acute is "a mind that nobleness made simple as a fire"? In describing "His Phoenix," Yeats was later to feature "the simplicity of a child," and in the "Long-Legged Fly," Helen is "part woman, three parts a child." In his *Autobiography*, Yeats notes that Maud's "face like the face of some Greek statue, showed little thought. . . ."[22] By the time that he was imagining ideal images for his own daughter in "A Prayer for my Daughter," Yeats is far more critical of Maud's capacity to distract men with her beauty, and to deliver her opinions and alleged "hatred" in arousing speeches:

> Have I not seen the loveliest woman born
> Out of the mouth of Plenty's horn,
> Because of her opinionated mind
> Barter that horn and every good
> By quiet natures understood
> For an old bellows full of angry wind?

"Why Should Not Old Men be Mad?" expresses Yeats's disenchantment that his "Helen of social welfare dream" should "climb on a wagonette to scream."[23]

Joyce's poems from *Chamber Music* feature a somewhat haughty, commanding female who is the subject of mystical adoration like the women of Yeats's early poems. Yet the female figure of *Chamber Music* lacks the powerful physical images and the sharp resentments of Yeats's best poems inspired by Maud Gonne.[24] In his late work, by creating Molly and ALP, Joyce would envision a mythic, monumental female to rival Yeats' Maudlike Helen. But the model was not the elegant Yeats, but the primitive grotesque forms closer to Rabelais, and to the ancient Celtic women, cited earlier. Like Yeats, young Joyce likes to ascribe simplicity to young fictional women like Bertha and Gretta, and to his real life's companion, Nora. In Beatrice and Miss Ivors, Joyce offers more intellectual types, however, and we will return to them. His ironic vision also acknowledges male mis-perception. Even supposedly "simple" women like Mrs. Dedalus and Gretta Conroy have secret interests and memories unsuspected by their intellectual men, Stephen and Gabriel.

In a recent article, Hugh Kenner suggests that Joyce may have had a sustained literary reaction against Maud Gonne as *Cathleen ni Hoolihan*, the "woman with the look of a queen" who demands the lives of Irishmen in service of their country. He finds throughout Joyce's work a rejection of the mythology of the revival and a warning about the dangerous consequences of the demanding female will. Kenner would see Mrs. Mooney of "The Boarding House," Mrs. Kearney of "A Mother" (a story that plays with the names Kathleen and Hoolihan), Mrs. Dedalus, and the mother of "Eveline" as devourers who work to the detriment and division of their nation, their families, and even themselves. Even ALP is suspected of self-destruction in this reading.[25] As usual, Kenner does an impressive gathering of evidence, but his thesis seems to be grounded on male-centered psychological theory, Freud's castrating mother. Stephen, in characterizing Ireland to his friend Davin, produces the degrading image of "the old sow that eats her farrow" (P, 203). But even in context, this line can assume a comic, ironic function for the reader in evaluating Stephen. Through Stephen, Joyce may represent the threatened male that he once had been. But even in *Dubliners*, he seems less fearful than amused and observant. Mrs. Mooney has comic heroic proportions that override any tragic implications to be found in her manipulations of Bob Doran. Miss Ivors has dignity and decency that are missed when she is summarized by Kenner as "aggressively patriotic." Though he was no great admirer of the literary revival, Joyce did not reject strong women as future models. Women of power, self-confidence, and humor enter the *Wake* repeatedly, their best representative being the Prankquean, modeled on a real Irish pirate woman, Grainne O'Malley. His depiction of nationalist women was more varied than Kenner suggests, as was his overall treatment of Maud Gonne.

Joyce was to have met Maud Gonne in Paris, early in 1903, but their appointment had to be cancelled because of a family illness and he made no further effort to meet her (JJ, 112, 122-123). Though Stanislaus reports that his brother had "some very unusual qualms regarding his shabby appearance" (MBK, 198), Ellmann is perceptive in linking Joyce's failure to reappear to the situation at home

(JJ, 122-123). He announces his decision not to return in the midst of one of his most self-pitying accounts to his mother (L II, 29-30). He would seem to prefer that she play his Mary, Mother of Sorrows, instead of offering practical advice that he keep all his friends, including Mrs. MacBride, since they may help him get on in his line (JJ, 123). The resistance to seeing Maud Gonne is in effect resistance to his mother and to the leading figures of the revival, like AE and Yeats, who had provided his introduction *via* letters to Gonne. At that time in his life, Maud Gonne was not the beloved goddess of Yeats's poetry, but a parental authority figure, to be resisted for the sake of his own egotism.

Joyce continued to react to Maud Gonne, at first scornfully, in letters to Stanislaus, and then more creatively in *Ulysses*. He would remark on her separation (not yet divorce) from John MacBride in 1905, "I have read in the *Figaro* of the divorce of the Irish Joan of Arc from her husband. Pius the Tenth, I suppose, will alter Catholic regulations to suit the case: an Italian comment says Irish genius is not domestic. Poor little U.I.: indignant little chap" (L II, 85). Among Joyce's victims in the brief passage are Maud Gonne, for her heroic nationalist posing, the Pope for his hypocrisy and political intervention, Ireland for its domestic malcontents, and Arthur Griffith for his defenses of Maud Gonne in the *United Irishman* (which the expatriate Joyce still read, when possible), and also perhaps for a frustrated love of Maud Gonne.[26] Stephen Dedalus would prove more interested in Maud Gonne's love life than her nationalist vocation: "Maud Gonne, beautiful woman, *La Patrie*, M. Millevoye, Félix Faure, know how he died? Licentious men" (U, 43).[27] Since he perceives himself as a sexual liberator of sorts, Stephen could be expected to respond to this aspect of Gonne, who had conceived two children out of wedlock by Millevoye, and later had a relationship with Faure before marrying MacBride.[28] Stephen shares Joyce's stereotypically feminine interest in gossip, which would become a major mode of discourse in *Finnegans Wake*, but which was already quite visible in the talk of Temple, Moynihan and Emma in *Stephen Hero* and *A Portrait*, in the *Dubliners* stories "Two Gallants," "Grace," and "The Dead," and in *Ulysses*, particularly concerning the reputation of another supposedly free lover, Marion Bloom.

In *Ulysses* Leopold Bloom takes Maud Gonne's nationalist mission a little more seriously than Stephen does. He recalls sympathetically "Maud Gonne's letter about taking them [British soldiers] off O'Connell street at night: disgrace to our Irish capital. Griffith's paper is on the same tack now: an army rotten with venereal disease . . ." (U, 72-73). A serious and continuing problem is exposed in Bloom's musings. He thinks women are attracted to the uniform. In the "Circe" chapter of *Ulysses*, the involvement of the British privates Compton and Carr with Irish women leads to violence when Stephen (acting more nationalistically than he usually does) tries to intervene (U, 587 ff). Today in Northern Ireland, IRA supporters intervene in such relationships with tar, feathers, and worse.[29] Later in the same chapter, female nationalistic enthusiasm and mob action are lightly mocked in a passage that mixes sexual with national passion, and has an undercurrent of violence. The executed national hero, the Croppy Boy, spouts "gouts of sperm" and "Mrs Bellingham, Mrs Yelverton Barry and the Honourable Mrs Mervyn Talboys rush forward with their handkerchiefs to sop it up" (U, 594). Interestingly, the executioner has in his possession a knife and a vial for poison; these had been used by other men he has hanged to brutally murder two women. These characters (bearing their husbands' names) obviously fall short of the women led by Gonne and Markievicz, both in object and manner.

Young Catholic as well as Anglo-Irish women of James Joyce's own age entered the nationalist movement through the women's organizations, *Inghinide na hEireann* and the slightly later *Cumann na mBan*. Women worked and learned side by side with men in the Gaelic League, founded by Douglas Hyde for the purpose of reviving the Gaelic language. Many also progressed to the stage. They began with historical *tableaux vivantes*, and some women acted an the early presentation mf Gaelic dramas. Sinéad Flanagan (later the wife of Eamon De Valera), for example, played the part of Maire in the first production of Hyde's drama "An Posadh," presented at the Gaiety Theatre in 1904. In *Stephen Hero*, Joyce offers a scene of a Gaelic League class attended by Stephen. He depicts young women who are brighter and less embarrassed by the presence of the opposite sex than some of the men in attendance (SH, 60-61). They also appear more serious about the subject matter. Clearly, Stephen attends only to have access to the physically alluring Emma Clery (a motivation that does not escape the maturing Joyce's irony). Emma seems earnest about her study, though Stephen insists on seeing affectation in this.

Arthur Griffith, leader of the Sinn Fein movement and editor of the journals *United Irishman* and *Sinn Fein*, provided young women with a forum for the publication of poetry, essays and prose, as did the poet AE in his economic journal *The Irish Homestead* and his anthology *New Songs*. Joyce has preserved the name of one of the less distinguished poets of this group, Lizzy Twigg, *via* the observations of Leopold Bloom in *Ulysses*. Bloom mentally admonishes a young woman, whom he mistakes for Ms. Twigg, for wearing wrinkled stockings and otherwise placing poetry ahead of personal appearance: "No time to do her hair drinking sloppy tea with a book of poetry" (U, 160).[30] Alice Milligan and Susan Mitchell are more formidable women writers whose careers were assisted by the openness of Griffith and AE. In the attitudes toward women of Sinn Fein and the Gaelic League, Hanna Sheehy-Skeffington sees "the renascence of the older Irish traditions, wherein women shared as a matter of course every phase of the community life," an exaggeration perhaps, but one with some truth in the ancient law we have noted.[31] But Sheehy-Skeffington is also cautious: "Sinn Fein is, theoretically at any rate, a revolutionary party, and as such disdains no enthusiasm, no help, whence-so-ever it comes. In revolutionary parties in their infancy . . . women have always been welcomed, possibly by reason of their inherent taste for martyrdom, a crown never denied their womanhood once it enters the lists. It is when parties grow circumspect through partial success and line up after the fight and the dust for the parade that woman falls naturally out of step and is duly left behind."[32] Joyce's suspicion of this sort of conventionality, even in the supposed revolutionary nationalism of his day, may well have affected his reaction to nationalist women.

Other groups, though they provided some opportunities to women, definitely had subsidiary roles in mind for them. Sheehy-Skeffington expresses impatience with the Young Ireland Branch of the United Irish League (the Parliamentary Party), of which she was once a member. She recalls that it was at first to have been called the "Young Men's Branch" and that young women were advised to form their own "Ladies' Branch." She humorously describes the "main duty" of these ladies groups as "being apparently to present valuable pieces of lace or Belleek ware, to the wives of leading politicians." This was obviously not the occupation for young women of her type. The difficulty had been overcome by a mass of spirited young women (probably led by Hanna) who "planked down our entrance fees to an amazed official," before excluding articles could be drawn up. Still, the United Irish League maintained leaders who wished to confine women to ornamental, social roles, and excluded a duly-elected woman from its convention.[33] It was a national problem that, in Hanna Sheehy-Skeffington's opinion, could be overcome only with female suffrage, one of the topics of our next chapter.

James Joyce was a privileged observer of young Catholic nationalist women in the home of Hanna Sheehy-Skeffington's parents, where her brothers provided his introduction. In a radio interview in the early 1940s she described the "good old Irish clan spirit" of the Sheehy family, especially the sisters, and the "strongly political" nature of the household. "Both my parents were Fenians. My uncle, Father Eugene Sheehy, the 'Land League Priest,' was one of the 'Suspects' in Kilmainham Jail with Parnell, Dillon, and Davitt. My Great-Grandmother in her youth knew Lord Edward Fitzgerald . . . Grandfather Sheehy was a native Irish speaker who was beaten at the 'National' school for every Irish word he spoke."[34] Nationalist background of this depth is difficult to pass off as affectation, though the young Joyce, recording his epiphanies at #2 Belvedere Place, would see it as such. This brief passage also demonstrates Hanna Sheehy-Skeffington's power as a political orator—an ability that was acknowledged and respected in Dublin.

There were three other lively sisters in the Sheehy household. Kathleen Sheehy was the most ardent nationalist—her name appropriately echoing that of the best-known personification of Ireland, Kathleen ni Hoolihan. Like Maud Gonne, Kathleen Sheehy helped prevent evictions in the west of Ireland.[35] Richard Ellmann traces the patriotic pin and austere bodice worn by Miss Ivors, the boldly nationalistic heroine of "The Dead," back to her (JJ, 246). Kathleen Kearney, scorned for her nationalist songs by Molly Bloom in *Ulysses*, may owe her name to this young woman as well as to Kathleen ni Hoolihan. The two other sisters have less nationalist significance, but still have an important relationship to Joyce. Margaret was the family performer and with Hanna wrote *Cupid's Confidante*, a play in which Joyce assumed the leading role with obvious enjoyment (JJ, 93). She seems to have possessed a certain boldness akin perhaps to Molly Bloom. The *Irish Figaro* reports that she gave a recitation of "Nothing to Wear" for the Literary Dramatic and Music Society, describing it as "very humorous," but "better suited to a male reciter."[36] Mary Sheehy, the youngest daughter, has gone down in history as Joyce's

The Sheehy Family (Hanna, second row, left;
Mary, second row, right; Margaret, second row, center;
Kathleen, front row, second from left).
Photograph courtesy of Andrée Sheehy-Skeffington.

secret infatuation and the inspiration for two of the poems in *Chamber Music* (MBK, 259), though recently this identification has been challenged.[37]

Joyce may have experienced some discomfort in the Sheehy household. He was a poet among more practical people, and his feeling of social inequality may have made him particularly critical of the manners of the young women. The latter he exaggerates to his eventual life partner, Nora, during their courtship: "I could never speak to the girls I used to meet at houses. Their false manners checked me at once" (L II, 237). Stanislaus Joyce suspected that Hanna Sheehy-Skeffington did not "understand those disattached personalities, the world's poets and artists and cranks," whose numbers implicitly contained his brother. She was a "practical animal" who found men who would not serve her purposes "worthless."[38] But her purposes were many, and included lecturing on literature and language. Hanna Sheehy-Skeffington offers her own picture of Joyce, which is much more tolerant than Stanislaus suggests:

> Yes, Jim Joyce and many of the U. C. D. and old "Royal" students came to our Sundays in Belvedere Place. . . . Joyce was then gay and boyish, flinging himself into topical charades. He loved to "dress up" and produce plays and parodies, and to sing old folk ballads in his sweet tenor.[39]

In this account, it is notable that Sheehy-Skeffington uses the reference "Jim Joyce," which resurrects one of Stephen's objections to the Daniels' household, described in biased detail in *Stephen Hero*: "In this house it was the custom to call a young visitor «by his Christian name» a little too soon" (SH, 44). A final note on the relationship of the nationalist-feminist Hanna Sheehy-Skeffington and James Joyce is that she visited him in Paris, and reports, with an attitude of cherishing it, "I have Jim Joyce's last card to me, written in September 1939."[40] Apparently Joyce never dismissed her type from his life, despite his early discomfort.

Their nationalism encouraged Joyce to see the women of his day in unconventional ways: in assertive roles, alongside his male peers, or in the context of Irish national history. A second popular movement—feminism—would attract active young women and probably become just as essential a subject as nationalism for the brooding Joyce.

Early Encounters
with Feminism
The Irish Feminist Movement
and the Literary Feminism of
Moore, Shaw, Hauptmann, and Ibsen

———————————— 3 ————————————

□ During Joyce's youth Irish nationalism became a liberating cause for young women, allowing them to work actively and seek education outside of the family circle. Although the term *feminist* existed, few women would have identified themselves as feminists. Even today, women's contributions to Irish nationalism are far better known and more widely respected than their contributions to the feminist movement. With the designation of International Women's Year in 1975, the Irish began to deliberately collect information on their own women's movement, which has proved invaluable to this study.[1]

In *Stephen Hero* and *A Portrait*, Joyce gives fleeting evidence of the major campaign among Irish, and indeed world, feminists of his day. As we have seen in Hanna Sheehy-Skeffington's essay "Women and the Nationalist Movement," the first step toward civic equality for women was considered to be female suffrage; the prevalent slogan was "votes for women." Ireland's first suffrage society, the Dublin Women's Suffrage Association (later renamed The Irishwomen's Suffrage and Local Government Association), had been founded by Anna Haslam of Youghal in 1876.[2] As in England, the movement was at first non-militant and constitutional in approach. Its petitioning of members of Parliament and educating of the Irish public *via* the press began to have effect twenty years later, at the time Joyce was at Belvedere and University College. In 1896, Poor Law Guardianships were extended to Irish women, and in 1898, Irish women were granted municipal franchise. The next goal became the Parliamen-

tary vote. MacCann (consistently labeled "the feminist") takes up
this campaign in both *Stephen Hero* and *A Portrait*, though, like his
original in life, Francis Sheehy-Skeffington, this was only one aspect
of his integrated effort for "equality among all classes and sexes" (P,
177).

In *A Portrait*, Moynihan mocks MacCann's enthusiasm for "Votes
for Women," renaming the campaign "votes for the bitches" (P,
195). The animal reference is comparable to a degrading epigram
on woman, quoted by Joyce to Stanislaus: "Woman is an animal that
micturates once a day, defecates once a week, menstruates once a
month, and parturates once a year."[3] It is notable that the excre-
mental epigram sacrifices accuracy for an artistic, temporal pattern.
Both the epigram and Moynihan agree with Aristotle's assignment
of woman to the lower orders of life. Moynihan is relentless in his
degrading of women. The physics lecture sets off his "What price
ellipsoidal balls! Chase me, ladies, I'm in the cavalry!" (P, 192), and
he is also partial to the verses, "Lottie Collins lost her drawers;/
Won't you kindly lend her yours?" (P, 197). The Moynihan attitude
was not unknown to Joyce. Stephen considers imitating the thought
and manner of this friend while sitting in the physics lecture, but
rejects the temptation: "—That thought is not mine, he said to himself quickly. It came from the comic Irishman in the bench behind"
(P, 193). Buck Mulligan's attitude toward women is similar to Moynihan's and is similarly rejected by Stephen in the "Oxen of the Sun"
chapter of *Ulysses*. Joyce also makes a comparable dismissal of Gogarty as an Irish character type in a letter to Stanislaus (L II, 187).
In *Stephen Hero*, Stephen is a bit more of the comic Irishman himself,
aiming supposedly "agile bullets" at the causes of equal rights for
women and bodily "purity" (SH, 49ff). Coarse remarks about women
and their aspiration for civic equality were an aspect of Joyce's male-
centered culture that he recorded, and in moments of bravado, even
participated in himself.

As suggested by MacCann's involvement in the cause of female
suffrage, Joyce's close friends were involved in the struggle for the
Parliamentary vote. Most notable in the group were Francis and
Hanna Sheehy-Skeffington and James and Margaret Cousins. Irish
feminists watched the militant techniques of protest of the Pankhursts and their Women's Social and Political Union with interest.
Gradually, they evolved their own cooperative but self-sufficient
movement. Much of this organizing occurred after Joyce left Ireland,

but he was aware of it and its English parallels through journals and friends. In 1908 Hanna Sheehy-Skeffington and Margaret Cousins would found the Irish Women's Franchise League, and from 1912 through 1916, James Cousins and Francis Sheehy-Skeffington would edit the incendiary, socialistic organ of that movement, the *Irish Citizen*. It is notable that another prominent Irish socialist, James Connolly, was also an outspoken feminist.

James Joyce had a complex set of reactions to Francis J. C. Skeffington, many aspects of which lie outside of the latter's advocacy of female equality and merit additional study. A man of individuality, ideas, causes, and propaganda, Skeffington was slightly ahead of Joyce at University College and, like Joyce, a frequent visitor at the Sheehy household. When he and Hanna Sheehy married in 1903, "each took the other's name as a gesture of belief in equal status for women."[4] James Joyce never acknowledged this change in name in any of his references to him. When Joyce fictionalized the Sheehys' gatherings as the Daniels' in *Stephen Hero*, he cast Stephen and McCann, their respective likenesses, very differently. However, Joyce and Skeffington tended to be grouped together as eccentrics in the University College student journal, *St. Stephen's*. In 1901 they cooperated in publishing *Two Essays*—"The Day of the Rabblement" by Joyce and "A Forgotten Aspect of the University Question" by Skeffington. Since the latter advocated admission of women to a reorganized Catholic university system, Joyce in effect collaborated in a feminist publication. Hanna Sheehy more appropriately recalls the endeavor as a mutual defiance of College censorship,[5] both essays having been rejected by *St. Stephen's*. Later the young men considered publishing their own newspaper, *The Goblin* (JJ, 140), a name which suggests continued mischief against the establishment. Both Joyce and Sheehy-Skeffington were rebels against external authority.[6]

Quite correctly, Joyce never seems to have felt any competition from Sheehy-Skeffington as a literary stylist, though he may have envied his easy access to print, especially in the role of editor of a series of journals. Sheehy-Skeffington became a journalist and propagandist, the immediate servant of political causes. "Women, Ireland, Labour, and Peace" are the ones listed in his obituary in the *Irish Citizen*.[7] Joyce requested copies of these publications from home and denounced one of his friend's "Dialogues of the Day" columns to Stanislaus as "three pages of puff," objecting especially to the journalist's "catch phrases" (L II, 153). The "Dialogues" featured

a rather outspoken "Mere Woman" along with such cultural stereotypes as the "Curate," the "Bookman," the "Barrister," and the
"Baronet," arguing over current political issues in an entertaining
but rather shallow and contrived manner. It is tempting to see precedent here for the political debates of "Aeolus," "Circe," and "Eu-
maeus" in *Ulysses*, though Joyce had abundant additional resources
in the nationalist press. Sheehy-Skeffington's best writing was a biography of his idol, Michael Davitt, a work that praises Davitt for
his feminist ideals.[8]

Joyce was less at ease with Sheehy-Skeffington's challenges to take
up moral action as a vocation and his personal criticisms of Joyce,
particularly relating to his elopement with Nora Barnacle. At times,
Joyce assumes a tone of light raillery. He labels his friend "hairy
Jaysus" in letters to Stanislaus, and has Cranly use this same epithet
and a similar tone toward McCann in *Stephen Hero* (SH, 113). Joyce
called him "the most intelligent man in St. Stephen's College after
myself," but also mocked his methodical nature and his "enthusiasm
that responded mechanically to all the more obvious appeals to justice, reason, and humanity" (MBK, 145). In *A Portrait*, the precise
ticking of a clock reminds Stephen of MacCann and the activist's
criticism of Stephen as "an antisocial being, wrapped up in" himself
(P, 177). Yet Stephen, while refusing to sign MacCann's petition for
international peace, is conciliatory: "You are right to go your way.
Leave me to go mine" (P, 198).

Privately, the young Joyce is unable to share Sheehy-Skeffington's
fundamental philosophy of cooperative, altruistic humanism—an attitude that has guided more women's lives than men's. He protests
to Stanislaus in letters written in 1905 and 1906 that Sheehy-Skeffington is a "stupid mountebank" (L II, 157) and "the bloodiest
impostor I have ever met," insisting that "there cannot be any substitute for the individual passion as the motive power of everything"
(L II, 81). Joyce seems to have dodged Sheehy-Skeffington's efforts
to involve him in political and philosophical arguments at the Sheehy
household.[9] But in *Stephen Hero*, Stephen plays a provocative role
with McCann, and a long dialogue is devoted to Stephen's attack on
McCann's feminism and his opposition to artificial stimulants. Stephen's refractory objections seem worn, rather than "agile." He
wonders about women in "the soldiery, the police and the fire-bri-
gade" as "doctors and lawyers" as well as in the role of confessors.
Though he says "certainly" to the doctor and lawyer, even McCann

cannot foresee women in the rest: "There are certain social duties for which women are physically unfitted," he responds to the first three occupations. On the priestly role, "You are flippant. The Church does not allow women to enter the priesthood" (SH, 50). As a pacifist, Skeffington would have sent no one to war, an attitude shared by many contemporary feminists. While Joyce knew him, Sheehy-Skeffington had not yet renounced the Catholic church, but he would later do so. Women have now responded to all of Stephen's challenges and entered all but the Catholic priesthood. Toward the end of their discussion, Stephen asks McCann whether his physical "wants" include women. McCann responds, "Never!" uttering the word "with a moral snap of the jaws" in a "business-like tone" that sends Stephen into "a fit of loud laughter." But he is annoyed because McCann's attitude "savored so strongly of *paterfamilias* and it stung him because it seemed to judge him incapable of that part" (SH, 51-52). Stephen's reaction here is fascinatingly complex. He has come to resent all that Simon, his own *paterfamilias*, represents. It is ironic that McCann, as a feminist, should fall into this role. Stephen would seem to have an aroused social conscience in detecting a hypocritical patriarchal tone in McCann. But Stephen wants to be deemed capable of the *paterfamilias* role himself. Perhaps he also wants McCann to realize that Stephen could have assumed the role but as artistic revolutionary has renounced it. Stephen is not the only one to be intrigued by McCann's sexual attitudes in *Stephen Hero*. Emma Clery gossips to Stephen about the likelihood that McCann will marry one of the Daniels' daughters. She is amused "that McCann should have a desire for matrimony" (SH, 153) and possibly unable to imagine him in the nuptial bed.

The ideal of sexual "purity" was embraced by a number of the Irish feminists of Joyce's acquaintance. It was a doctrine that "nauseated" him and that he intended to address in his writings, as he discloses to Stanislaus in 1906:

> . . . If I put down a bucket into my soul's well, sexual department, I draw up Griffith's and Ibsen's and Skeffington's and Bernard Vaughan's and St. Aloysius' and Shelley's and Renan's water along with my own. And I am going to do that in my novel. . . . I am nauseated by their lying drivel about pure men and pure women and spiritual love and love for ever: blatant lying in the face of truth. (L II, 191-192)

Reticence and naïveté about sexuality were typical of the young upper-middle class Catholic women of Joyce's acquaintance, whose manners Joyce protested. Describing the months before her marriage to James Cousins, Gretta Cousins recalls, "I knew nothing of the technique of sex, but I had utter trust in his knowledge, his will and his integrity. . . . Jim and I had realised that our surest unity was in our similar aspirations to build purity and beauty into our lives and into the world."[10] Still, she grew "white and thin during our first married year. People thought this was due to the problems of adjustment to the revelation that marriage had brought me as to the physical basis of sex." Cousins apparently never adapted. "Every child I looked at called to my mind the shocking circumstance that brought about its existence. . . . I found myself looking on men and women as degraded by this demand of nature."[11] Joyce had need of a more natural woman and found one in the lower-middle class Galway woman, Nora Barnacle. Gretta Cousins's case, though perhaps not typical, was probably not unusual in barely post-Victorian Ireland. Francis Sheehy-Skeffington, on the other hand, does not seem to have been quite so cold as Joyce suggests, though he may have shared his warmth with very few. Love poems he wrote to Hanna Sheehy have survived. One of 1903 displays a degree of ardor, idealizing Hanna's voice, both as the tool of a effective female orator, and as an instrument of love:

> I've loved the tones that voiced Love's vow—
> Aye Sweetheart!—though I never said it!
> Or ringing angry-clear for right
> 　Or softly, whispering word-caresses,
> Or rippling into laughter bright
> 　Your voice delights whom it addresses
> And if a high-pitched word I blame,
> 　Forgive, O dear the reason this is
> That mere monopoly's my aim
> 　I'd share no more your voice than kisses![12]

In a fragment of another poem, Sheehy-Skeffington moves from an appreciation of physical beauty to intellectual and abstract beauties.

> Thus through a graceful outline, tresses fine,
> Complexion fair, hands shapely, lustrous eyes,
> With faultless features all in you combine
> Not these could win for you could conquer beauty's prize
> Disjoined from what within they symbolize.

Hanna Sheehy-Skeffington.
Photograph courtesy of the National Library of Ireland.

Refined thought, acute perception, heart
Pure, sympathetic, void of all disguise
Sweet gentleness; when sudden these out-start
Before the eye, there lines your beauty's truest part.[13]

Joyce never looked for good voice or "acute perception" in a beloved woman. In capturing the idealist and activist in MacCann, Joyce seems to have missed some outstanding qualities of love that Sheehy-Skeffington could express. Probably he could never place himself in a position to observe them, or found them inimical to his artistic purpose, if he did. Stanislaus Joyce, however, refers to Hanna Sheehy's "nice little hand" and "beautiful voice" in his diary.[14]

Sheehy-Skeffington wrote a letter to Joyce on October 6, 1904, that was critical of his proposed elopement with Nora Barnacle. His concern, like that of poet-economist AE (George Russell), was for Miss Barnacle's welfare (L II, 73n). In his early letters home to Stanislaus, Joyce refers repeatedly to Nora as "the companion," a term for her coined in Sheehy-Skeffington's letter. Puzzled by his own inability to fathom this new companion and her lack of regard for his art, Joyce mockingly suggests, "Ask hairy Jaysus what am I to do? He ought to know" (L II, 73). Joyce also seems to enter into reproductive competition with his former friend. The game may have had special appeal because of Sheehy-Skeffington's de-emphasis of sexuality. In 1905 Joyce receives reports from his bawdy and treacherous acquaintance, Vincent Cosgrave, about "Mrs Skeffington's antero-posterior diameter" (L II, 125), and Stanislaus reports with delight that Cosgrave will deliver news of the birth of Joyce's son, Giorgio, "in person to Skeffington " (L II, 103). He also expresses the intention of making Sheehy-Skeffington Giorgio's godfather (L II, 81)—a sure way of bringing attention to the event. During his 1909 visit to Ireland, Joyce reports, without mocking comment, the news that "Skeffington has a son two months old" (L II, 238). In a letter written at the start of that trip, he made the rather stilted remark, "Mr and Mrs Skeffington met me and invited me to their house: I did not go" (L II, 230). It is implicit that Stanislaus knows of a tension Joyce is maintaining with Sheehy-Skeffington, probably in response to the admonishing letter of 1904. Though it may have resulted in a personal snub, Sheehy-Skeffington's letter may have had the positive effect of challenging Joyce to fidelity and to the achievement of the welfare of Nora Barnacle. Joyce definitely wanted evidence of his success in this reported.

Joyce's connection with James and Gretta Cousins was neither as strong nor as preoccupying as his relationship to the Sheehy-Skeffingtons. Yet, as we have already seen, their memoirs are instructive about the experience of young women of Joyce's era, and they also touch upon Joyce himself. Stanislaus Joyce records his brother's negative impression of the couple, whom he stayed with for two nights in September 1904: "Cousins and Mrs. Cousins, especially, invited Jim to stay for a fortnight, but Jim found their vegetarian household and sentimental Mrs. Cousins intolerable, and more than this he did not like their manner to him."[15] The complaint about "manner" is a usual one, visible also in Joyce's dealings at the Sheehys' and attributable in part to his self-consciousness about his family's social decline. Furthermore, the Cousins were at that time favored by the literary powers who seemed to be slighting Joyce. James Cousins was embraced by AE's circle of theosophical poets and the Fays had chosen two of his plays for the first program of their National Theatre Society in 1902. James Cousins had encountered Joyce shortly after his visit with them, and was seemingly pleased with the notoriety they had attained from their visitor.[16] In her memoirs, Gretta Cousins calls Joyce "a favorite of mine though he was reputed to be a 'bad boy.' " Mrs. Cousins, who had a Bachelor of Music degree from the Royal University, also reports, "I delighted in his lovely tenor voice especially when I accompanied some of his Irish songs with nobody but ourselves to hear in our little drawing room."[17] Gretta Cousins, whom he charges with sentimentality, must have represented to Joyce the epitome of artificiality in upper-middle class young Catholic women. She was still a relative newlywed (married 16 months) and may have unconsciously displayed some of her sexual anxieties to Joyce, who by then had met the very natural Miss Barnacle. But her memory of making music together with Joyce has a suggestion of intimacy and delight that is warm, if not sexual.

The Cousins's resented vegetarian menu was an aspect of their belief in theosophy, a popular philosophy that Joyce had given consideration to himself. It is notable that the Cousins found feminism compatible and even necessary to theosophy. The theosophical movement gave prominence and power to many women of the era, including Annie Besant (a close friend of George Bernard Shaw) and Madame Blavatsky,[18] whose works Joyce read during his own period of interest in theosophy. Dora Marsden, editor of *The Egoist*, which later serialized *A Portrait*, was also a feminist and theosophist. The

Margaret Cousins.
Photograph courtesy of the National Library of Ireland.

Cousins's feeling of equality and mutuality is visible in their cooperative memoir, *We Two Together*, which furnishes one of the best contemporary accounts of Irish feminism in the early century.

Despite her supposed "sentimentality," Margaret Cousins was one of the first Irish women to be imprisoned for feminist protest, in her case for the breaking of windows on Downing Street in London in 1910. Both Margaret Cousins and Hanna Sheehy-Skeffington shattered Dublin windows and endured Irish prisons and hunger strikes in their efforts to have suffrage included in the Home Rule bills for Ireland, but to no avail. Gretta Cousins eventually carried her campaign for female suffrage and education to India, where the couple settled permanently.

One feminist appears, rather appropriately, in a mass demonstration in the "Circe" chapter of *Ulysses*. She is a praiser of Bloom, "the world's greatest reformer." She serves a comic purpose, joining a series of his female adulators: a millionairess who responds "richly," and a noble woman who answers "nobly." Her praise of what Bloom has "done" is delivered "masculinely" (U, 481). Joyce does not appear to scorn her. She forms a part of his human universe, and is just as laughable, just as real, and just as fictional as the rest of the "Circe" cast.

The near-dissolution of the feminist movement in the 1920s, both in Europe and in America, has been blamed on the excessive concentration on female franchise by many of its conservative members, including the Pankhursts.[19] The feminists closest to James Joyce in turn-of-the-century Ireland and later in England had much more comprehensive, radical goals for women than the vote. Just as important to Francis and Hanna Sheehy-Skeffington was equal education. In February 1900 Francis presented a paper titled "The Progress of Women" to the Literary and Historical Society of University College. His principal plea for equal education was contained in "A Forgotten Aspect of the University Question," the essay published cooperatively with Joyce's "The Day of the Rabblement." In June 1904 Sheehy-Skeffington resigned as Registrar of the Royal University over the issue of women's admission to University College. He had been criticized for circulating a petition in favor of co-education by the President of the College, William Delaney, and found it impossible to have his "freedom of action with regard to [the issue] hampered."[20]

Catholic women of Joyce's era stood at the end of the line for opportunities in university education—a fact which convinced most feminists that the only solution was to obtain co-education in the

Catholic universities of the future. This issue became an adjunct to the very visible argument of "the University Question" for nearly twenty years spanning the turn of the century. It was clear that an educational double standard existed between Protestant and Catholic men, and that this inequity should be remedied in planning for the future. Protestant Trinity, "the grey dull block . . . set heavily in the city's ignorance" (P, 180) was a true lecturing institution, with an excellent faculty, a library, athletic fields, rich extracurricular activities, and a three-century tradition. Catholics had never been happy with the non-denominational character of the Queen's Colleges, established by Robert Peel. The twenty-year-old "Royal University," set up in 1879, supplied largely Catholic member colleges with limited building funds; it administered examinations, gave cash awards for high examination grades, and issued university degrees to students who prepared at these colleges or on their own.[21] Although it lacked a dining hall, library, and athletic fields, Joyce's own University College was better off than most of the men's colleges of the "Royal." It had a fifty-year tradition dating back to its founding by Cardinal Newman and a campus consisting of three stately eighteenth-century mansions facing attractive St. Stephen's Green. There were active, reasonably stimulating extracurricular groups like the Literary and Historical Society and the student journal, *St. Stephen's*, and the Jesuits' instruction commanded respect. But there is no question that Trinity offered men a sounder program of studies, more extensive lectures, and a more prestigious and competent faculty.

Alexandra College, founded in 1866 as the female counterpart to Trinity, was officially non-denominational, but was predominantly Protestant once Catholic women's colleges were founded. It depended on Trinity for borrowed faculty, but the male institution resisted all attempts at alliance made by the women's college.[22] The two Catholic women's colleges in Dublin that affiliated with the Royal University were St. Mary's University College, started by Dominican Nuns at 28 Merrion Square in 1885, and Loreto College, established by nuns of the Loreto Order at St. Stephen's Green in 1895. St. Mary's was the college attended by Hanna Sheehy and provides the backgrounds needed to understand the contexts of Emma Clery and Molly Ivors, the two Catholic university women represented in Joyce's fiction. Both the Dominican and the Loreto nuns have a long and eminent history in Irish education; in prestige they most nearly compare to the Jesuits, whom John Joyce was proud to have educate his son. It is worth noting that the elder Joyce did not take corresponding pains with his daughters. None attended the university and they received at least part of their primary education at a national school on Mount Joy Street, boarding at St. Joseph's Orphanage, where the Irish Sisters of Charity (an order devoted to the poor) provided religious instruction.[23]

St. Mary's and male Catholic university colleges were alike in many ways. Gabriel Conroy asserts in "The Dead" that his career and that of Miss Ivors "had been parallel, first at the University and then as teachers" (D, 188). Similarly, Mary Colum, an alumna of St. Mary's, asserts that she and James Joyce "had been educated in the same way."[24] The curriculum of St. Mary's University College, as set by its founder, Mother Patrick Shiel, included the ordinary subjects of the university courses plus vocal and instrumental music and an advanced course of religious instruction. As time went on, St. Mary's became particularly distinguished for its teaching of the Gaelic language—a fact which may have given young women a head start on the men in Gaelic League classes. The nuns of St. Mary's set as their aim "the maintenance of higher education and the advancement in life of the orphan daughters of the upper and middle classes." Although they were never limited to orphans, they remained committed to women who needed to or planned to make their own way in the world.[25] The university college of St. Mary's was founded three years after its secondary school, St. Mary's High School. Although both levels of St. Mary's were oriented toward the relatively modern examination system, which had been opened to women in the 1870s, they also partook of the nineteenth-century convent-school traditions exemplified by Sion Hill, founded by the Dominicans in 1836. At these older institutions "cultural and moral education was accompanied by the teaching of music, needlework, art, and elocution . . . and the task of turning girls into young ladies was effectively accomplished through the teaching of Christian values and social aptitudes."[26] As a remnant of her education by Ursuline nuns, Joyce's grandmother on his father's side had kept French language prayer books (MBK, 22). Education for girls had until very recently been pious and home-oriented, with aspects of the finishing school, and continued to be that way for many upper-middle class Catholic girls. Stephen thinks along these lines when he watches a group of women students "returning to the convent—demure corridors and simple dormitories, a quiet rosary of hours" (SH, 184). He is probably referring to one of the inexpensive hostels run by nuns for women students. Mary Colum reports that curfews and restrictions against attending the theater greatly limited her freedom during her time of residence in one of these hostels, probably the Dominican Hall, St. Stephen's Green.[27]

The teaching staff of St. Mary's was largely drawn from its cloisters and the graduates of Sion Hill. Even if the curriculum had shifted toward comparability with male education, this staff obviously provided very different role models from the Jesuits of Joyce's University College. In recalling her convent education, one alumna of St. Mary's High School, Mary Colum, contrasts the "self-sacrificing" nuns who administered her education with the occasional learned Jesuit brought in to explain important issues.[28] St. Mary's used as faculty some eminent female graduates like Mary Hayden (B.A., Alexandra College, M.A., St. Mary's) and Katherine Murphy (who had won first place honors for the B.A. in Modern Languages in 1890). But like Alexandra College, St. Mary's depended heavily upon faculty borrowed from male institutions.

Father William Delaney, President of University College during Joyce's time there, strenuously opposed admitting women to his university's lectures; women were first admitted to University College at the end of Joyce's years there, but were relegated to separate lecture rooms. Though Emma Clery in *Stephen Hero* expresses interest in hearing the paper Stephen was due to deliver in the Literary and Historical Society, she would have been barred from attending. Starting in 1889, the women had St. Mary's Literary Academy, a society comparable to the men's Literary and Historical Society at University College. Many of their topics compared to the men's: "Nationality *versus* Cosmopolitanism in Literature," "Some Moral Aspects of the Drama" (Hanna Sheehy's topic), and "Young Ireland." Other subjects suggest their special concerns: "What Women Can Do for the City Poor," and "The Last Four Generations of Women."[29] If a Catholic woman had a contact (usually a brother), she might be asked to write in a column called "Girl Graduates' Chat" for *St. Stephen's*. Francis Sheehy-Skeffington considered the title (derived from Tennyson), and the column's trivial content affronts to women.[30] Stephen is scornful of women's contributions to a similar column in *Stephen Hero*, where Emma's friend writes for the column, "The Female Fellow"—a Joycean title that adds an ironic example of male-centered language to insult. "Glynn's sister" contributes an article in Irish (SH, 187, 182), demonstrating the female role in the nationalist movement, and perhaps the capable teaching of Gaelic at the women's college. The women of St. Mary's University College never had a publication comparable to *St. Stephen's*, though starting in 1913, *The Lanthorn*, the year book of the Dominican College, Eccles St., gave their successors in a different educational arrangement an organ for publication.

Despite these limitations, the "female fellows" of Joyce's era were already distinguishing themselves as scholars. In "A Forgotten Aspect of the University Question," Francis Sheehy-Skeffington uses women's performances on national exminations to argue their rights to equal advantages in any reformed scheme for Catholic higher education. His tabulations show that by 1900, women were earning 28.5% of all the honors granted, a figure that had climbed steadily since 1884. In the 1894 competitions, St. Mary's had come in a very presentable third behind Queen's College, Belfast, and University College, Dublin.[31] Especially in the modern languages—Joyce's specialty, but usually the area chosen by the women instead of the "masculine" classics—men were feeling pressured by women. Joyce's awareness of this is recorded in *Stephen Hero*, where Stephen is as untroubled as Joyce probably was himself:

> Stephen who did not care very much whether he succeeded or failed in the examination was very much amused observing the jealousies and nervous anxieties which tried to conceal themselves under airs of carelessness. . . . Their excitement was so genuine that even the excitement of sex failed to overcome it. The girl students were not the subject of the usual sniggers and jokes but were regarded with some aversion as sly enemies. Some of the young men eased their enmity and vindicated their superiority at the same time by saying that it was no wonder the women would do well seeing that they could study ten hours a day all year round. (SH, 130-131)

Stephen's lack of academic insecurity here does not qualify him as a feminist. He is primarily a scrupulous observer of human interactions, including sexual politics. Elsewhere, Stephen refuses to take Emma Clery's bid for equal education seriously. The report of this conversation with Emma is tinged with his own biased interpretations of her motivations:

> She coquetted with knowledge, asking could he not persuade the President of his College to admit women to the college. Stephen

told her to apply to McCann who was the champion of women.
(SH, 66-67)

Sheehy-Skeffington in fact resigned as Registrar of University College rather than concede to the administration's request that he with-
draw a "memorial" petition he had circulated on the issue of female
admissions.[32]

In advocating co-education for the Catholic University of the future, Francis Sheehy-Skeffington joined outstanding graduates of the
women's colleges, who had convened as the Women Graduates' Association. The campaign had been initiated by Alice Oldham, who
touched off a series of articles by different people in the *New Ireland
Review*, titled "Women and the University Question." One propo-
sition favored a separate women's college that would specialize in
"feminine" arts like embroidery, domestic science, and likely future
occupations for women, especially teaching. Mary Hayden and Hanna
Sheehy looked forward to wider professional opportunities and
pointed to successful ventures in co-education in the United States.[33]

In *Stephen Hero*, McCann offers his arguments for co-education,
which are in fact a condensation of Francis Sheehy-Skeffington's, first
presented in "A Forgotten Aspect of the University Question," published jointly with Joyce's essay in 1901:

> He believed that the sexes should be educated together in order
> to accustom them early to each other's influences and he believed
> that women should be afforded the same opportunities as were
> afforded to the so-called superior sex and he believed that women
> had the right to compete with men in every branch of social and
> intellectual activity. (SH, 49)[34]

In addition to claiming the justice of equal education, the discussions
in favor of co-education assessed typical male and female behaviors
as they related to the educational system, suggesting that both sexes
would benefit from a combination of these qualities; in effect it is
an appeal for androgyny. Undoubtedly aware of the arguments, Joyce
may have benefitted from their content for future portrayals of the
sexes. Co-education did prevail with the advent of the National University in 1909, bringing to an end the women's colleges, and the
distant relationship between the sexes at the University that Joyce
had known. Early university women like Mary Hayden, Alice Oldham, Hanna Sheehy-Skeffington, Maud Joynt, and Louise Gavan Duffy

were models of strong, independent, intelligent, purposeful Irish womanhood that Joyce only hints at in his writing.

In addition to his personal experience of Irish struggles for female suffrage and equal education, Joyce could find in modern Irish literature one writer deeply concerned with women's lives—George Moore.[35] Other Irish writers should perhaps be mentioned. AE has been commended for his support of women writers. Yeats sketched Maud Gonne in memorable and epic proportions in his poetry, but always with regret that he could not master her and with a faintly patriarchal tone. His intellectual relationship with women like Augusta Gregory and especially Olivia Shakespear may have been superior to anything Joyce achieved in his mental life with women. But surely, Yeats does not merit the title "feminist." John Millington Synge imagined the strongest of the modern Deirdres and the powerful outcasts in Widow Quinn of *The Playboy of the Western World* and Mary Byrne of *The Tinker's Wedding*. But these works came too late to affect the young Joyce, and an older Joyce protested Synge's language, preferring Ibsen.[36]

James Joyce schooled himself in George Moore, reading and commenting upon every novel he could obtain to his brother Stanislaus (MBK, 98). He translated Moore's *Celibates* into Italian. Moore's cosmopolitan education in Paris and London and his debt to Joyce's idol, Ibsen, made him especially appealing to the rebellious young Irishman. Moore's *A Drama in Muslin* and *The Untilled Field* anticipate the naturalism and social sensitivity of *Dubliners*, including the pervasive theme of Irish urban paralysis. *A Drama in Muslin* features a heroine, Alice Barton, and sympathetically views women caught in conventional traps, a subject that would later interest Joyce, in slightly different focus. The rituals Moore studies involve Castle society, not the Catholic middle class that Joyce would concentrate upon. But the marriage game he studies is just as confining and demeaning to women. In the 1915 preface to *Muslin* (a reworking of the earlier novel), Moore recognizes that his theme is identical with that of Ibsen's *The Doll's House*.[37] Women claim the center and the title of a number of Moore's novels— *A Drama in Muslin, Evelyn Innes, Esther Waters, Sister Theresa*. Two novels with important heroines, *Vain Fortune* and *Esther Waters*, receive what sparse praise Joyce has for Moore in his anti-literary-establishment essay, "The Day of the Rabblement" (CW, 71). It is interesting that, unlike Joyce, Moore casts women characters like Mildred Lawson (a title character of *Celibates*) in the role of artist.He grants them vivid internal monologues and dreams, some of which may have served as models for Joyce's young artist, Stephen Dedalus. Alice Barton of *A Drama in Muslin* is, like Stephen Dedalus, engaged in a struggle against social conventions:

> Since she had left the convent she had begun to feel that her life must correspond to her ideals and she had determined to speak to her mother on this (for her) all-important subject—the conformity of her outer life to her inner life. The power to prevail upon herself to do what she thought was wrong merely because she did not wish to wound other people's feelings was dying within her.[38]

Evelyn Innes's remorse about her dead mother takes a form comparable to Stephen's hallucinations of his own mother in *Ulysses*:

> Evelyn drew back as if she felt the breath of the dead on her face, as if a dead hand had been laid upon hers. The face she saw was grey, shadowy, unreal, like a ghost; the eyes were especially distinct, her mother seemed to be aware of her . . . She looked always like a grey shadow; she moved like a shadow.[39]

Like Joyce's story "Eveline," Moore's *Evelyn Innes* involves a young woman's decision to leave home and family for a man of the world, and in moments of crisis, the thought patterns of Eveline and Evelyn are even similar.[40] Kitty Hare, a young victim of rape in the *Celibates* story, "John Norton," has a nightmare very strongly like Stephen's nightmare of goatish creatures, thrusting human, terrific faces at him as they circle, with swishing tails besmeared with stale shit. "The claws of the hyena are heard upon the crumbling tombs, and the suffocating girl strives with her last strength to free herself from the thrall of giant lianas. But there comes a hirsute smell; she turns with terrified eyes to plead but meets only dull, liquorish eyes, and the breath of the obscene animal upon her face."[41] Like Stephen in another part of *A Portrait*, Kitty also imagines her own funeral. Although he greatly improves upon the original, Joyce also seems to owe a debt to George Moore's *Vain Fortune* for the characterization of Gretta and Gabriel Conroy and for the final scene of male disillusionment in that story.[42]

Joyce's literary contexts also included modern Europeans who were interested in many aspects of women's emancipation, including such issues as sexual and intellectual freedom. The writers of problem plays concerning these subjects are particularly notable. Joyce's greatest resource was Henrik Ibsen, whom both he and George Moore idolized.[43] Similar problems are treated by Gerhart Hauptmann, whose plays Joyce translated as a young man. Joyce was also an interested reader of George Bernard Shaw's *The Quintessence of Ibsenism*, and later had the English Players of Zurich present Shaw's *Mrs. Warren's Profession*, a play which stimulates thought on new women, female economic survival, and mother-daughter conflicts. When asked to subscribe to a first-edition copy of *Ulysses*, Shaw declined but quipped that he would like to force every *male* in Ireland to read it (JJ, 506), perhaps suggesting that Joyce offered criticisms of the male establishment that he approved.

It has never been the fashion to say that Joyce derived feminist ideals from Ibsen. In examining Joyce's youthful essays on the Norwegian playwright, both Björn Tysdael and Richard Ellmann find that Joyce was attracted to Ibsen's aesthetic "truth" and his dramatic technique, rather than his viewpoint on women. While they acknowledge Joyce's reading of *The Quintessence of Ibsenism*, they find Joyce's interpretation less female-centered (JJ, 54).[44] In his review, "Ibsen's New Drama," Joyce claimed that "what primarily rivets our attention" in the play is "the perception of a great truth, or the opening up of a great question or a great conflict which is . . . of far-reaching importance" (CW, 63). The woman question, the problem of male-female relationships in the new century, seems to qualify eminently for Joyce's criteria. In the essays "Drama and Life" and "Ibsen's New Drama," Joyce shows distinct interest in women's experience by repeatedly using the phrase "men and women" instead of the typical, generic "men" (CW, 40, 41, 44, 49, 50, 51, 61). He closes "Drama and Life" with a quotation from one of Ibsen's heroines, Miss Hessel from *Pillars of Society*: " '. . . what will you do in our Society, Miss Hessel?' asked Rorlund—'I will let in fresh air, Pastor.'—answered Lona" (CW, 46). Here Joyce is willing to adopt the point-of-view of one of Ibsen's heroines as his guide to the future role of art in society. Joyce's admiration for Ibsen's feminism and his sense of its importance to his art are also evident in a late exchange with Arthur Power, which is becoming a favorite text for feminist critics of Joyce:

> . . . you do not understand Ibsen. You ignore the spirit that animated him. The purpose of *The Doll's House*, for instance, was the emancipation of women, which has caused the greatest revolution in our time in the most important relationship there is—that be-

tween men and women; the revolt of women against the idea that
they are the mere instruments of men.
   —And the more pity, [Power] replied, for the relationship between the sexes has now been ruined; and intellectualism has been
allowed to supersede a biological fact, and the result is that neither
is happy.
   —The relationship between the sexes is now on a different basis,
but I do not know whether they are happier or unhappier than
they were before; I suppose it depends on the individuals.[45]

In addition to granting importance to the theme of "the emancipation
of women" in Ibsen, Joyce also admits the importance of intellect
as well as biology in male-female relationships, and sees the emancipation of women itself as "the greatest revolution in our time."

   Henrik Ibsen ranks high in feminist criticism for his depiction of
independent-minded "new women" who question the social norms
of a country which, like Ireland, was very conservative socially. Ibsen's new women can sometimes exercise mystical and destructive
power over their men. Hilda Wangel (*The Master Builder*), Irene
(*When We Dead Awaken*),[46] Rebecca West (*Rosmersholm*),and Hedda
Gabler (*Hedda Gabler*) all lead men to death, though that death has
an aspect of societal protest and escape. Women like Mrs. Alving,
Maja (*When We Dead Awaken*), and Nora Helmer (*The Doll's House*)
can display determination and resourcefulness in reaction to change.
Hedda wields a gun and Irene a knife, threatening themselves and
their men alternately. Ibsen writes memorable dialogues between
men and women in which both parties (but especially the women)
explain their present and remembered frustrations, make charges,
and react either with candid truth or renewed questioning—a strategy that evades hypocritical submission to the male's view. This is
an aspect of style that Joyce definitely attempted in *Exiles*, and recent
performances of the play may demonstrate that he was more successful with emotionally arousing dialogue than has generally been
recognized.[47] He may have tried something similar in the dialogues
between Stephen and Emma Clery, which are so deliberately posi-
tioned throughout the surviving pages of *Stephen Hero*. Gabriel's
exchanges with Gretta and especially Miss Ivors in "The Dead" are
also reminiscent of the form.

   Another important aspect of Ibsen for Joyce is his presentation of
many male artists in relationship to the women who have served
them: Rubek and Irene, his model in *When We Dead Awaken*; Eilert
Lovborg and Mrs. Elvsted, his writing assistant (*Hedda Gabler*); and

Halvard Solness and Hilda Wangel, his youthful encourager (*The Master Builder*). Ibsen repeatedly notes the male artist's victimization of his female inspirer or amanuensis. Both Irene and Mrs. Elvsted regard the work of art as their child, a mutual creation with the artist. But in both cases, the artist has betrayed them by seeming to destroy the child. In "Ibsen's New Drama," his review of *When We Dead Awaken*, Joyce takes special interest in the Rubek-Irene relationship. In his plot summary, he is aware of Rubek's "unquiet conscience" and records Irene's characterization of the statue she posed for as "the child of her soul" (CW, 57). Joyce also congratulates Ibsen for his understanding of women:

> In Irene's allusion to her position as model for the great picture, [sic] Ibsen gives further proof of his extraordinary knowledge of women. No other man could have so subtly expressed the nature of the relations between sculptor and his model, had he even dreamt of them.
>   IRENE. I exposed myself wholly and unreservedly to your gaze [more softly] and never once did you touch me. . . .(CW, 54)

Joyce commends Ibsen for his variety in depicting women, but himself clearly prefers the mystical, spiritual Irene to Rubek's alienated young wife, Maja, whom he describes as "a difficult little person" early in the analysis (CW, 50). Still, he has an appreciation for the note of "free, almost flamboyant life" which she contributes to this play, much as Hilda Wangel does to *The Master Builder*. "Her airy freshness is a breath of keen air" (CW, 65). One suspects that Joyce preferred to inject keen air into society himself, or through a male persona, instead of creating young women characters to do so. Polite middle-class women move in stale conventions, display polished manners, and augur a marriage trap to Stephen in *Stephen Hero*. Only occasionally is a young girl allowed a brief injection of life—the flower-seller in *A Portrait*, Lily with her cynical view of contemporary men in "The Dead," and Dilly Dedalus buying her French primer in *Ulysses*.

James Joyce may have looked to Gerhart Hauptmann for milder versions of the new woman than the ones who figure centrally in Ibsen. James T. Farrell noted years ago that Joyce's women in *Exiles*, in contrast to Ibsen's female characters, lack the inner impulse that allows the mto strive for freedom and a sense of personal worth.[48] Jill Perkins compares Helen of Hauptmann's *Before Sunrise* to Bertha of *Exiles*.[49] Stephen Dedalus, of course, has reveries, not of Hedda

Gabler or Nora Helmer, but of "the girls and women in the plays of Gerhart Hauptmann; and the memory of their pale sorrows and fragrance falling from the wet branches mingled in a mood of quiet joy," memories of them evoked, "as always" by the "rainladen trees in the avenue" (P, 176). Joyce describes Rosa Bernd and her lover emerging from opposite sides of a bush and finds Hauptmann's treatment of Rosa's type "altogether to [his] taste (L II, 163). He would situate Emma Clery of *Stephen Hero*, Mangan's sister of "Araby," and Beatrice of *Exiles* in similar wet surroundings and an aura of fallen shame. He also liked to imagine his life's companion, Nora, in attitudes of sorrow (L I I, 49, 256).The Hauptmann type merges here with the pale, downcast Irish colleen, both lacking the spirit and intelligence of Ibsen's women.

Joyce's female characters do avoid two contemporary ideals of women that George Bernard Shaw warns against in a chapter titled "The Womanly Woman" in *The Quintessence of Ibsenism*. Like Shaw, Joyce repudiates the self-sacrificing, submissive "womanly woman" and questions the ideal of "purity" in human relationships. Interestingly, Shaw attributes both ideals to William Stead, Editor of *The Review of Reviews*, whose image is featured beside the Csar's in the peace rescript scene of *Stephen Hero* (SH, 112), and whose name is mentioned in the analogous scene of *A Portrait* (P, 196). Stead was the hero of Francis Sheehy-Skeffington and his fictional counterpart, MacCann, and his doctrine of "purity" appeared in Sheehy-Skeffington's philosophy, as mentioned above.

The "womanly woman" became a well-known term, surely echoed in Leopold Bloom's appearance as "a finished example of the new womanly man" during one of the hallucinatory passages of the "Circe" chapter of *Ulysses* (U, 493). As Elaine Unkeless has pointed out, this is not one of Bloom's best expressions of androgyny. His "womanly" attitudes at the hands of the manly woman, Bello, include submissiveness, masochism, and willingness to be victimized—the worst aspects of the supposed feminine ideal.[50]

Joyce's most fully developed, realistic portrayal of the womanly woman is Mrs. Dedalus of *Stephen Hero*, *A Portrait*, and *Ulysses*. She offers peace and food, not arguments, for Christmas dinner. She scrubs her college-aged son's neck and ears, and he answers her protest "calmly" with "it gives you pleasure" (P, 175). He vividly recalls her shapely fingers, reddened by the blood of squashed lice from the children's shirts (U, 10). Her threatening aspect after her death results from Stephen's guilt over using her in life and from his unconscious projections. Like most mothers, she was a first authority figure, and may have therefore remained an unconscious threat.[51] She cannot be established as a devouring mother from behavior she has displayed.

Joyce's attack on the "lying drivel about pure men and pure women," referred to earlier in this chapter, has Ibsen as one target, in addition to Joyce's Irish friend, Sheehy-Skeffington (L II, 191-192). Advocacy of "purity" was not in fact limited to Irish nationalists and feminists of Joyce's era. The English feminist Christabel Pankhurst offered two solutions to the problem of venereal disease—votes for women and chastity on the part of men as well as women. Joyce may well have read one rebuttal to this proposal, since it was written by Dora Marsden in the same issue of *The Egoist* that carried the first installment of *A Portrait*.[52] Marsden does not consider the threat of disease strong enough to offset the disadvantages of "purity," which is itself a form of sexual obsession, and creates a "dull" atmosphere akin to "death in life." Paralysis, Joyce might have termed it. Shaw also admits in his "Womanly Woman" chapter that passions do exist and that romantic love only disguises the sexual "appetite" in both sexes.

In *Stephen Hero*, it is McCann who interprets Ibsen as an advocate of purity. According to him, the "teaching of Ibsen" and the "moral of Ghosts" is "self-repression." "—O Jesus! said Stephen in agony. . . . You have connected Ibsen and Eno's fruit salt forever in my mind" (SH, 52). It should be clear that McCann offers an inadequate "moral" for *Ghosts*. Joyce admired Ibsen for his ability to represent the "complexities" of life (CW, 49), and surely *Ghosts* has complexities that McCann does not appreciate. In *Ghosts*, impurity is a problem. The sins (or indulgences) of the father are visited upon the syphilitic artist-son, Osvald. But much of the drama treats sympathetically Mrs. Alving's passion for the misguidedly self-repressed Pastor Manders. Osvald's foreign experiences also suggest that in less provincial parts of the world, young people love freely, responsibly, and happily.

If *Ghosts* bears a warning about the future consequences of sexual freedom, Gerhart Hauptmann's *Before Sunrise* displays a comparable wariness of alcohol in the attitudes of supposed feminist characters. The hero, Loth, as if an amalgamation of Joyce's two activist friends, Sheehy-Skeffington and Thomas Kettle, is a socialist and a student of political economy. Pertaining to the "Woman Question," he declares that his future wife "may ask . . . anything . . . everything that has been denied her sex so many years." He dismisses the barbs of Hoffman (his future brother-in-law) about smoking and trousers for women as "mere trifles." Hoffmann's criticisms are similar to the ones Stephen uses in his confrontations of McCann's feminism in *Stephen Hero*. Loth does still want somewhat of a womanly woman who will sacrifice herself "in so far as I am busy in the life of my work." Finally, he demands purity. She must have "bodily and mental sanity." The latter requirement proves Helen's undoing, since she comes from a family of alcoholics. Loth's decision against marrying her is encouraged by a Dr. Schimmelpfennig. A "Specialist for Diseases of Women," he claims to have dedicated himself to solving the "Woman Question," and asserts that he does not "think badly of woman," only "badly of marriage." The argument against "instinct" or passion as the basis for "life-long marriage" resembles some of Joyce's objections expressed to Stanislaus and Stephen's arguments in favor of a night of free love, posed to Emma Clery in *Stephen Hero* (SH, 198). But Schimmelpfennig seems to have sworn off all attachments in the degenerate society where he is practicing. His disgust and clinical detachment anticipate the celibate Mr. Duffy of "A Painful Case." Jill Perkins also compares Loth's disengagement with Helen to Duffy's fleeing from Mrs. Sinico in the same *Dubliners* story.[53] The issue of women and alcohol is a concern of society in Joyce's story as well as Hauptmann's play. The Doctor's aloof, critical, clinical observations on women seem most suggestive of young Joyce himself, in his medical phase.

George Bernard Shaw questions the institution of marriage in "The Womanly Woman," as do Hauptmann in *Before Sunrise* and Ibsen in numerous dramas, including *Ghosts*, *Rosmersholm*, *The Doll's House*, *Hedda Gabler*, and *When We Dead Awaken*. This is a position which, as we shall see, Stephen assumes in *Stephen Hero*. Joyce, of course, avoided marriage himself, explaining his reasons rather abstractly in letters to Nora, which will be treated in chapter 4.

Joyce makes an especially interesting claim of merit for Ibsen in his review—one that serves to close this chapter.

> Ibsen's knowledge of humanity is nowhere more obvious than in his portrayal of women. He amazes one by his painful introspections; he seems to know them better than they know themselves. Indeed, if one may say so of an eminently virile man, there is a

curious admixture of woman in his nature. His marvellous accuracy, his faint traces of femininity, his delicacy of swift touch, are perhaps attributable to this admixture. But that he knows women is an uncontrovertible fact. (CW, 64)

The editors of *The Critical Writings* compare this to Carl Jung's statement on Joyce's "Penelope" chapter of *Ulysses*: "I suppose the devil's grandmother knows so much about the real psychology of a woman, I didn't" (CW, 64). The congratulations men offer one another for their understanding of women are controvertible. Nora Joyce was not reluctant to challenge Jung's judgment of her husband's knowledge of women (JJ, 629). Joyce's interest in crossing sexual boundaries as a writer is significant, however. There is androgynous potential in Joyce's sense that the male artist may beneficially take on an admixture of the female, as there is in Jung's theories of animus and anima.

It is remarkable that aside from daily experience with Irish feminist women (and this was probably not very intense), most of James Joyce's early education on feminism came from men: Sheehy-Skeffington, Moore, Shaw, Hauptmann, and Ibsen. This is more a comment on Joyce's era than on Joyce. With time, he would meet a second set of feminist women who were more approachable because of his increased maturity and their greater interest in literary, rather than political action.

The Female Family
of Joyce

------------------------------- 4 -------------------------------

□ So-called women's magazines know what to do with the mothers, sisters, wives, and daughters of famous men. They cater to an audience's supposed curiosity about the great male, emphasizing the romantic and sexual aspects of his life, ferreting out secrets about his tastes for food and relaxation, and usually placing their female subject in a decidedly supporting role.[1] Mark Shechner suspects scholars of having related propensities:

> *Ulysses*, like most autobiographical novels that are based on the private lives of artists, solicits our prying. It may be, in fact, that what we honorifically call the critical temper is really a kind of nosiness on our part and fiction is a sort of formalized gossip.[2]

While it makes many positive contributions, Shechner's own extensive Freudian analysis of Joyce's relationship to Mary Jane Murray Joyce and Nora Barnacle Joyce casts them in roles that have become the standards of male-centered Joyce criticism—"virgin," "whore," and "temptress," to which he adds another male projection derived from Jung and Neumann, the "phallic mother."[3]

This chapter strives to consider the women of Joyce's family as much as possible in their own right, as persons, and as part of a female world or tradition. It is essential to work with sensitivity to the problems of achieving these aims and attention to the reasons for such difficulties. Feminist criticism, as the creation, for the most part, of intellectual, middle-class American, English, and Continental

54

women, has had its own biases, and it is only in the last few years
that they have been acknowledged. Joyce's female family tests the
feminist critic by demanding that s/he deal fairly with women whose
lives (probably unlike her or his own) were home-centered; Nora
Barnacle's humble Galway origins offer further tests of class and
cultural biases.

Joyce's female family were what Tillie Olsen calls "silent" women.[4]
Pressed by the demands of an enormous family, or an unconventional
one suited to a sensitive and demanding artist, disinclined to writing
by their socialization, or by inborn personality traits—for whatever
reasons—the female family of James Joyce left few recoverable traces.
We are concerned with Mary Jane (May) Murray Joyce, the mother;
Josephine Murray, an aunt; Nora Barnacle Joyce, the wife; Margaret,
Eileen, May, Eva, Florence, and Mabel Joyce, the sisters; and Lucia
Anna Joyce, the daughter. These women did not use "silence" deliberately, as Joyce had in assuming the triple formula of Stephen
Dedalus: "silence, exile and cunning" (P, 247). It was their nearly
inevitable female heritage. They wrote no diaries that have survived;
very few of their rare letters have been preserved, and they seem
to have had relatively few intimate confidantes to recollect their
inner lives.

There exist a few useful accounts that partially break the silence.
Richard Ellmann arrived on the scene soon enough to interview three
of Joyce's sisters—Eileen, Eva and May—and two of Nora's—Mary
and Kathleen. With the help of Kathleen, he obtained a long, unrestrained and unpunctuated account of Nora's girlhood escapades
from her friend Mary O'Holleran (JJ, 157-159). Stanislaus Joyce's
memoirs reveal strong resentments, particularly of his father, John
Joyce. They display a bewildered adolescent's attitude toward women
and male-female relationships. But they are revealing about the world
of his mother and sisters, including John Joyce's occasional violence
to them (MBK, 35, 56), which the sons tried to prevent. Stanislaus
saw his sisters as individuals and sensed the desperate nature of the
girls' situation following his mother's early death at age 44.[5] Joyce's
niece, Bozena Berta Delimata, has recently published memoirs that
concentrate on Joyce's female family, and are especially illuminating
about the fate of the sisters.[6] Nora and Lucia Joyce have been described by members of the Joyce circle. But loyalty to Joyce has
understandably tempered remarks. Reports cover mainly Joyce-centered social occasions, and not the countless hours his female family

filled while Joyce wrote or met separately with friends. Joyce's sensitivity about Lucia's psychological symptoms imposed its own lasting censorship. Harriet Shaw Weaver considered that Mary Colum's memoirs were rather "injudicious in some details she has given, in particular as to Lucia's illness."[7] Weaver burned much of her correspondence from Paul Léon on this subject and the British Library collection contains her note that she destroyed letters with intimate family news. This eliminated important evidence about the women in Joyce's life, Nora Joyce in particular.

Joyce provides some evidence about the lives of the Joyce women, in letters that have been saved. These display probing interest and concern for their happiness. Joyce's letters are, of course, tricky resource materials, requiring close analysis of his focus and attitude. Joyce's transformation of his essential family women into characters has had its own limiting effects. As May Murray Joyce has become Mrs. Dedalus, she has been loaded with the burdens of a son's Oedipus complex, unshakable guilt, and embitterment.[8] Nora ,as Molly Bloom or ALP, is considered sexually promiscuous or an archetype in the flesh. Lucia, as Issy, has been implicated into patterns of family incest. In effect, the original, living women have been further obscured.

We know very little about Mary Jane (May) Murray Joyce. In his Alphabetical Notebook, James Joyce reconstructs a happy girlhood from the remnants found in a drawer:

> The drawer in her bedroom contained perfumed programmes and old feathers. When she was a girl a birdcage hung in the sunny window of her house. When she was a girl she went to the theatre to see the pantomime . . . and laughed when Old Royce the actor sang. . . .[9]

Some early charm and determination are implied in her ability to attract the reputedly handsome, relatively better-off John Joyce, and her defiance of paternal disapproval to marry him. Stanislaus imagines that a fine young lady preceded the already fading beauty he first knew as a child:

> . . . Mother had little left of what had once made her a figure in drawing-rooms, little except a very graceful carriage and occasional brilliancy at the piano. She had a small, very feminine head, and was pretty. . . . It is in her favour that in the middle of worries in which it is hard to remain gentle or beautiful or noble, Mother's

character was refined as much as Pappie's was debased, and she gained a little wisdom.[10]

Mrs. Joyce had received training in manners and music until the age of nineteen from two aunts, recreated by Joyce in "The Dead" as Julia and Kate Morkhan, whose gifted niece is also named Mary Jane. These same parlor accomplishments were evidently encouraged in Joyce's sisters. Stanislaus remarks on Eileen's "good tuneful contralto" (for which he and brother James even financed a few lessons in 1909 [JJ, 285]), and complains about her practicing the "Rakes of Mallow" on the piano one day when he was ill. The eldest sister, Poppie, he describes as having a "good and strange to say strong touch on the piano."[11] Her music gave Mrs. Joyce an activity to share, first with her tenor husband, and then with her children, particularly James. John Joyce seems from Stanislaus Joyce's accounts to have rather enjoyed showing off his voice and his dancing and to have ignored his wife on some social occasions (MBK, 381). Mrs. Joyce certainly lingers behind Mrs. Dedalus, who "played on the piano the sailor's hornpipe for [Stephen] to dance," (P, 7)—another subordination of female talent for male show. May Dedalus occasionally accompanied James' singing in the Sheehys' parlor gatherings.[12] On the back of a letter sent from Paris, Joyce copied for her the music of a Pierre Loti air, " Upa-Upa."It is unclear whether this was intended to mitigate the tone of an otherwise rather severe missive, as Ellmann suggests (L II, 30, 30 n.2), or whether Joyce simply wanted her to learn it (L II, 21-22), perhaps to accompany his singing. Music could be a loving gesture toward his mother. He sang "Who goes with Fergus" to his own accompaniment as she lay dying (JJ, 135-36).

Mary Jane Joyce also entered into her son's academic and artistic life. Stanislaus recalls his brother's habit of having her test him on his lessons, even into his teen-age years (MBK, 45). Her own early intellectual bent may be reflected in Mrs. Daedalus' revelation in *Stephen Hero* that she "once read all kinds of new plays," but gave them up when her husband did not share her interest (SH, 85-87). Amid their adolescent demands for love and respect, Joyce's letters home from Paris also hint of interests shared by the two of them, somewhat exclusive of the rest of the family: "I hope that you will write to me and if you do write also about the things that interest us" (L II, 26; Jan. 25, 1903). But Mrs. Joyce's letters accept intellectual inferiority on her part. She writes, apparently repeating Joyce's own evaluation, ". . . as you so often said I am stupid and cannot grasp the great thoughts that are yours much as I desire to do so" (JJ, 114).

Into his naturalistic masterpiece, *Dubliners*, and the at-home scenes of *A Portrait* and *Ulysses*, Joyce infused the all-too-typical problems of urban Irish Catholic households like his own: a long procession of births, a pious and compliant mother, and a garrulous, frequently drunken, free-spending father figure. Describing his early family life in a letter to Nora, Joyce attempts the analytical frame of the social scientist, but emerges as a rebel against the "system." His mother plays the central role of victim in the summary and may have been the impetus for his social rebellion:

> My mind rejects the whole present social order and Christianity—home, the recognized virtues, classes of life, and religious doctrines. How could I like the idea of home? My home was simply a middle-class affair ruined by spendthrift habits which I have inherited. My mother was slowly killed, I think, by my father's ill-treatment, by years of trouble, and by my cynical frankness of conduct. When I looked on her face as she lay in her coffin—a face grey and wasted with cancer—I understood that I was looking on the face of a victim and I cursed the system which had made her a victim. We were seventeen in family. My brothers and sisters are nothing to me. One brother alone is capable of understanding me. (L II, 48; Aug. 29, 1904)

"Home" as Joyce knew it from his early family life—especially from his adolescence onward—was indeed a net to fly by, but the family members most needing escape were the ones least likely to achieve it: the women. There had been some reasonably happy years when the family lived graciously at Bray, and a growing tribe of children was tended in a nursery and surrounded by servants and nursemaids, in good Victorian style. There had been Mrs. Conway (Dante) to assist with the early education of the children, available because she had been deserted by an opportunistic spouse. John Joyce tried to avoid his wife's relations, thereby depriving her of some of the richness of typical female Irish family life. Still Josephine Murray, her brother's wife, managed to become an essential resource for May Joyce and her children. Although the high style of the first years did not continue, Mrs. Joyce remained a patient, competent, self-sacrificing wife and mother. She bore thirteen children. Three

of them, among them her firstborn, a son, did not survive infancy;
two died at age fourteen. Stanislaus describes the quality of his mother's relationship to each of the children:

> An ever-watchful anxiety for her children, a readiness to sacrifice
> herself to them utterly, and a tenacious energy to endure for their
> sakes replaced love in a family not given to shows of affection. She
> was very gentle to her children though [sic] she understood them
> each. It is understanding and not love that makes confidence be-
> tween Mother and children so natural though unacknowledged, so
> unreserved though nothing is confessed (there is no need of words
> or looks between them, the confidence that surrounds them like
> the atmosphere). Rather it is this understanding that makes love
> so enduring.[13]

Like James, Stanislaus uses the word "love" with difficulty, but finally
his mother's anxiety, sacrifice, understanding and confidence amount
to enduring love. In death "for the first time . . . she had the importance that should always have been hers," Stanislaus decides.[14]

Although May Joyce was undoubtedly an important figure to her
children and although there were more females than males in the
household, [15] the family Joyce grew up in was decidedly male-centered. John Joyce wielded the power and was indulged in his wishes
by his angelic wife. With the partial exception of James, who is
usually considered his father's son (JJ, 22; MBK, 57), John's children,
especially Stanislaus, present a very negative picture of the family's
patriarch.[16] John Joyce's character and habits of spending, drinking,
engaging in invective, and holding grudges created many victims,
most of them women. A spoiled only child, as Stanislaus reports, he
had adored his spendthrift, handsome father and carried on a "By-
ronic" relationship with his mother, whom he dropped from his life
after his marriage (MBK, 24, 32). His temper and sobriety degen-
erated as the bright prospects of his family background and personal
charm faded. Stanislaus reports the darkest moments. Once, in a
drunken stupor, John Joyce attempted to strangle his wife (MBK,
57), and near the end, he raged at the slowly dying woman, "If you
can't get well, die. Die and be damned with you" (MBK, 233). After
her death, he shifted the verbal and even physical abuse to his most
available victims—usually the youngest children, all female (JJ, 144).
John Joyce had, from the start, adored James. He lavished both his
verbal approval and the early stages of a fine education upon him.
This came at the expense of the other children, both emotionally

and educationally. Though sisters outnumbered brothers, the boys had an advantage in birth order. Margaret ("Poppie"), the second surviving child, was the only female among the oldest five children. Stanislaus makes a strong case for the injustice Poppie suffered, even at the hands of her mother, who seems to have vented her frustrations upon this daughter instead of attacking their more obvious masculine and cultural sources:

> Mother's treatment of Poppie is unjust, not nearly so unjust but of the same kind as Pappie's treatment of her, and perhaps due a little unconsciously to that example. These women of Nirvana who accept their greatest trials with resignation, letting worries be heaped like ashes on their heads and hoping only in one thing— their power to live them down, vent themselves in irritability about ridiculous annoyances. . . . Mother's temper was only lately of this kind . . . and . . . was directed against Poppie from a habit begun when Poppie was young and very obstinate.[17]

Ironically, it was Poppie who assumed May Joyce's burdens after her death, learning to pry funds out of her father and securing a place for her younger sisters in a national school on Mountjoy Street, supervised by Sisters of Charity. In all of this, John Joyce gave her "no help, but abuse."[18] Stanislaus Joyce is clearly troubled by Poppie's "hopeless life," like his own in its being "without purpose and without interest." He sees her in "a forced virginity," despite the fact that she has "a woman's attractiveness."[19] Poppie seems to have been as determined a Catholic as her mother, and when it became possible to send one of the sisters to Trieste to be with James's family, she chose the pious Eva over the youngest sister, Mabel, probably considering her a better influence for her brother (JJ, 285).

In his diary, Stanislaus lavishes the greatest attention upon James, and writes at some length about his younger brothers, the beloved Georgie and the bungling Charles. He is less expansive about his sisters but offers sketches of each one. Poppie is usually analyzed for her sense of duty and clearly seems a victim of circumstance. May (the third sister) merits his highest regard. She avoids heavy household labor and seems unlikely to remain a Catholic. May has "an observant sense of humor," which she even directs at priests. Of all the girls "she is the only one who has any intellectual curiosity." Stanislaus senses her maturing as a self-conscious process he calls "beginning to live."[20]

Joyce's proclamation to Nora that "my brothers and sisters are nothing to me" is undoubtedly an exaggeration, used partially to fend off guilt over leaving them in dire need. In casual jesting with friends, Joyce would speak of "my twenty-three sisters" (JJ, 44). The possibly more caring Stanislaus reacts with a sense of injustice to the fact that James "always had an ascendancy over the girls of the family because of his cleverness, his talents, his good looks and that even temper which was in striking contrast to mine" (MBK, 237).

James Joyce eventually used several of his sisters as sources for literature. May probably contributed to the intellectually curious Dilly Dedalus of *Ulysses* (who is named for one of Nora's sisters). The name "Isabel" may be borrowed from one of the middle names of Eileen Joyce, though Eileen seems to have had a great deal more humor and spirit than the fictional Isabel. Stephen's thoughts about Isabel's hopelessness in *Stephen Hero* come straight from Stanislaus's diary account of Poppie. That Joyce discovered the importance of his sisters as material through Stanislaus was hardly unusual; he readily admitted that some of his best ideas came from his younger sibling. Joyce also uses Poppie's situation to create "Eveline," who copes with younger children and an irascible father after her mother's death. Oddly enough, Poppie, rather like the priest in the faded photograph in "Eveline" who is said to have emigrated to Melbourne, became a nun and removed to New Zealand. It is worth remarking that Joyce follows her no farther. He never makes positive use of nuns, though they represent a powerful female force in Ireland. In the "Circe" chapter of *Ulysses*, the nymph that threatens Bloom is portrayed in the guise of a nun, and it is recalled that a nun was the inventor of barbed wire (U, 553). Joyce seems to resist seeing female celibacy as a solution to family problems or seeing the church as a refuge for women.

Two of Joyce's youngest sisters, Eva and Florence, remained single and lived together in Dublin. Eileen and May both married, had three children each, and were widowed early. All four worked in clerical positions for the remainder of their lives to support their children and themselves.[21] Their stories are anticipated by "Clay" and "The Sisters" in *Dubliners*. But the experiences of the working mother and the woman outside the home, especially in the workplace, are never depicted in Joyce's works.

Both Stanislaus and James Joyce regretted the Irishwoman's supposed alliance with the Catholic Church, and wished that May Joyce had rebelled, not just against the verbal and physical brutality of her husband, but also against the control exercised over her by her confessor (MBK, 36, 231, 234-5). "My mother had become for my brother the type of the woman who fears and, with weak insistence and disapproval, tries to hinder the adventures of the spirit. Above all she had become for him the Irishwoman, the accomplice of the Irish Catholic Church, which he called the scullery-maid of Christendom, the accomplice, that is to say, of a hybrid form of religion produced by the most unenlightened features of Catholicism under the inevitable influence of English Puritanism. . ." (MBK, 238). In *Ulysses* and the close of *A Portrait*, Stephen expresses resentment of his mother's submission to the priest, but chiefly for its impact upon his life, not hers.

Stanislaus Joyce notes that his brother appeared to be less affected by scenes of family brutality than himself. But he suggests that family problems were pervasive in their culture, and that this had its effect upon his brother's earliest fiction:

> Half hushed-up stories reached us of somewhat similar things happening in the families of friends of ours whose material position, at least, was assured. . .; poverty cannot, therefore, have been the roots of the evil. The main struggle of the various Mrs. This-bodies and Mrs. That-bodies . . . was to conceal carefully what went on at home, but not more than a couple of years later it became his set purpose to reveal it. (MBK, 56)

It is interesting that Stanislaus sees the silencing mission as a female one, perhaps again focusing upon woman as victim, as he clearly does with his mother and Poppie. He goes on to mention that James Joyce's first stories, written in his school days, were "Silhouettes." The title suggests both an art of shadows, displayed in the parlor, and the vague forms that play upon the window, behind drawn shades. The one sample that Stanislaus recalls concerns a domestic squabble, where "the burly figure of a man, staggering and threatening with upraised fist, and the smaller sharp-faced figure of a woman" are silhouetted upon a window blind. A blow is struck. There are also children caught in the unhappy situation, their heads later silhouetted as their mother warns them not to waken the father (MBK, 56, 90).

Joyce's later *Dubliners* stories frequently deal with unhappy marriages in a largely off-stage fashion. The Conroys' marriage in "The Dead" seems perfectly happy until very late in the story, when Gretta weeps over the memory of her lost lover—a crisis which forces Gabriel to revise his whole view of himself and their relationship.[22] Other stories offer more obviously inadequate marriage partners than Gabriel. In "Eveline," we look back at the Hills' marriage as echoed in Eveline's experience. We visit the Chandler and Farrington homes after viewing the public lives of the husbands. We recollect with Mrs. Mooney the dissolution of her marriage to her father's foreman and look forward to the Dorans' unpromising future in "The Boarding House." Mrs. Kernan of "Grace" had found "a wife's lot irksome" and, though "there were worse husbands" had apparently experience a "violent" spouse when her boys were younger (D, 156). The blame for these tragedies cannot simply rest upon the male figures. The Chandlers have different fantasies of a happy life—Chandler's centering upon modest artistic acclaim; Annie's, upon the popular media's concept of house beautiful. Both are delusions in which one spouse fails to participate. The Farringtons have a relationship summarized by Joyce's authorial remark in "Counterparts": "His wife was a little sharp-faced woman who bullied her husband when he was sober and was bullied by him when he was drunk" (D, 97). The Mooneys of "The Boarding House" evidently had problems with alcohol and bullying like those in "Silhouettes" and "Counterparts." Being a strong personality, however, Mrs. Mooney had obtained a separation from her husband. It was a measure that May Joyce had also considered.

The "sharp-faced" women of "Silhouettes" and "Counterparts" may show again a debt to Stanislaus's observations of women. Stanislaus detects in his diary "a sharp look" in Katsy, the cousin admired first by James and then by Stanislaus: "This look is common in a certain class and I dislike it most in woman." Stanislaus goes on to detect the look in actress Marie Walker, slightly in his own mother, and oppressively and constantly in a neighbor, whom he avoids at all costs.[23] Although the responsibility for the difficulties in their parents' marriage was largely John Joyce's, both brothers sensed sources of trouble in women as well. After two years with Nora, Joyce would write Stanislaus, "I am no friend of tyranny, as you know, but if many husbands are brutal the atmosphere in which they live (vide Counterparts) is brutal and few wives and homes can satisfy the desire for happiness" (L II, 192).

Joyce had expressed a more positive view of family to his mother, which was an indirect affirmation of her role and a manifestation of his dedication to the family theme that would culminate in *Finnegans Wake*: "... no one that has raised up a family has failed utterly in my opinion. You understand this, I think" (L II, 39; March 20, 1903). Though Stephen Dedalus resolutely defies his mother's Catholic religion and pious devotions at the end of *A Portrait*, and though he smashes the haunting image of her in her graveclothes in *Ulysses*, it is important to detach these fictions from Joyce's actual behaviors, feelings, and motivations toward May Joyce. That he termed her a "victim" in his letter to Nora suggests that Joyce felt little personal bitterness toward her after her painful, early death at the age of forty-four. That she died a victim of personal, economic, and social circumstances is an indisputable assessment, but also a partial one that may obscure personally-viewed successes that escaped her son's appreciation.

James Joyce took all of Dublin by surprise when in 1904 he fell quite frankly and somewhat awkwardly in love with Nora Barnacle, a young woman from Galway who was working in Finn's Hotel. Miss Barnacle's willingness to respond to the young man who encountered her on Nassau Street was characteristic of the adventurous temperament recalled by her best Galway friend, Mary O'Holleran. As girls, Nora and Mary had "pinched" candies of various descriptions, gone out at night dressed up in men's clothing, and participated in practical jokes. There had been a strong interest in forecasting the boys they would marry, which was assisted by the ancient rituals and charms still prevalent in the lively folk culture of the west of Ireland:

> ... We would fill our mouths with wheat and then go round the house listening at the doors to hear if a boys name mentioned as he would be our supposed future husband and we would burst out laughing and run like the dickens for fear the boys would catch us but they could never catch us we would then go to another house and buy a pennyworth of pins we would stick 9 pins into the red part of the apple and throw the 10th pin away we would put the apple with the pins in, in our left foot stocking and tie it with our right foot garter and put it under our head when we would go to bed to dream of our future husband. (JJ, 158)

Such divination would appear in Joyce's works—in "Clay" where a game of fortunes is played on All Hallows Eve and in *Ulysses*, where Molly considers her romantic future with the aid of tarot cards. Nora's previous walking out with a young Protestant named Willie Mulvey had led to "a bad beating" by her uncle Tommy Healy, of whom

Nora was "terribly afraid." Her removal to Dublin shortly after seems to have been an effort to escape his paternal control. She wrote Mary, "here I am in Dublin and my uncle Tommy won't follow me any more" (JJ, 159).

That James would unite with a young woman in 1904 was the last thing that his brother Stanislaus seemed to expect in the diary entries of early that year. Stanislaus himself shows great responsiveness to the manners and appearance of several young women—his cousin Katsy Murray, Mary Sheehy (his brother's former interests), and even Hanna Sheehy-Skeffington. But he finds his brother a "prig" about women. The indecent talk he records befits a Buck Mulligan, and may have been encouraged by Mulligan's original, Oliver St. John Gogarty, James Joyce's frequent companion during that period. "He talks of them as soft-skinned animals. 'That one'd give you a great push.' 'She's very warm between the thighs, I fancy.' 'She has great action, I'm sure.' " A remnant of this attitude survives in *Stephen Hero*, where the girls of Dublin are referred to as "marsupials" (SH, 176, 210), an emblem which suggests stupidity, but also may evoke womb structure in the marsupial's pouch. James Joyce also told Stanislaus he had "an instinct for women." But Stanislaus has observed, in attending social evenings with his brother, that despite the fact that "they flatter him with pressing attention," the "wise virgins" of their middle-class society "will not meet him on the highways alone, nor will they marry him."[24] Nora is described in Stanislaus's diary: "Miss Barnacle has a very pretty manner, but the expression on her face seems to me a little common. She has magnificent hair." He also reports that "she calls [Jim] 'my love,' though he is not a clerk."[25] By late August, Stanislaus despairs at his brother's amorous and perhaps too common, clerk-like responses, "I never saw Jim manage any affair so badly as he has managed his affair with Miss Barnacle."[26]

Joyce's early letters to Nora Barnacle are better read than quoted here. He too admired her "magnificent hair," mentioning in his first note, "I looked for a long time at a head of reddish-brown hair and decided it was not yours," and soon calling her "dear little brown head" (L II, 42-43).[27] He soon moved on to the more intimate region of her stays and the mischievous demand that she leave them off (L II, 43-44). Nora Barnacle not only met and walked with Joyce, she treated him as "my love" and not as my genius, demonstrating a lively and real instinct for the man. It seems from later correspondence that, in the course of their walks from Merrion Square to Ringsend, Jim Joyce and Nora Barnacle probably went as far physically as Harry Mulvey and Molly Tweedy did in Molly's recorded memories of *Ulysses* (SL, 159; U, 760). Nora may have felt some uneasiness about this physical intimacy, which Joyce tried to dispel (L II, 44). Joyce went through both literary and philosophic struggles in their correspondence. As Ellmann notes (JJ, 159), he apparently worried over how to sign himself and whether to use the word "love." In keeping with Ibsen, or challenged by social revolutionaries like the feminist Sheehy-Skeffington, Joyce tried to spell out the terms of their future together. He visualized himself as a combatant against the establishment, with a new code of honesty in male-female relationships:

> It seemed to me that I was fighting a battle with every religious and social force in Ireland for you and that I had nothing to rely on but myself. There is no life here—no naturalness or honesty. People live together in the same houses all their lives and at the end they are as far apart as ever. Are you sure you are not under any misapprehension about me? Remember that any question you ask me I shall answer honourably and truly. But if you have nothing to ask I shall understand you also. The fact that you can choose to stand beside me in this way in my hazardous life fills me with great pride and joy. (L II, 53; Sept. 16, 1904)

Nora had trouble comprehending the revolutionary manifestoes contained in some of Joyce's love letters (L II, 53; Sept.12, l904). The usual theme of her letters was her loneliness in his absence. What Ellmann has taken for "self-possession" may have been bafflement, tolerated for the sake of love, on her part (JJ, 159).

Once they were living together in Pola and then Trieste, Joyce began to learn more about Nora's past and to generalize from her to womankind—observations which he typically reported to his younger brother back in Dublin. Nora had fended off a cleric, who suggested that she tell her confessor, "it was a man not a priest." "Useful difference," comments the anti-clerical Joyce to his equally anti-clerical brother (L II, 72). He reacts matter-of-factly to Nora's meetings with Mulvey. "She says she didn't love him and simply went to pass the time." But he is outraged at the brutality of her uncle's efforts to prevent the meetings:

> She was opposed at home and this made her persist. Her uncle got on the track. Every night he would be at home before her. "Well,

my girl, out again with your Protestant." Forbade her to go any
more. She went. When she came home uncle was there before
her. Her mother was ordered out of the room (Papa of course was
away) and uncle proceeded to thrash her with a big walking-stick.
She fell on the floor fainting and clinging about his knees. At this
time she was nineteen! Pretty little story, eh? (L II, 72-73; Dec.
3, 1904)

The relation of the story again shows Joyce's repugnance to family
violence. Nora's uncle is represented as brutal, authoritarian, and
perhaps even lecherous, in the absence of "Papa." Joyce recognizes
and admires the persistence in Nora's character that made her defy
the uncle. The same quality may have enabled her to elope with
him. Sympathy with the female side of the Barnacle family is also
visible in a card he wrote to Nora in 1909 from "your mother's
house" in Galway, addressing her as "my dear little runaway Nora":
"I have been here all day talking with her and I see she is my darling's
mother and I like her very much" (L II, 240). Nora's mother had
separated from her hard-drinking husband, perhaps showing greater
strength than May Joyce. In his ability to charm and get along with
his mother-in-law, Joyce had precedent in his own father, who had
received the blessings of Mary Jane Murray's mother.

Nora Joyce's first few years as "the companion" were difficult, and
the strain on her is apparent in Joyce's reports to Stanislaus and Aunt
Josephine. When she met Joyce, Nora Barnacle had already begun
her removal from the familiar surroundings of Galway and from a
troubled family. But life in Pola and Trieste meant an end to easy
female companionship and even to conversation with more than a
few people. Almost immediate pregnancy deprived her of her usually
excellent health and high spirits; she entered the physical and emotional transformations of maternity with no preparation and little
support from female society.

In a letter to Stanislaus in July 1905, Joyce describes the rudeness
of Triestines to Nora—their sniggering at her "short four crown skirt,"
hair style, and "distorted body"—her inability to purchase necess-
ities without his help, her fatigue in the one hundred degree heat,
and her crying spells. "She has nobody to talk to but me and, heroics
left aside, this is not good for a woman." When we read his description of her as "really very helpless and unable to cope with any kind
of difficulties," we should remember that Joyce himself was at the
time depressed and that Nora was being severely stressed by her

new environment and physical state. Joyce also makes the frank admission, "As a matter of fact I know very little about women and you, probably, know less." He sends Stanislaus to the family wise woman, "Aunt Josephine who knows more than either of us." Joyce also considers the idea typically offered to young couples that one of the pair is not worthy of the other. He had earlier sought his sisters' opinions of Nora from Stanislaus and reports that one of the Berlitz English teachers thought Nora unworthy of him, but refuses to enter into the "self-stultification" involved in forming such a verdict. Still, had the judgment really offended his own sense of things, he might not have mentioned it to Stanislaus. Implied here is the possibility that he might have found another woman who would have coped as well as he. Another, chauvinistic notion that he entertains is that women really are inferior at coping with the world. He confides to Stanislaus, "After all, it is only Skeffington, and fellows like him, who think that woman is man's equal" (L II, 93-96).

Joyce hoped for himself and Nora that "we may live happily," avoiding the extreme of Harriet Shelley's "douche in the Serpentine," and the more typical, but equally abhorrent, "spectre" of "mutual tolerance" offered by Aunt Josephine (L II, 96). In 1906 Joyce rejected a German bank clerk's formula for a wife: "She should be able to cook well, to sew, to housekeep, and to play at least one musical instrument" (L II, 157). Although, during his later travels, he occasionally wrote home with orders to Nora regarding furnishings, food, and her grooming, especially when he was planning for visitors, Joyce's ideal of mutual happiness was to prove consistent, and to be more important than the functions performed by either partner.

Despite its placing further limits on Nora Joyce's freedom, the birth of Giorgio Joyce in late July 1905 seems to have cleared the air briefly for the couple. In Ireland it became Joyce's (not Nora's) personal triumph among his family and friends (most of them young, unsettled men). In his letters, Joyce is extremely eager to have news of Skeffington, maybe because he now feels that he has vindicated himself, disproving the feminist's dire predictions about Nora's future. Perhaps with Skeffington still in mind, he makes the egalitarian statement, "I think a child should be allowed to take his father's or mother's name at will on coming of age" (L II, 108) (a notion he failed to resurrect twenty-one years later). As noted earlier, Joyce tells Stanislaus that he wants his feminist friend to be his son's god-father (L II,), but this is either a joke or another unpursued idea.

Nora's problems in adjusting to the dual burdens of James Joyce and motherhood were still evident in letters written some months after Giorgio's birth. Joyce was moved to tell Aunt Josephine, "I imagine the present relations between Nora and myself are about to suffer some alteration" (L II, 128). In assessing himself as a spouse he admits, "I daresay I am a difficult person for any woman to put up with but on the other hand I have no intention of changing." He feels that Nora should realize the difference between him and "the rest of the men she has known." He is "not a very domestic animal." He supposes he is an artist and fantasizes that he has (or had) "every talent to live" a "free and happy life." If so, he had not demonstrated this in Paris in 1902-1903. But Joyce is not too hasty. He waits for better understanding, not wishing "to rival the atrocities of the average husband." Making allowances for other people (Nora in this instance) was an unaccustomed, wearying burden, but one which would prove invaluable (L II, 128-1 29). Hélène Cixous has seen another side of this story and suggests that Joyce was having even greater difficulties than Nora in adjustment to marriage—an institution that his Dublin experiences had taught him to fear. Cixous suspects him of typical paternal jealousy of his new offspring and an additional artist's sense of rivalry between the child (to whom Nora was devoted) and his works (to which she was indifferent). Cixous is also suspicious of Joyce's rejection of convention:

> He needs always to feel free, within a certain constancy; and it is necessary for Nora to be always a woman met casually, to remain like a little blue flower one picks after the rainstorm. Joyce must eliminate "duties" and "rights," so that she may never be able to call upon the occult powers of the Church or of motherhood. Nora has to be as submissive, within the framework of this imitation freedom whose yoke she alone bears, as May Joyce was to John.[28]

Despite Joyce's revolutionary professions against marriage ceremonies and his criticisms of conventional husbands, his life with Nora was in practice not so different from the conventional bourgeois norm, as Cixous has detected. The bachelor Frank Budgen concurred.[29]

Aunt Josephine did respond indirectly to James's troubled letter, and to many other diverse pleas from her gifted nephew. With maternal fondness and belief, she carried out the opposite role to the artist's selfish one; like May Murray Joyce, her motto was *serviam*. Aunt Josephine sent everything from patterns for baby clothes to copies of *The United Irishman* to the Joyces in Trieste. Unfortunately, though many letters from her are mentioned in Joyce's correspondence, only one is available in published form. Josephine Murray is reported to have written Nora a "kind letter" just before Giorgio's arrival, and is the only family member noted to send Nora a special "Bravo" upon the birth (L II, 100, 102). In the one published letter of June 1906, Aunt Josephine clearly sides with Jim in the continuing family difficulties:

> . . . I cant understand Nora surely it is a monstrous thing to expect Jim to cook or mind the Baby when he is doing his utmost to support both of them surely she can make as good an attempt as Jim it seems very soon for her to be so disappointed I wonder does she know what it is to be with a person with a scurrelous [sic] tongue from which you are never safe there is some excuse for Jim drinking it is the old story of finding forgetfulness. (L II, 138-139)

Aunt Josephine has seen worse men (her own husband was one of the models for Farrington of "Counterparts") and has a conventional notion of male-female roles. Nora could expect little sympathy from her. Aunt Josephine's letters offered more than advice, however. They would become an important literary model, as did other unlikely writings for Joyce.

Aunt Josephine's run-on sentences resemble Molly Bloom's diction in the "Penelope" chapter of *Ulysses* and indeed are typical of the slightly educated women in Joyce's family. Nora writes similarly, as many have noted in connection with Molly, and Mary O'Holleran's account of Nora's youth, written down by Kathleen Barnacle Griffin, has the same feature. Joyce generalized in a letter to Stanislaus, "Do you notice how women when they write disregard stops and capital letters?" (L II, 173). The remark is prompted by an interpolated note to Stanislaus from Nora. After one has read a number of letters displaying this fluid style, a certain appropriateness asserts itself. The long sentence quoted in part above is not the only sentence in Aunt Josephine's letter, but it does isolate her impressions about what Nora can expect in her relationship with Jim. Shorter, less complicated ideas receive more stops in both Aunt Josephine's and Nora's letters: "I would like to write to Jim but I dont know what to say to him." or "You must be tired of me now and I hope both you and I will have better news next time" (L II, 139). Nora Joyce does not seem to have liked letter writing nearly as much as Aunt Josephine, but she kept up amenities with Joyce's friends, especially when he was incapacitated by illness. Her most routine letters expressing thanks for a courtesy extended or reporting the nature of an illness are punctuated fairly conventionally. This might lead one to suspect that she had benefitted from her husband's educating, or perhaps only from his editing over the years. Yet as late as 1930, in a letter to Harriet Weaver, Nora Joyce was still using her own rules of punctuation. She begins with two long but end-stopped sentences expressing sympathy about the illness of Miss Weaver's sister-in-law and comparing her surgery, from which she had a lasting improvement. Nora then launches into a lengthy personal and domestic unit about the rigors of Miss Weaver's winter, the mild weather she has been experiencing, and her delight at escaping from housekeeping for morning walks in the *bois*. The main housekeeping burden is serving afternoon teas to the many men who come to assist Joyce with revisions. These related subjects call for flow, rather than punctuation. She surfaces for a period at the mention of another specific individual, Stuart Gilbert, who is remarkable for his consumption of tea cakes.[30]

Mary Jane Joyce's letters to her son also featured run-on sentences. These were most apt to occur in the personal sections, parts of her letters that were (by her own description) "simply talking just as we would do at the fire here" (L II, 33). That this style was self-consistent and worthy of his own artistic use was one of Joyce's most important discoveries from his female family.[31]

The crisis of the first years passed in the Joyces' relationship. Joyce's sisters Eva and Eileen were brought to Trieste, largely as company for Nora. Eileen's daughter reports that Nora, being "still conscious . . . of the fact that she and Jim had been 'spliced by the blacksmith of Gretna Green,' not formally married . . . welcomed companionship" (see FW, 212.10). Mutual fondness may be found in the fact that Eileen named her second child Nora. Nora seems also to have gained confidence. She no longer felt that she was being talked about. Her niece suggests that "Aunt Nora had developed a discriminating taste, and her interesting life with Uncle Jim had broadened her mind."[32] For his part, Joyce learned to be amused by Nora's sayings and doings. He tells Stanislaus about her ability to blow huge soap bubbles with the one-year-old Giorgio, and accepts the fact that she will never share his form of culture, education and initiative, though he had probably hoped at first that she would. He interpolates Nora's one-sentence letter about Giorgio's acquisition of appetite, teeth, and singing voice and observes:

> You will see from this interpolated letter the gigantic strides which Nora has made towards culture and emancipation. The evening before last I found her stitching together skins of apples. She also asked me to teach her geography! (L II, 173)

Although he had expected the opposite, Joyce became a fairly domestic man, working in a room at home instead of withdrawing to a separate work realm, as most men did and do. He was not one to get on the floor and blow bubbles with children, and he was intolerant of their noise. But he did play games with his small nieces, and was less formal than Stanislaus with them.[33] In the final years of his life, he would qualify as "the most memorable man" in the life of his grandson, Stephen, to whom he recounted tirelessly the same myths that ran throughout his works.[34] Hélène Cixous's likening Joyce's marital arrangement to John Joyce's is too simplistic. Though Joyce's home style posed its own severe limits and implied his superiority, Joyce avoided the atmosphere of brutality experienced in his father's house and represented in many of the families of *Dubliners*.

While Nora became more independent after their first year, she continued to receive Joyce's help in their domestic affairs—the seeking of food, flats and clothing, the making of appointments, and hopeful plans for their children's careers. Nora seems to have been a careful housekeeper, despite Joyce's messes of paper and ink. She prepared many teas, but few dinners. She wrote requisite letters when Joyce's health prevented him from doing so. But she did this reluctantly; she was not to be made literary. While Nora went along with Joyce, she maintained her own set of rules and world priorities—to his eternal fascination. Even the most discreet of the inner circle around Joyce seem to have delighted in the couple's differences—Nora's charm and warmth beside Joyce's formality, her occasional outburst against his attitudes, and her habitual undercutting of his foibles.

The erotic love letters Joyce wrote to Nora in 1909 were first published in unexpurgated form in 1975 (in *Selected Letters of James Joyce*). One thing they disclose is that Nora was not a reluctant sexual partner. She had in fact initiated genital contact "long ago at Ringsend"—the site of their early walks in the summer of 1904. Joyce also recalls fondly that she had sought the active coital position during their early days together in Pola (SL, 182). In many ways, Nora's inclinations seem the fulfillment of male erotic fantasies. Joyce was eager to improve upon the past when he returned to Trieste, after his visits to Dublin, and had a multitude of fantastic suggestions for Nora, which he later reused in *Ulysses*. It may be an extension of Joyce's religious and social rebellion that he likes to combine in his imagination Nora's saintly expressions or little-girl innocence with "dirty," "naughty," or "animal" behaviors.

Although Joyce had cautioned in 1909, "Our children (much as I love them) *must not* come between us" (L II, 242), Nora appears to have remained quite devoted to them.[35] Her report to Stanislaus about Giorgio's growth is touched with fondness. A letter she wrote to Eileen Joyce from Galway in 1912 reveals her enthusiasm for visiting family and her pride in her children, particularly Lucia who looked "rosey," charmed her grandfather Joyce, and persisted in singing in various locations, according to her mother's report (L II, 302-303). It was a cruel twist of fate that, when Lucia became afflicted by schizophrenia in her mid-twenties, she occasionally turned on her mother, while she remained more dedicated to her father. It was a belated exaggeration, of course, of a preferential attitude displayed by many adolescent daughters toward their fathers. Although James Joyce was deeply affected by Lucia's illness (which he described as "heart-pilfering");[36] and sought gifts, projects and medical treatments to alleviate it, it was Nora who bore the brunt, Nora who managed her tedious daily care and suffered her disheartening outbursts; she felt "deep maternal distress" over Lucia long after Joyce's death.[37] Lucia recalled their relationship positively in memoirs she wrote in 1961. "She was like a sister to me and we were the best of friends. She never scolded me and allways (sic) wanted me to be happy and have a good time."[38]

Nora Joyce paid a price in isolation and experience for the unique and often happy companionship she had with James Joyce. Their mutual dependency in maturity is evident in Joyce's need to remain with Nora throughout her hospitalization and operation for cancer in 1928 (JJ, 607). Nora Joyce's happiness seems to have ended with her husband's death. In a letter to Harriet Weaver in December 1941 Giorgio reports that his mother sees no one and "spends most of her time going to the cemetery.''[39] In October 1947 (nearly seven years after Joyce's death), Maria Jolas writes to Miss Weaver that ''almost [Nora's] only interest'' is in ''the books and articles now being written,'' and expresses her own opinion, ''after all, he did so entirely dominate all their lives, didn't he?''[40]

From birth, Lucia Joyce was overshadowed by the unpredictable irregularities that became a norm of the Joyces' existence. The family was overwhelmed with debts and Joyce was confined to a hospital with rheumatic fever when Nora presented herself at the paupers' ward of a Trieste hospital to give birth. In striking contrast with the much-heralded arrival of Giorgio, this event barely went noticed. A second son would not necessarily have been better received. But Stanislaus had remarked upon Giorgio's birth, ''I am very glad it is a son and so I suppose are you'' (L II, 102). Lucia's childhood development was interrupted repeatedly by the family's moves between flats, countries, and languages. The Joyces' emotional energies would be sapped incessantly by Joyce's crises over money, publishing difficulties, bad reviews, and personality clashes; most taxing were his illnesses and eye operations, many of which Lucia reported patiently in letters to friends like Miss Weaver, letters that contained much of her father and little of herself. As is also Nora's case following her liaison with Joyce, there are few traces of Lucia's having long or deep friendships with women; to date, there are no accounts of Lucia by her contemporaries.

Lucia Joyce's identity, from her twenties until her death in December 1982 was further obscured by mental illness and its various treatments. Her responsiveness in interviews varied greatly over the years. At times, her recollections seemed clear, and she was capable of responding to questions about her youthful interests. Sometimes she seemed to test the wits of the interviewer.[41] Her guardian, Jane Lidderdale (who inherited her charge from her godmother, Harriet Weaver), made it a policy to cultivate Miss Joyce ''for herself, as an individual,''[42] and this effort seems to have met with some success over the years of her confinement at St. Andrew's in Northampton, England. Lucia Joyce differs from her mother and grandmother in that she has left remarkable, written traces, the principal gathering being a collection of letters, drawings, notebooks, and clippings preserved in the Sylvia Beach Collection at the University of Buffalo. Lucia Joyce also has a much more complicated cultural context than the older members of the Joyce female family. She came of age in

Lucia Joyce.
This photograph and the one of Lucia Joyce dancing are by
Berenice Abbott, permission of the Poetry/Rare Books Collection of
the University Libraries, State University of New York at Buffalo,
and Berenice Abbott.

an intellectually charged, modern environment—Paris of the 1920s—
and in the family of a man hailed as one of its greatest geniuses.

Starting in her teen-age years, Lucia Joyce was enlisted as a letter-
writer for the family. A thank-you note to Katherine Sargent, written
in English in January 1922, expresses gratitude for a box of fruits
and lively news. Lucia also reports that her mother narrowly escaped
being hit by a bus that veered into a footpath, and she describes a
Christmas celebration enjoyed by Giorgio and herself: "I dressed
myself up in 'Charlie,' we had a lot of fun and I had a great succes,
we danced and played and sang and I don't know what else."[43] Lucia's interest in Charlie Chaplin was also manifested in a short article
she wrote on him, which Joyce mentions in a letter to Valery Larbaud
(L III, 88; Feb. 1924). This enthusiasm was both modern and in
keeping with her involvement in the dance. At age seventy, and after
years in institutions, Miss Joyce still recalled being "thrilled when
Ulysses came out."[44] She was helpful at that eventful time, reading
to Joyce and writing letters for him during one of his eye ailments.
The Buffalo archive and the British Library contain many business
letters written by Lucia to Sylvia Beach and others providing lists of
books to be ordered, reviews to be sought, and instructions about
press copies. There is occasional humor, though it is difficult to de-
termine whether its source is Joyce or Lucia: "He is sorry to hear
that Mr. DuBois is following the two Misses Ottensooser and Miss
Fernandez herself down the road to starvation. He thinks however
that as the publisher of Ulysses you have the right to inquire what
notice Mr. DuBois and Mrs. Ciolkowska have written in return for
their press copies."[45]

Though Lucia, like Giorgio and all of Joyce's close acquaintances,
was drawn into the business end of Joyce's writing, she also had
pursuits of her own and was sometimes impatient with the James
Joyce-centered home environment, with its hordes of devoted male
writers and scholars. Joyce did not desert his family to pursue his
career, but the surroundings he shaped clearly bored Lucia, even at
age thirteen. There is some recognition of this in a note to John
MacCormack: "My wife wishes me to say that if your daughter finds
any afternoon too boresome Lucia (who finds every afternoon boresome, I am afraid) would gladly keep her company" (L III, 34;
Dec. 17, 1920). Later, on the same theme, Joyce reports to Miss
Weaver in March, 1931, that "most of the males between twenty
and thirty-five who float around me seem to be from the point of

view of the opposite sex, completely worthless."[46] Lucia Joyce's interest in Samuel Beckett and his inability to respond (JJ, 649) are unfortunately considered the main items in Lucia Joyce's biography by many.[47] Stuart Gilbert was a member of the male scholarly group that assisted Joyce, but in the company of his wife, Moune, was also a family friend who sensed Lucia's frustrations and even discussed them with her, starting when she was about twenty-one.

> Lucia always seemed a little out of place in the *milieu* centring on her father. . . . The atmosphere must have been rather uncongenial to a young, vivacious girl and, though devoted to her parents, she welcomed occasions of escaping from it. Several times, when I had persuaded her to come with me to the nearby *Chez Francis* . . . I was struck by the change in her manner when I switched the conversation over to ordinary topics and encouraged her to talk about herself. Her ambition was to strike out on her own. . . . "I want to *do* something," she would say. (L I, 33-34)

There is a more desperate personal plea in Lucia's cry, "Mais, m'sieu. C'est moi qui est artiste," recorded by Molly Colum shortly before Lucia was institutionalized in 1932.[48]

The artistic pursuit Lucia recalled most clearly in a 1977 interview was her dancing, particularly her work in modern dance with Margaret Morris and the "goldfish dance" that she did to the music of Debussy, wearing an unusual costume of her own design.[49] Joyce fondly reports this event, part of an international competition at the Bal Bullier, to Miss Weaver:

> Lucia's disqualification for the dancing prize was received by a strong protest from a good half of the audience (*not* friends of ours) who called out repeatedly "Nous reclamons l'irlandaise! Un peu de justice messieurs!" She got the best notice, I think. (L I, 280; May 28, 1929)

Stuart Gilbert explains that Miss Joyce lost because of the current "vogue of negroid dancing" (L I, 33). Miss Joyce also studied dance with other schools, including Lois Hutton and Helen Vanel in Paris and at the Duncan School in Salzburg. Joyce apparently attended a rehearsal of Lucia's "faunesque" dance with the Hutton-Vanel company at a time when he was rather distracted by difficulties he was experiencing with Miss Beach. His self-centered attitude registers, but so does his admiration for Lucia: "She dances through it all. She was very good I think" (L III, 171). Both Frank Budgen and Stuart

Lucia Joyce dancing.

Gilbert compare Lucia's lithe grace to her father's impromptu dancing—his *"pas seuls* at the end of a festive evening" that were "a
diverting blend of eccentricity and elegance" (L I, 33).[50] Ellmann
summarizes Lucia's promise: "Lucia, tall, slender, and graceful, attained a style of some individuality" (JJ, 612). Critic and family friend
Louis Gillet, probably at Joyce's prompting, was more sentimental
and nostalgic in retrospect: "The dancer's steps wove no fantasies
more unseen than when she danced on the stage in moving figures
of herself to delight the spectators. . . . Let us leave her on her lawn
swaying like a sylph amid those veils of mist floating from the ponds
that drink the moonlight above the meadow. . . ."[51]

More practically, dancing provided Lucia Joyce with some female
friends, among them Kathleen (Kitten) Neel, whom she still mentions
frequently,[52] and Dominique Gillet, daughter of Louis Gillet. The
latter friendship was encouraged by Louis Gillet in the early 1930s
"when [Lucia] had difficulties with her family," according to Ms.
Gillet.[53] The family's acquisition of friends in Paris was one reason
why James Joyce was reluctant to move again, even when he was
finding living conditions in Paris difficult.[54]

The programs and publications of the "Rhythme et Couleur" dance
group, collected by Lucia Joyce to represent the "artiste pur,"[55] and
included in the Buffalo collection, reveal a consciously theoretical
approach to dance as an art form. A publication of the group, *Cahiers
Rhythme et Couleur*, includes poetry and the aesthetic of the group
in a series of articles titled "La Danseuse Artiste et Educatrice."
Helen Vanel (one of the group's two female leaders) suggests th at
the artist seeks perfection which s/he knows exists because of an in-
terior harmony, reliant on the rhythm of the universe. S/he participates in "nature" through the power and richness of his or her
instinct, contrary to popular conceptions of the artist, the dancer is
not "disequilibrated" or mentally imbalanced. "The artist is also a
missionary, especially to the young, and with the purpose of transforming the world."[56] The form of the dance practiced by the group
was designed to disengage dance from convention. Instead of seeking
individual success and using feminine charm to appeal to the sensuality of the public, true artists of the dance become abstract forms,
part of the ensemble of the composition. Dance unites rhythms of
space, color, line, and volume (as does painting) but synthesizes these
in time through movement. The human body injects into this a mag-

netic current. To this is added auditory rhythm. The essay ends with an assertion of the primordial importance of color.[57]

That Lucia kept these materials suggests that their philosophy of dance as an art form and the dancer as artist may have been important to the identity Lucia Joyce was forming, before she lost self-direction in her twenties. The ethics of disengagement from convention and the missionary impulse are comparable to Joyce's philosophy at a comparable age. Lucia Joyce reports that when she used to talk to her father, he would frequently take notes on little slips of paper.[58] It is tempting to assume that some of this modern philosophy of the dance, including the emphasis on color and rhythm, may have worked its way into *Finnegans Wake*—particularly in the "Mime" chapter (which I discuss further in chapter 9) in which Issy, as dancer in colorful costume, plays a central role.

In 1977, Lucia Joyce recalled her dancing much better than the lettrines she turned to later, with Joyce's encouragement. According to Jane Lidderdale, Lucia gives various reasons for ending her dancing career, some more convincing than others. One she offered in 1977 was that Joyce did not want her to continue since she used to become very nervous over it.[59] Stuart Gilbert suggests that "constant practice imposed too great a strain on her rather delicate physique" and so her parents decided (with her approval) that she should cease at least temporarily" (L I, 33). Jane Lidderdale notes that Lucia Joyce seems to have believed herself more fragile than she seemed to be, and that this self-perception may have been fostered by her parents.[60] They did, perhaps unintentionally, shelter her from experience. Gilbert notes that at 25, she "had still the inexperience of half her age" (L I, 34). Dominique Gillet Maroger has suggested to Miss Lidderdale that Joyce's apparent feeling that the dance was an inferior art form may have discouraged Lucia from pursuing it.[61]

Joyce followed his daughter's efforts to find a career with concern, seemingly eager to encourage anything that would prove congenial. Joyce reports the variety of her attempts to Miss Weaver:

> She having given up dancing began to attend drawing classes and seems to have astonished her master by her designs, then she gave that up and began to write a novel. Lately she seems to be attending dress shows, she is full of energy to do something but I do not know how to direct it.[62]

It is interesting that Lucia Joyce titled the drawing-book in the Buffalo collection "Rhythme et Couleur," in echo of her dance group's name and aesthetic philosophy.

The drawing and coloring of initial letters, which she considered combining with bookbinding, was Lucia Joyce's second major attempt at a vocation.[63] Her elaborate, richly colored lettrines in Joyce's *Pomes Penyeach* and *A Chaucer A B C*, like *Finnegans Wake*, feature flowers and trees, including leaves and berries. They are reminiscent of the initial letters of the *Book of Kells*, so treasured by Joyce, in their use of cross-hatching and sinuous, snaky lines. Their dots and scallops go beyond the Irish pattern, however. There are daggers and arrows, a razor, and even a firecracker. Miss Joyce does not always confine herself to conventional letter shapes but fractures the alphabet for the sake of aesthetics. In the lettrines, more than in her sketches and surviving scraps of prose, Lucia Joyce shows original talent. In happier circumstances she might have become an artist-craftswoman in the tradition of William Morris.[64] Press clippings with very positive notices on her lettrines are included in the Buffalo collection, indicating her interest in their reception. Joyce actively sought appreciaton of the work, for example, writing Frank Budgen repeatedly about English shops where he might see the initial books (L III, 264, 320).

Even as Lucia Joyce made these last attempts at art, she became menaced from within. Miss Weaver's archive in the British Library contains a fragment written in French in Lucia's hand which describes a vision of large, grimacing masks.[65] Joyce expresses concern to Miss Weaver over the lack of "even casual connections" in the overall letter (L III, 254). He responded to Lucia's style in his own silly and disconnected letters back to her—grim levity which may have helped him continue *Finnegans Wake*. Joyce marveled at his daughter's supposed capacities for prophecy and clairvoyance to friends like Gilbert, who has also described her travel to Ireland in 1935 as a mission, designed to reunite Joyce with Ireland (L I, 34; see also L III, 330, 331n).

That visit is generally considered by the Joyce circle to have gone badly, although Lucia emerged from the supposed "squalor" (L III, 371, 372n) stronger and happier, by Joyce's own admission (L III, 369). The uncertainty proved too much for Joyce, who called in Nora's relatives and Maria Jolas to review the situation and arrange Lucia's return. He also perceived a female conspiracy, which he blamed primarily on his sister Eileen Schaurek. Lucia was cared for during part of her stay by her seventeen- and nineteen-year-old Schaurek cousins, while their mother worked (L III, 362). During the English stage of the travel, Miss Weaver was in charge. Joyce complained to Giorgio of Miss Weaver's being "for months past in collusion with Eileen 'not to write this to Paris,' " keeping him ignorant of "the sordid squalor of the case" and of "the warning of the authorities that their next step would be to commit her or intern her." He felt that "Miss Weaver, as with her other female charms, walked blue-eyed and prim-mouthed into my sister's booby trap" (L III, 369). Although Eileen seems to have been the least predictable of the Joyce sisters (Ellmann describes her as "flighty," and found some of her memories unreliable),[66] there seems to be no evidence of personal gain from the supposed "trap." Indeed, Lucia's care was quite difficult and may have been complicated by Joyce's eager acquiescence to her requests.[67] Eileen left a job at the Irish Sweep for a modest £2/week remuneration from Joyce (L III 344), and she and all the women involved retained Lucia's fondness. It seems that these well-intentioned women were working against two strong opinions of Joyce's—that he would always be betrayed by Ireland and that he was one of very few people who could keep Lucia out of an institution, which he wanted to do at all costs.

Lucia Joyce was also fond of Sylvia Beach. Her gift of embroidery sent from Ireland was probably an effort to reforge this connection for her father, but he reacted, "Why send vases to Samos?" and referred to Beach coldly as "my ex-publisher" (L III, 356, 356n). She wrote frequently to Miss Beach and received careful replies until the latter died.[68] Lucia also attempted to affect her father's medical future. She wrote Miss Weaver expressing her concern about an approaching eye operation, and also her self-critical identification with some of his character traits:

> Could you not persuade my father to cut out his operation he is going to have? I do believe the doctor but I think that this time they have gone too far with him. Giorgio is of the same opinion and you know how much we are fond of him in spite of the fact that he is sometimes a little difficult to get along with (for that side I resemble him unfortunately).[69]

Although his loyal friends like Stuart Gilbert and Maria Jolas have reported Joyce's deep concern over Lucia, his efforts and worries about her were too late and too simple in conception. A fur coat, lessons, the recruitment of a fiancé, even a publication—all failed to address the complex and talented woman who could never come to be. Many gifted women are never let out into the world, as it was then and is now constituted, but this one turned inward and lost what little consciousness and power she had gained.

James Joyce wrote two memorable poems to his family. The more celebrated is "Ecce Puer," an occasional poem prompted by the nearly simultaneous death of John Joyce and the birth of Stephen, son of Giorgio and Helen Joyce. The second poem is "A Flower Given to my Daughter," written in 1913 in Trieste, when Lucia was five or six years old and published in 1917 in Harriet Monroe's periodical, *Poetry*. Joyce also sent a typed copy of it to Miss Weaver in 1927.[70] "Ecce Puer" is cyclical and patriarchal, a lineage of men, reaching "out of the dark past," and a prayer extended to the father, who seems a masculine deity as well as a lost human parent:

> A child is sleeping:
> An old man gone
> O, father forsaken
> Forgive your son!

Joyce named his son to make a lost brother live. Giorgio, in naming his own son Stephen James gave flesh to his father's fictional personification and actual self. Stanislaus Joyce would name his own son James. The male family of Joyce are bound in family history.

Lucia Joyce was named not for history or dynasty, but for the greatest of physical essences, light. In the poem, Joyce associates her with a flower. His erotic letters to Nora had also likened Nora to a wild blue flower, plucked from the hedges, the flower and the hedges serving as emblems of the west, and of his taking her in love. In his poem for his daughter, the frail white rose is not plucked but given, an action which casts the child in a different role from Nora's. Thus the poem does not directly suggest incest, as some have suggested.[71] The giver is unidentified, a female "whose soul is sere and paler/ than time's wan wave." Ellmann suggests that she is Amalia Popper, Joyce's young Jewish student in Trieste, the inspiration for *Giacomo Joyce* and one of the models for Molly Bloom (JJ, 342-346). Her half of the poem is inferior to the daughter's:

> Rosefrail and fair—yet frailest
> A wonder wild
> In gentle eyes thou veilest
> My blueveined child.

Here Lucia receives the emblem of Joyce's love for Nora from another fantasized lover, Amalia. But the poem itself ennobles Lucia as "fair" and "blueveined." The frail quality belongs to her physical self, but also to the "wonder wild," which is rendered more private and mysterious by the child's veiling of it in "gentle eyes." It is a poem of almost fearful cherishing.[72] Lucia has the blue and the veil so often associated with the Virgin Mary by Joyce, as in tradition. But her "wonder wild" is her most precious and delicate essence. Joyce detected it early but also saw it become hopelessly obscured.

New Free Women
in the
Company of Joyce

5

□ Robert McAlmon remarks of the era and cultural environment he shared with James Joyce, "It is some kind of commentary on the period that Joyce's work and acclaim should have been fostered mainly by high-minded ladies, rather than by men."[1] During his Trieste, Zurich, and Paris years, by mail and through literary and publishing circles, Joyce formed relationships of great benefit to himself with cultured, intellectual women attuned to his works. They not only fostered him; they provided an enriched human context for, and a new range, to his conception of woman and feminism.

In *Finnegans Wake*, Joyce records an early publishing debt: "I'm so keen on that *New Free Woman* with novel inside" (FW, 145). As Ellmann recognizes, the novel was *A Portrait of the Artist as a Young Man* (JJ, 351), first published in 1914 in *The Egoist* (1914-1919), a recently renamed little magazine which had evolved from *The Freewoman* (1911-1912) and its successor, *The New Freewoman* (1913). At the time that Joyce's novel appeared, the company that produced *The Egoist* was still named "The New Freewoman Limited." While the *Finnegans Wake* allusion can be read as fact or double entendre or both, it is also appropriate to see in it a metaphor of female gestation which befits the role of the women editors of the journal.

The original editor of all these journals, Dora Marsden, the assistant editor of *The New Freewoman*, Rebecca West, and the honorary secretary and later editor of *The Egoist*, Harriet Shaw Weaver, were all feminists of intellectual depth and conviction. Weaver was originally attracted to *The Freewoman* instead of *Votes for Women*, the first organ of the Pankhursts' Women's Social and Political Union, because *The Freewoman* exceeded what she considered the "narrowly propagandist" nature of the W.S.P.U. journal. Dora Marsden was a graduate of Manchester University and a veteran of suffragette hunger strikes and forced feeding. She had been in succession a district organizer for W.S.P.U. and a worker for England's second militant feminist organization, the Women's Freedom League, but she had managed to offend both groups with her impulsive, independent planning.[2] She continued to use her journal as a corrective to other forms of feminism, while still advancing the equality of women in her own way. Her attack upon Christabel Pankhurst's advocacy of a single standard of chastity as a solution to venereal disease shares the pages of *The Egoist* with Joyce's *A Portrait*.[3]

As illustrated in the subtitles of her periodicals, Marsden's interests were not limited to women—she was concerned with whatever restricted the spiritual freedom of both sexes, as was Joyce. In May 1912, the original subtitle "A Weekly Feminist Review" was altered to "A Weekly Humanist Review," in the words of the editor, "to show that the two causes, man's and woman's, are one."[4] Later both *The New Freewoman* and *The Egoist* carried the subtitle "An Individualist Review." This phrase links these London journals in philosophy to *Dana*, the Irish publication, named for a goddess, which had published Joyce's early poem "My Love is in a Light Attire" in 1904. *Dana*'s editors, John Eglinton and Frank Ryan, had favored independence and freedom of the human mind in their opening editorial. Rebecca West describes the "programme" of *The New Freewoman* as "the revolt of women, philosophic anarchism, and a general whip-round for ideas that would reform simultaneously life and art."[5] West had interested Ezra Pound in *The New Freewoman*, and soon Richard Aldington, H. D. (Hilda Doolittle), and T. S. Eliot were making it a more literary publication. It was Ezra Pound who brought James Joyce's work to Dora Marsden's attention. The women editors worked cautiously with Pound, aware that he might usurp their journal for his own purposes but also appreciative of his ability to scout for talented new writers.[6] With the increasing importance of literary content, the feminist tone of the original journals was muted. According to Harriet Weaver, it was "the new masculine element which had allied itself with the paper" that "before long raised objections to the title *The New Freewoman*."[7] Rebecca West regrets that there never was a true feminist literary movement or journal in the early part of the century.[8]

In their enthusiasm for Joyce, scholars tend to overlook the fact that through much of her life, Harriet Shaw Weaver was supportive of a woman who she originally thought had great promise—Dora Marsden .She generously assisted in Marsden's study of what could be termed feminist philosophy. Dora Marsden worked throughout her life on a series of philosophical treatises, some of them constructed around male and female principles. Weaver once compared the female principles of her two protégés: ". . . you speak of Molly Bloom having been called the all-time female principle (I don't myself think she is big enough for that, but that is by the way). . . . My friend Miss Marsden. . . . held that the world had gone wrong because of the "shedding of a God," the Great Almighty Mother Space: the Magnetic Ocean. . . ."[9] Both Rebecca West and Harriet Shaw Weaver found Dora Marsden enormously attractive as a young woman; West describes her as "brilliant in mind and saintly in character and . . . exquisitely glamorous."[10] Marsden, like Joyce, was a free spirit, but in her middle years she was incapacitated by physical and mental illness. Weaver's compassion was a major force behind the appearance of Marsden's books, *The Definition of a Godhead* (1928), *The Mysteries of Christianity* (1930), and *The Philosophy of Time* (1955), the last of these an unfinished work.[11]

Marsden praised sections of *A Portrait* when they first appeared in *The Egoist*, finding "the four sermons and the Parnell passage . . . unsurpassable." She anticipated trouble from "the authorities" about "the passage over the relative merits of Christ and Tsar as icons . . . without counting the fruity 'languidge,' " and praised Weaver for "dispersing the spoil well in time."[12] Marsden found Joyce "appalling" in *Ulysses*, but was willing to fight for its publication by a public press.[13] Joyce, for his part, inquired after Miss Marsden in several of his letters to Harriet Weaver; he shared Weaver's concern for Marsden's health and empathized with her fatigue:

> I hope Miss Marsden's book will come out soon, after such a long strain in solitude and want of recognition. It is incredible how certain states of fatigue and depression can act on the body, though I did not feel my brain wandering beyond a desire to indicate an object when I alluded to it.[14]

When *The Definition of a Godhead* finally appeared, Joyce declared, "I am looking forward to thieveries on an unheard of scale as soon as I find an accomplice as rascally minded as myself,"[15] but there is no further evidence of his referring to this work, which Marsden had dedicated to "the great name, hushed among us for so long of her, heaven, the mighty mother of all."[16]

It was Harriet Shaw Weaver who took an early interest in Joyce's writing for its own merits. Weaver was the quiet, backstage kind of social reformer. She came to *The New Freewoman* after a brief career in East End social work, focused upon the needs of poor children and the establishment of the South London Hospital for Women. She had wanted to attend a college, but her family thought such a course was useless; they also prevented her sister from pursuing medical studies. Harriet Weaver's reverence for her family was to affect her public style throughout her life—Miss Weaver not wishing to embarrass them with her liberalism. Throughout her life, she responded to family needs for help, visiting an aged aunt or nursing an ailing sister or niece. Jane Lidderdale, her goddaughter, describes her style as follows:

> It was not in her nature to give public testimony or engage in open controversy, but she loved those who did. She wanted to help them, unostentatiously, whenever help was needed. For herself, she sought to enlarge her experience by listening, and to protect her integrity by silence.[17]

Miss Lidderdale reports further that she "never had an open and sustained conversation with Miss Weaver about Joyce," that Miss Weaver never really "opened up." Such reticence was a family trait, but one which Weaver carried to her own extreme.[18] Richard Ellmann, who worked with her repeatedly in preparing his biography of Joyce, observes, "She avoided self-consciousness, almost as if she didn't want to admit she had a self."[19] Robert McAlmon, given the delicate mission of describing Joyce's drinking habits to Miss Weaver, reports his own bewilderment at Weaver's silence (perhaps greater than usual because of her company and his troubling subject):

> She is – – – reticent or shy? Difficult to get at in any case. She would let me talk and answer with a short-gasped "yes" or "no," and looked into space. Whether she heard or was bored stiff, I couldn't say. At last she came through with a confession: She had never faced life with sufficient courage to know reality. She had been afraid from her childhood days of people who drank.[20]

Harriet Shaw Weaver.
Photograph copyright by the British Library.

Weaver admitted her fears, and characteristically declined to dictate others' behavior, accepting McAlmon's reassurances about Joyce.[21]

Despite her ladylike demeanor, Weaver had unconventional, even anarchistic ideas that she acted upon. Her philanthropy to *The Egoist*, Dora Marsden, and James Joyce was based upon the Marxist-style belief that her inheritance "tainted by usury, was hers in trust."[22] She had rejected her family's evangelical Church of England faith as a young woman.[23] Some of her objections to the family's style of faith can be seen in the observations she makes about her aged aunt in a letter to Sylvia Beach. Finding the old lady more "sweet and gentle" than she had ever known her to be, Weaver remarks, "I think it must be her true nature coming out, rid at last of the hard ultra-protestant poison with which she was infected in her youth and which narrowed her mind and whole outlook."[24] When she became editor of *The Egoist* in the midst of the publication of Joyce's serial, she fought with her printers to assure the integrity of the author's text, and regretted when this was impossible.[25] Late in life, Weaver joined the Communist Party (a fact which she kept typically quiet). She felt a distaste, furthermore, for American foreign policy, a factor which may have affected her selection of libraries to receive her manuscripts.[26]

Harriet Weaver has been described as "asexual" by Rebecca West, and her biographers explain that she felt "a total lack of interest in the other sex, except as human beings." Jane Lidderdale adds that, unlike Sylvia Beach, Harriet Weaver was not a lesbian, that she liked men, though presumably this liking was of a sisterly or collegial sort; as another relative adds, there was "never a flicker of flirtation."[27] Like Virginia Woolf, Weaver lost a well-loved brother in young womanhood. Her lack of sensuality and her close control of her emotions make Weaver the opposite of Joyce's most celebrated female character, Molly Bloom. However, her celibacy had important elements of freedom—in action and thought—that were rarely available to married women of her era.

Harriet Weaver, like her mother before her, had a keen aptitude for mathematics, which is visible in her account books. She had good powers to systematize, as can be seen in the 224-page "Symposium on Time," which she wrote to free Dora Marsden for "the more creative side" of her philosophical writing. It is interesting that "time," the male-associated entity in Marsden's philosophical scheme, was settled upon Weaver, while Marsden maintained full responsibility for the female concept, space. In this "Symposium," Weaver classifies abstracts she has selected from 152 philosophers into twenty-one different attitudes toward "time," carefully listing philosophers and cross-listing their ideas.[28] This same capacity for organization is shown in the careful notes she submitted to the British Museum to accompany the *Finnegans Wake* manuscripts.

Miss Weaver was not a "creative person."[29] She avoided creative writing, except for letter-writing, where she followed the time-honored formula of addressing first her correspondent's recent concerns, then business, and last her own news. The few essays she has left us were usually written in support of someone else's work. She assumed heavier duties at *The Egoist* to free Dora Marsden's time, and was driven to writing for the paper herself only when Marsden's copy failed to appear. Her obvious distaste for the editorial tasks is contained in the mock threat of verses titled "With Apologies to Caliban," a set of curses sent to Miss Marsden.[30] Marsden tried hard to encourage Weaver's writing, hailing her as "a new poet" and "a live prophet" when her first essay appeared.[31] Marsden also combatted Weaver's tendency to rely upon quotations: "*You* are a horror: a villain: a _____!!! It is imperative you should produce an article: 'quotes' won't do unless you have interlarded them with remarks. . . ."[32] But Weaver resisted, writing only four articles, and repeating herself somewhat, even in them.

Weaver's four leading columns for *The Egoist* reveal much of her philosophy and suggest sympathies similar to Joyce's.[33] Like Joyce she was wary of journalistic methods and of the judgments of masses and popular movements. Two of her essays deal with the dangers of theories and suggest in rather militant language that the proper fate of a theory is to be destroyed, not to become a lifelong hobby. It is liberating language, befitting to *The Egoist*, but also appropriate to Miss Weaver, to feminism, and to a spokesperson for James Joyce and his vow: *non serviam*:

> It has skirted all movements and caught on to none. That is its distinction and one which we aspire to retain. *The Egoist* is wedded to no belief from which it is unwilling to be divorced. To probe to the depths of human nature, to keep its curiosity in it fresh and alert, to regard nothing in human nature as foreign to it, but to hold itself ready to bring to the surface what may be found, without any predetermination to fling back all but welcome facts—such are the high and uncommon pretensions upon which it bases its claim to permanence.[34]

Weaver's model of human nature, constructed in response to pro-pagandists who would appeal to humans' "higher nature," supports her personal style of self-control, and also Joyce's interest in the ordinary. Her stream metaphor has Jungian tones; furthermore, it is perhaps prophetic of the fluid, female power of Anna Livia herself:

> Once having accepted the suggestion of current speech that per-sonality comprises a higher and lower, we must necessarily assume the existence of the "middle nature," which presumably has es-caped a label because it is just "ordinary." All the fuss and fury naturally attach themselves to the surfaces. Likening human nature to a stream, it might be said that at the top we are frothy, at the bottom muddy, while in the middle flows the mass of clear water wherein lies the full power of the unified personality: the self at its strongest and most firmly poised, the critical and discriminating Ego: a power to be reckoned with who cannot be easily moved hither and thither at the will of another. It has frequently been noted how readily of these three "natures" the highest and the lowest will interchange and dovetail into one another.[35]

As was the case in Dora Marsden's reactions to Christabel Pankhurst's doctrine of "purity," Weaver finds that avoidance of lower subjects only serves to heighten them—an attitude that clears the way for her acceptance of Joyce's full subject matter: "The kind of sombre maj-esty with which the Unknown is invested spreads a protecting veil of mysteriousness and importance over the region of "Vices," and actually constitutes their main fascination. . . . Arrest them, scruti-nize them, and size them up, and vices are commonly quite pitifully small things."[36] This attitude was undoubtedly helpful to her in ac-cepting Joyce's personal style and subject matter. It is notable that the letters to the editor of *The Egoist* frequently addressed problems of sexuality and marriage in a liberal and open manner. A married couple that wrote in frequently, offering their own observations and ones garnered from Havelock-Ellis were Beeban and Noel Teulon Porter—a happy coincidence with the name of the leading family of *Finnegans Wake*.[37] Announcing that *The Egoist* will publish *A Portrait* in book form, Weaver congratulates Joyce for "having won for the critical understanding intellect standing-room on a portion of the territory now held specially sacred to exhibitions of a vapid senti-mentality trapped but with a furtive salaciousness."[38]

In the last number of *The Egoist*, Weaver offered a revolutionary manifesto to usher in her future work in publishing books: "It seems to us that, in establishing on non-commercial lines an enterprise limiting itself to the production of works either of original matter having a general philosophic bearing or to works of exposition giving the philosophy of new departures in art-works, we should be making operative an influence capable of transforming our entire world of form-thought and action."[39] The Egoist Press, run nearly exclusively by Harriet Weaver, went on to publish three editions of *A Portrait*, and one each of *Ulysses*, *Exiles*, *Dubliners*, and *Chamber Music*, in addition to works by Wyndham Lewis, T. S. Eliot, Ezra Pound, Jean Cocteau, Marianne Moore, H. D., Richard Aldington, and Dora Marsden.

As her biographers attest in titling their work *Dear Miss Weaver*, it is as a writer of letters that Harriet Shaw Weaver is most memorable, and best recorded. Her correspondents included many of the distinguished writers associated with the *Egoist*, as well as Dora Marsden, Sylvia Beach, and members of her family. As a writer of considerate, critical, motivating letters, she upheld and extended an important literary tradition associated strongly with women.

Our best evidence of the growth and nature of the relationship between James Joyce and Harriet Shaw Weaver is provided by the letters they exchanged from 1915 until Joyce's death.[40] The maturing, more reserved, and always faintly genteel Joyce could respond to this extraordinary woman, whose need for personal privacy outmatched his own, but whose reliability, common sense, fair-mindedness and calmness met needs that patrons rarely perceive.

Maria Jolas (who like all those who were Joyce's friends in his later years holds Miss Weaver in high regard) evaluates their correspondence as follows:

> He wrote to her just as if he were writing to another man, and an intelligent one in whom he had confidence. Of course he wrote more guardedly from the language standpoint than he did to Budgen, but the letters to Miss Weaver are really, are absolutely to an equal, and her replies are extremely intelligent.[41]

It was probably the finest group of letters Joyce wrote, surpassing those to his friend of the Zurich interval, Frank Budgen, which were often written hurriedly, and rivaled only by the open, often highly opinionated early letters to Stanislaus. Joyce honored Budgen with the curses that had adorned the early letters to Stanislaus, and with his memories of important shared experience in Zurich. With the exception of his guidance of Budgen's reading of the "Nausicaä," "Oxen of the Sun," and "Penelope" chapters of *Ulysses* (all episodes focusing on women and male-female difference, interestingly enough) the literary content of the letters to Miss Weaver is richer. Stuart Gilbert had described the Budgen letters as "Rabelaisian," but observed, "the letters to Miss Weaver, different in tone, are even more interesting."[42] These offer Joyce's most complete and direct explanations of all of *Ulysses* and *Finnegans Wake*. They assume an intelligent, committed reader with a good memory. Other parts of letters describe Joyce's family life and provide a diary of Joyce's physical and mental health for nearly a twenty-five year period.

From the start, the tone of Weaver's letters to Joyce was highly rational and business-like, but she was also capable of concern, or humility and gracious apology, when her actions and evaluations caused Joyce any form of distress. Thus her letters offer an interesting combination of stereotypes of masculine order and feminine sympathy. Like Joyce, Weaver used verbal formality to achieve a safe distance—to retain or retreat into her more temperate nature, in the case of Mr. Joyce. This formality characterizes her earliest letters. Their business partnership established, Weaver indirectly gratified a desire to know Joyce more personally, almost as a friend. The queries of Ben Huebsch, the American publisher of *A Portrait*, give her an excuse to request biographical information and photographs that she had not sought for herself. She also looked to *Exiles* for autobiographical content.[43] Joyce was more direct in his questions about her family background.

As time went on, Weaver began to venture more personal remarks—at first proper concern for his health and other worries, but gradually she made these in a less formal tone and with reference to herself. In 1917 she wrote, "You are indeed unfortunate in being troubled with such a number of illnesses: they seem to have a conspiracy not to let you alone. I suppose there are not many people who have the good fortune to be always well like me."[44] She was willing to make herself an object of humor or a perpetrator of mischief. She wrote that after reading the "Cyclops" chapter of *Ulysses*, "it was difficult to speak straight and to avoid interlarding one's words with the favorite and unladylike adjective" (bloody) of the narrator.[45] When she finally sent Joyce photographs of herself in 1919, she made light of being "so weak as to allow myself the pleasure of being credited still with something of youth." She admits her willingness to delude Ezra Pound about her age, but to Joyce confesses that she is forty-three.[46] The photograph displays, not just youth, but beauty as well (JJ, plate xxxi), though to claim that was beyond Weaver's slight vanity. She teased Joyce about her having Belfast relatives "who are violent Orangemen" and about his burning of the early draft of *A Portrait*: "In view of what happened to the 'original' original it is fortunate that the chapters of *Ulysses* are typed out as soon as they are written and the typescript dispatched to safer keeping in England and America."[47] A spirit of playfulness is also detectable in Weaver's willingness to participate in *Finnegans Wake* games with Joyce. She, like his Paris friends, guessed at the title of the work from riddles provided by its author. She accepted his invitation to order a portion of the book, using appropriate *Wake* language to request "one full length grave account of his esteemed Highness Rhaggrick O'Hoggnor's Hogg Tomb as per photos enclosed" (JJ, 581-582).

Weaver was reluctant to enter Joyce's personal affairs at first and only did do so after Sylvia Beach convinced her that Joyce's problems with finances and domestic arrangements had begun to interfere with his writing.[48] By corresponding with third parties and using the offices of her solicitor, Weaver tried to make her personal and financial interventions as unobtrusive as possible. She was reluctant to allow financial power or personal philosophy to impinge upon the freedoms of an individual—an attitude that went back to her *Egoist* days. As her biographers have indicated, once Weaver's "loyalty had been given, to whatever cause or person, she was incapable of withdrawing it."[49] This was the only area, it seems, where she lacked control. Because of it, she accepted Joyce's spending, drinking, and the obscurities of *Finnegans Wake*. She also involved herself in the care of Lucia Joyce. As her late correspondence shows, after Joyce's death, she sent funds she had intended for his resettlement in Switzerland to cover the funeral, and patiently oversaw the resources of his estate, responding to the needs of Nora, Giorgio, and Lucia Joyce. She fulfilled her plan of expending her "tainted" inheritance, living in her final years on very modest means. Harriet Weaver visited Lucia Joyce regularly while Miss Joyce was at an institution in Northampton and was the one who broke the news of Nora Joyce's death to her daughter. On one of her last outings, Miss Weaver took Lucia a box of watercolor paints, still fulfilling Joyce's wish that Lucia should never feel abandoned.[50] There is little need to justify the title Lucia had given her years before, "Saint Harriet."[51]

Along with her capacities for fun and personal compassion, Harriet Weaver maintained a sense of order and purpose in her transactions with Joyce. She was at times both his personal and his literary critic. She wonders if he has suffered from "absent-mindedness" about an address or details already sent him in previous correspondence.[52] Weaver had opinions of Joyce's works. The positive ones she volunteered; the negative ones were offered more reluctantly, and always in an apologetic tone. She especially liked his poetry, *A Portrait*, and the more lyrical portions of *Ulysses* and *Finnegans Wake*. An early letter offered her appreciation of "A Memory of the Players in a Mirror at Midnight," and "Bahnhofstrasse," the latter "especially in moods in which the thought of my great age oppresses me." In early correspondence about *A Portrait*, she wrote with implied personal agreement, "A reviewer at last speaks of the beauty of the book."[53] Perhaps due to her interest in individual psychology, she was "spellbound" by the "Circe" chapter of *Ulysses*.[54] Of "Nausicaä," she remarked somewhat personally in March 1920, "You are very good for the soul, I think, medicinal, you are so unflattering to our human nature: so though you are neither priest nor doctor of medicine, I think you have something of both—the Reverend James Joyce S.J., M.D."—a perceptive character analysis of him that the author appreciated (JJ, 475). "Penelope" she described as "prehuman," to which Joyce responded, "Your description of it . . . coincides with my intention—if the epithet 'post human' were added. . . . In conception and technique I tried to depict the earth which is prehuman and presumably posthuman." His observation that the "name" of the chapter "Penelope" (as weaver) "by other strange coincidence is your own" (SL, 289) was an after-the-fact tribute to Miss Weaver's reading and herself. She also reacted to the Anna Livia Plurabelle section of *Finnegans Wake* "with flawless pleasure."[55] But as Ellmann has indicated, these reactions were qualified by others. The first few episodes of *Ulysses* which she read for publication in *The Egoist* were "bitter to me at least—difficult too, the third section—but of vital interest."[56] She finds "Sirens" lacking in Joyce's "usual pitch of intensity" and rather maternally attributes this to his "worries" instead of his intentions.[57] Her boldest and (to Joyce) most troubling statement came in reaction to *Finnegans Wake*,

at a time when he felt that everyone was reacting negatively to that
work:

> Some of your work I like enormously—as I am sure you know—
> especially the more straightforward and character-analytical parts
> and the (to me) beautifully expressed ghost parts. . . . but I am
> made in such a way that I do not care much for the output from
> your Wholesale Safety Pin Factory nor for the darkness and un-
> intelligibilities of your deliberately-entangled language system. . . .
> (JJ, 590)

Incapable of flattery, Harriet Weaver provided an invaluable, though
sometimes frustrating, gauge of the future reception of his work.
Particularly with *Finnegans Wake*, where she read manuscripts as
they were produced, she became the reader who wrote the book.

What did Harriet Shaw Weaver represent to Joyce? She was too
regarding of freedom to become a financial lord or mother figure.
Her biographers suggest that by choosing to support Joyce, she may
have fulfilled his personal myth of election, confirming him in the
greatness he had claimed for himself.[58] The match was so unusual
and yet so workable that a supernatural explanation certainly serves
better than a practical, and especially a monetary one. Weaver was,
in fact, only the first example of female election of Joyce; he was
similarly magnetic to other helpful intellectual women of his day.

As a quiet observer, schooled, as Virginia Woolf puts it, in the
sensibili ty of the sitting room,[59]a patient correspondent, loyal friend,
amanuensis and saint, Harriet Shaw Weaver was like the self-sacrificing angelic woman who pervades Victorian women's history. In
her apparent selflessness, however, she had intellectual discretion
and she developed personal approaches and methods that maintained
her private, individualist stance and fostered her own growth, as well
as Joyce's. Richard Ellmann has beautifully summarized Harriet Shaw
Weaver's qualities as a "Jamesian epitome of feminine intelligence
and sympathy" (L II, xxviii). This evokes her nineteenth-century
manners, restraint, and discrimination. But it may divert our attention from the tensions between old order and new freedom, between
criticism and loyalty, English and Irish, and masculine and feminine
that made her help and criticism so valuable to Joyce. This he acknowledged when he inscribed a book to her in 1926 as "Enrichetta
Weaver."[60]

Sylvia Beach was the second extraordinary woman to become an
essential benefactress of Joyce. She and her inseparable associate,

Sylvia Beach with her sister Cyprian.
Photograph courtesy of the Princeton University Library.

Adrienne Monnier, are more difficult to represent than Miss Weaver, and have been less well comprehended by Joyce scholars. For Weaver, we have a fine biography; for Beach, until very recently we had only a collection of brief tributes, *Sylvia Beach (1887-1962)*, and her memoirs, *Shakespeare and Company*. The latter masks the young Sylvia in the old, and seems to have been written with mixed emotions that sometimes benevolently added to existing myths, and sometimes fretted over unrevisable and not necessarily regrettable acts.[61] Miss Beach has been seen mainly in her role as intrepid publisher of *Ulysses*, and in the 1931 episode of withdrawal from her massive services to Joyce. While Joyce's late friend, Maria Jolas, has consistent praise for Miss Weaver's unwavering support of Joyce, she continues to mildly disparage Beach and Monnier, who (unlike herself) go back to Joyce's first days in Paris. Adrienne Monnier did write Joyce in May 1931, detailing the ways that she felt he was taking advantage of them (JJ, 651-652). Jolas has termed it a "tactless accusation which angered" Joyce,[62] and "proof, if proof were needed, that the Sapphic heart can harbour monsters with eyes as green as any other"—a rather tactless accusation of jealousy, couched with an allusion to the lesbianism of Beach and Monnier. Jolas describes herself in a role of conciliator between the dead Joyce and the aged Beach. She reports that, in the late 1950s, she had repeated to Beach Joyce's own reaction to criticism of her: "All she ever did was to make me a present of the ten best years of her life." As Beach's eyes filled with tears, Jolas sensed "a deep mutation was possible, one that would purge her heart of all bitterness—a bitterness she had paid for with years of incorrigible migraine—and leave only awareness of having been elected and privileged to share in a unique undertaking."[63] This account probably tells more about Jolas' own sense of election to service of Joyce than it does about Beach, whose commitment to James Joyce, while deep and generous, was certainly not the only important thing in her life, nor did it consume even the "ten best years" of it, as claimed by Joyce.

As photographs taken of her around her bookshop, Shakespeare and Company, show, Sylvia Beach was a slight, sprightly woman. She encouraged a jaunty pose from James Joyce and the antics of climbing to a second-story balcony from young composer, George Antheil.[64] Beach had a chirpy, bird-like manner,[65] and seemingly boundless cheer, energy, and initiative. These qualities are evident in a RTE film interview of her, made when Joyce's Tower was opened as a museum. The first stanza of Joyce's playful adaptation, "Who is Sylvia," captures some of these qualities:

> Who is Sylvia, what is she
> That all our scribes commend her?
> Yankee, young and brave is she
> The west this pace did lend her
> That all books might published be[66]

Other elements of Beach's personal style can be understood in the contexts of her upbringing and her need to cope with the male world. Noel Fitch cites Beach's childhood in the parsonage and reactions to her father, Rev. Sylvester Woodbridge Beach, D.D., as the source of several stereotypically feminine traits—her hospitality, self-effacement, and ego-building flattery of her visitors.[67] Throughout her film interview, Beach uses the modifier "little" to describe her bookshop, as if needing to insist upon its modest proportions. She was skilled in conversation and facilitation, her graciousness occasionally relieved by sharp or even biting exercise of wit—a classic coping mechanism of the bright female. Beach was especially close to the women of her family. Her mother, like herself, had loved the artists of Paris and operated a lively salon for students when the family lived there during Sylvia's adolescence. She painted, wrote articles, and supported her daughters' aspirations. Sylvia was the second of three daughters. Her long-term sympathy with the feminist movement of her era is evident in her letters, particularly the ones to her sister Cyprian, who eventually moved to Paris to pursue a film career. Sylvia was pleased when, in 1913, Cyprian identified herself with "Votes for Women," and revealed her efforts to get their Cousin Mary to subscribe to the *Suffragette*.[68] Sylvia recommended that Cyprian should read John Stuart Mill. While working with her sister Holly in Serbia after World War I, Beach expressed impatience with her American colleagues. The American women display a "clinging" femininity, in contrast to the rugged and self-sufficient British women: "I wish our women were keeping pace with the rest all over the world."[69] Sylvia had the backing of $3,000 from her mother's savings to set up her bookshop in 1919, and numerous smaller financial contributions from her mother, Holly, and Cousin Mary over the years. Mrs. Beach and her sisters also helped keep the shop stocked by obtaining English and American books requested by Sylvia.

Sylvia Beach should be appreciated as the co-leader of a literary network conceived of and operated by women, according to their own, unorthodox principles. Beach instinctively bonded with Adrienne Monnier, French seller of modern books, publisher, and author. Beach's bookshop, Shakespeare and Company, was modeled largely on Monnier's La Maison des Amis des Livres, which the young Monnier had opened in 1915. Neither woman had been trained as a bookseller, and Monnier admits self-critically her own eschewal of the profit motive: "We were so afraid of passing for paltry tradespeople that we pretended without end to neglect our own interests, which was childishness besides."[70] Unlike Harriet Weaver, Beach and Monnier did have to earn a living, so finances could not be disregarded totally. The names of these bookshops suggest something of their spirit. Monnier's was a *house* of *friends* of books, a commercial enterprise rendered domestic and amicable. The "Company" of Beach's shop was an association of people (authors and readers) with one another; Beach took the dead language of conventional incorporation and enlivened it with a sense of hospitality. Earlier, Beach had considered calling the shop The Little Book Club, a name with similar connotations of intimacy and fellowship.[71] As Richard McDougall has suggested, these women made the Rue de l'Odéon, where Monnier's shop was located from its inception, and where Beach's relocated in 1921, into Odéonia, a center for intellect and joy in life and words, despite the outer world's "time of destruction" (Monnier's own phrase). [72] The two bookshops complemented one another, and in all of their history, there is no suggestion of competition.[73] Monnier specialized in modern French literature, the writing which had originally drawn Beach to Monnier's shop. Beach's shelves made modern writing in English available in Paris, her shop attracting both the French and the postwar English-speaking expatriates, who made it their club. Bookselling, as practiced by Beach and Monnier, was not a lowgrade service to literary genius. It was a chosen, psychological, and even mystical operation involving spirit and human relationship. Said Monnier, "A shop seems to us to be a true magic chamber: at that instant when the passer-by crosses the threshold of the door that everyone can open, when he penetrates into that apparently impersonal space, nothing disguises the look of his face, the tone of his words . . . and if we know how to observe him at that instant when he is only a stranger, we are able now and forever, to know him in his truth. . . .This immediate and intuitive understanding, this private fixing of the soul, how easy they are in a shop, a place of transition between street and house."[74]

To enter the spaces organized by Beach and Monnier was a self-election. It entitled the stranger to much more than the purchase of books. Recognizing the limited finances of their customers, and the importance of circulating books, Beach and Monnier offered secondhand copies, and opened the select resources of their circulating libraries for a modest subscription fee. The shops housed special displays, readings, and lectures to familiarize the public with new writers, and the writers with one another. The walls of Shakespeare and Company became a large album, and its drawers, an archive of its members. As an organization, it was comparable to the notable female institution, the literary salon. But it was more accessible, egalitarian, and diverse than typical salons, including the nearby, contemporary menage of Gertrude Stein and Alice B. Toklas.[75]

There was a loving and probably sexually passionate relationship between Beach and Monnier.[76] Their lesbianism admitted warm friendships and a lively social life with literary men as well as women. Among their best friends were the notable Frenchmen Valery Larbaud, Leon-Paul Fargue, Jules Romains, Paul Valéry, and André Gide. Bryher was a friend and supporter of both women, and Sylvia Beach had the much-noted devotion of Ernest Hemingway. All of these relationships were less formal and more joyful than the alliance struck with Joyce.

Janet Flanner (one of the many female writers in Sylvia Beach's fold) has summarized Beach's abilities as follows: "Sylvia had a vigorous clear mind, an excellent memory, a tremendous respect for books as civilizing objects and was really a remarkable librarian. She loved the printed word and books in long rows." Flanner also suggests that Beach "did not have a literary mind or much literary taste."[77] These last qualities are difficult to assess. Beach certainly was not a literary critic, not even informally, like Harriet Weaver. She wrote little besides her autobiography, an account of her internment during World War II, and spirited personal letters. Beach did have abilities as a translator and undertook several projects along these lines. Ellmann describes her longest translation, of Henri Michaux's *A Barbarian in Asia*, as "very capable."[78] Together with Monnier, she also translated T. S. Eliot's *Prufrock*, and according to Valery Larbaud, provided valuable assistance in early French translation work on *Ulysses*.[79]

Adrienne Monnier was more notable as a contributor to literature itself. She edited several reviews issued from her bookshop at wide

intervals, and wrote several volumes including fabliaux, poetry, and
articles (which she called her *Gazettes*). Even her memoirs of friends
have a dimension of literary criticism. Monnier's *Gazettes* include an
article on "Joyce's *Ulysses* and the French Public" that qualifies her
as a feminist critic. Of special interest are her remarks on the "Nausicaä" chapter:

> This chapter up to Bloom's final monologue, preserves the tone of
> articles and famous little announcements of fashion magazines.
> Everything that the ordinary woman places at her own feet, the
> whole flattering murmur that a crowd of others like herself pro-
> duces in her, all the beauty advice, the dictates of fashion, the
> insipid poetry, the tame mystery, all-purpose religion, recipes, et-
> iquette and, hovering over all, impregnating the least detail, love
> like the atmosphere—yes everything is there; that devil of a Joyce
> has left out nothing. The masculine public keenly enjoyed this
> chapter.[80]

Monnier lightly distances herself from "the masculine public," and
the "ordinary woman," but also recognizes the depersonalizing effect of mass appeal on the Gerties of the world. Joyce is a "devil"
for so thoroughly immersing Gerty in this blight, and also for so
relentlessly exposing the poverty of stereotypical female preoccu-
pations. Her enthusiasm for this aspect of the chapter resembles
Weaver's, though Weaver had considered it "human" rather than
"female" nature. Monnier also sees Joyce as a new type of mystic,
a "mystic of the human" with an uncommon female ideal. Instead
of expressing his truth in beautiful images, Joyce "chooses . . . that
which has been sacrificed, shamed, cut off, mistreated—that which
nobody had ever dared to present as it really was, that which had
always been regarded as outside of the law, outside of love. Nothing
to him appears useless or unworthy. Everything feeds the belly of
his Our Lady of the Underworld."[81]

In publishing, Beach and Monnier joined other avant-garde women
publishers of Joyce—Dora Marsden and Harriet Weaver of *The Egoist*
and Margaret Anderson and Jane Heap of *The Little Review*. Beach
recognized the pattern and quipped in her RTE film interview, "It
was always women who were publishing Joyce." Although she did
not accept the manuscript, another woman, Virginia Woolf of the
Hogarth Press was identified by Weaver and Beach as a likely publisher for *Ulysses*, and her press was noted for taking risks with avant-
garde writers. Beach had some personal benefit in mind when she

published *Ulysses*. In letters to her family financial backers (who might desire such news), she expressed her "hope to make money out of it, not only for Joyce but for me" and the belief that "*Ulysses* means thousands of dollars of publicity for me."[82] In her autobiography, Beach describes herself as the "midwife" of *Ulysses*,[83] typically a female role, and one that demands attention to the mother (in this case, Joyce) as well as the literary product. Not only did she take on a venture that no commercial press would risk, but she also granted Joyce the unusual and expensive right to revise proofs in very late stages, an arrangement that facilitated its revolutionary stylistic elaborations. In an essay titled "Great Amateur Publisher," Janet Flanner is critical of Joyce's treatment of "the amateur woman publisher" of the "modern masculine classic": "All Joyce's gratitude, largely unexpressed, should have been addressed to her as a woman. For all the patience she gave him was female, was even quasi-maternal in relation to his book."[84] Not only did Beach see the first edition of *Ulysses* to press; she also published *Pomes Penyeach* and *Our Exagmination Round his Factification for Incamination of Work in Progress*, and turned her office into a clipping bureau and clearing house for reviews and articles on Joyce. She scheduled publicity events, like Valery Larbaud's celebrated lecture on *Ulysses*, held at Monnier's bookshop in December 1921—its revenues returned to Joyce (JJ, 520-524). Adrienne Monnier became the publisher of the important first French edition of *Ulysses* as well. Simone de Beauvoir, who frequented La Maison des Amis des Livres as a student, has testified to the importance of Monnier's French edition of *Ulysses*: "a door was opened for us to a new world of foreign writers. . . ."[85] As time went on, Beach became in effect Joyce's agent and executive secretary.

That there were limits to Beach's tolerance of Joyce is evident in her memoir *Shakespeare and Company*, where she criticizes his "way of life," including the lavish hotels and restaurants he patronized, and his heavy tipping, in contrast to her simple living with Monnier.[86] She did have, and gently insisted upon, a style of her own—a dog, a car, and weekends away that Joyce apparently disapproved. "Joyce, as Saturday approached, always thought up so many extra chores for me that it usually looked as if he were going to win. But Adrienne and my own doggedness to hold on to my Sabbath in the country armed me for resistance."[87]

Sylvia Beach's autobiography is, in the main, positive concerning Joyce. As if accepting one of the female roles described in Virginia Woolf's *A Room of One's Own*, Beach serves as a magnifying mirror.[88] In what seems to be an overstatement, she describes her attitude toward Joyce at the time of their meeting as one of worship. "I imagined James Joyce up in the sky with the Gods." She frequently refers to his "genius." In their first, solitary meeting, she recalls greeting him, "Is this the great James Joyce?"[89] The half-sincere, half-teasing remark is comparable to ones that Emma Clery makes to Stephen Dedalus in *Stephen Hero*. It seems a typical tactic for bright and bold young woman of the period to get a man's attention. Beach finds Joyce more democratic and gracious than do most memoir writers, stating that he "was a great mixer—never at all standoffish," that he "treated people invariably ashis equals," and that he had told her he had "never met a bore." [90]

Perhaps more interesting than her clouded memories of their first meeting are Beach's social comments in the autobiography. She makes an interesting contrast between male-female relationships in France, as exemplified in Monnier's bookshop, and their gatherings in other parts of the world. While Joyce quaintly refrained from mentioning "certain things in the presence of ladies," a Frenchman did not. "The ladies themselves, in a country where men don't go off by themselves, were not at all disturbed." His own books, Joyce had no reluctance about: "Joyce had no objection to putting *Ulysses* into the hands of ladies, or to ladies publishing it."[91] Beach was amused by Joyce's family life, and especially by Nora's poking and pushing of him: "Joyce enjoyed being called a good-for-nothing by Nora; it was a relief from the respectful attitude of others."[92] She calls him "patriarchal," but has a less-than-repressive trait in mind—his regret "that he didn't have ten children."[93] She goes on to remark on his devotion to Giorgio and Lucia.

Although she is less notable as a correspondent than Harriet Weaver, Sylvia Beach provides the best access to her personality in her letters. According to people who knew her, her autobiography gives a misleading impression of her. She seems to have been distressed by the pressures of writing it and still very ambivalent about the sacrifices she had made for Joyce, as well as their rupture. She was also bewildered by the experiences of the depression and the German occupation, and by old age.[94] A much more jubilant and witty woman emerges in the letters she wrote to her mother and sisters and to

Harriet Weaver—their mutual concern for Joyce growing into an enjoyable female relationship in their later years. Sylvia Beach had strong opinions about what the Joyces needed, and sensed the power of Miss Weaver as an arranger and a persuader of Joyce (the same power sensed by Paul Léon when he replaced Beach as Joyce's Paris agent.) In letters written in 1922, Beach reports to Weaver, "Douglas' article quite made [Joyce] forget the pain in his eyes for the moment but he seems to be somewhat too excited at present. I think it is good for him to have something to think of that takes him out of himself however."[95] A few days later, she suggests that Joyce might have avoided the current attack of iritis if he had followed the doctor's treatment patiently and adopted "a more comfortable and wholesome mode of living." In this letter she was orchestrating Miss Weaver's major gift to Joyce, given with the aim of making wholesome living possible for the Joyce family.[96] On the more humorous side, Beach has her own formula of health: "I don't believe much in doctors except for setting broken bones and calming acute attacks of maladies. I think that plenty of sleep, food, work, and outdoor exercise and perhaps to see one's family as little as possible is the only way to be healthy."[97] Beach speaks here to another sane celibate. Their behind-the-scenes arrangements to help Joyce have a touch of the goddess about them, Sylvia Beach taking on her more spritely aspect.

Sylvia Beach's saddest episodes had to do with money and time—precious resources that she was not confident in handling. By nature an open, enthusiastic person, she spontaneously gave of herself and her ability to raise money for artists. Experience, reflection, and the well-meaning advice of friends like Jackson Mathews made her wary of generous first impulses,[98] causing her to contradict her own actions or promises. She began collecting Joyce materials for the love of it, and was uncertain but also wary of their value, which mounted unpredictably during the years. Miss Weaver gave her invaluable Joyce collection to the British Museum, influenced in the choice by the Joyce family's wish that Joyce's materials should not go to Ireland. Miss Beach got the reputation of selling to the highest bidder. She was also warned that the value of her collection would be reduced if scholars were allowed to "scoop" it before its sale. What she really needed was confidence in receiving the kind of benevolent advice and concern that she and Miss Weaver had provided for Joyce. While she retained many friends, her final years may have been more lonely than Joyce's. Adrienne Monnier became plagued with Ménière's syndrome and took her own life; Beach died alone.

Harriet Weaver, whom Beach addressed as "Dearest Josephine," offered a calming influence when Beach brought up her suspicions of scholars, and when both women were dragged into a bizarre dispute over Joyce's death mask.[99] Joyce's two chief benefactresses exchanged visits half a dozen times between 1924 and 1960, and Beach reported more than once an easing of terrible migraine headaches experienced since childhood when she was with "Josephine." But, though Miss Weaver brought about a final conciliation, Beach's memoir writing had reminded her of an old resentment toward even this exemplary woman. The subject was the proposed release of a cheaper Egoist edition of *Ulysses* before Beach's Paris edition was exhausted. Beach could not be sure, even in this late friendship.

Sylvia Beach was responsible for Joyce's introduction to Eugene and Maria Jolas, and the latter also deserves a place among the women who served as midwives to his life and works. The Jolases had just started the review *Transition* and soon began publishing selections from *Work in Progress*, along with Jolas's revolutionary statements on "the word," and Jungian investigations of the collective unconscious. The American-born Mme. Jolas refuses to call herself "a Joyce student," but prefers to be considered a "former friend." [100] She has been his protective friend from the time of their meeting in 1927, until the present. In addition to performing secretarial tasks for *Transition*, she ran a school, École Bilingue, first in Paris and then in Neuilly, which Joyce's grandson attended briefly. Sylvia Beach reports Joyce's admiration of Mme. Jolas's singing—especially the American songs and she fondly recalls their duets.[101] Like May Joyce and Margaret Cousins, Jolas accompanied him on the piano. She arranged the convivial holiday dinners and the teams of typists and proofreaders and participated in the good conversations that were essential to Joyce's happiness and progress with his work. Her most significant contribution to his well-being and his ability to write *Finnegans Wake*, however, was her maternal care of Lucia Joyce, throughout her heightening mental illness. Mme. Jolas also strove to protect the interests of Nora and Giorgio Joyce following Joyce's death. She maintained a correspondence with Harriet Shaw Weaver which reveals these efforts. She enterprisingly undertook exhibitions of Joyceana to provide income for the survivors, and demonstrated deep concern for all of them, particularly for Lucia.[102]

Although she displayed some discomfort with "women's lib" during an interview at the 1973 Joyce Symposium, Jolas also pointed with pride to Harriet Weaver's feminist backgrounds, and in 1980 contributed the article, "The Joyce I Knew and the Women around Him" to a special number of *The Crane Bag*, "Images of the Irish Woman." In this article, Jolas observes that "as far back as he could recall, Joyce had known a dominantly feminine world, composed as it was of his harassed, parturition-prone mother (15 pregnancies), the strict, bigoted 'Dante,' a swarm of sisters—six—a maid-servant, little girl playmates in the neighborhood."[103] She finds that "neither the family man nor the professional writer provides a clear reply" to the question "need the man-woman relationship be a conflictual one?"[104] She notes further that Joyce's attitudes varied from "his appreciation of the fact that biological difference need not exclude common interests and parallel action" to his instinctive embracing of Hamlet's "Frailty, thy name is woman."[105] This last seems a canny perception of Joyce's range of reactions to women.

Djuna Barnes, American journalist and, like Joyce, an experimenter in several literary genres, was among the young women who knew Joyce in Paris in the 1920s. One of the "lost generation," she was frequently in the company of Robert McAlmon. Her impressions of Joyce are recorded in two articles written in 1922, when she had been in Paris for only four months. They suggest that Joyce treated her a little more like the young male writers who surrounded him than is usually the case in his relationships with women. Furthermore, her accounts have a refreshing spirit compared to the usually awed, reflective memoirs, owing perhaps to their contemporaneity and to Barnes's tendency toward satire. She is placed here, in the chapter on Joyce's female acquaintances, but was also, at an early age, his critic as well.

In her article for *The Double Dealer*, "Vagaries Malicieux," Barnes treats Joyce as one of numerous experiences of Paris—a city so universally built up in the imagination that it was bound to receive a critical response from the young journalist, writing home. One of the most extraordinary moments in the article comes when, in the midst of Joyce's anecdote about a series of engravings illustrating the *Odyssey*, Barnes allowed her mind to wander—behavior quite out of accord with the usual vigilant attention accorded the master.[106] Barnes makes several frank, yet not really malicious observations on Joyce that present him in a different light. She says, for example, that she had little chance to find out whether Joyce had the "perfect" memory attributed to him, saying instead, "it has some of the slow dragging quality of an inland mist," and that in conversation Joyce "drifts from one subject to the other, making no definite division."[107] It is a trait in which he resembles the female voice he has created for Molly Bloom and ALP. The samples of conversation Barnes provides suggest that Joyce felt free to range in subject with her, the topics including a cynical observation on George Moore's sexuality ("He spoke, too, of Moore 'The Playboy of the Western World,' ") and a spicy baroness, who supposedly offered Joyce her "trunkful of pornographic plates . . . collected throughout many years of a roving, dissatisfied life, the life of a lover of mine, a Greek." In an observation that may also have been advice to Barnes, Joyce remarked, "But I did not write her story. . . . It was too extraordinary and a writer should never write about the extraordinary, that is for the journalist."[108]

A second article written for *Vanity Fair* was exclusively about Joyce, "James Joyce: A Portrait of the Man Who is, at Present, One of the Most Significant Figures in Literature." Barnes is still a keen and original observer of Joyce. Her descriptions of his physical features are comparable in quality to those of his friend Budgen, who viewed him with the painter's eye. The tone of the article, though frank, is less cynical and more direct, as suits the *Vanity Fair* audience. We learn that the usually shy Joyce had approached Barnes at the café Deux Magots, "out of the fog and damp, a tall man, with head slightly lifted and slightly turned, giving to the wind an orderly distemper of red and black hair, which descended sharply into a scant wedge on an out-thrust chin." Joyce had a plausible motive for meeting her: "Because he had heard of the suppression of *The Little Review* on account of *Ulysses* and of the subsequent trial, he sat down opposite me, who was familiar with the whole story. . . ."[109] In addition to having American publishing contacts, Barnes seems to have struck a congenial note by admiring "the most delightful waistcoat it has ever been my happiness to see. Purple with alternate doe and dog heads. The does, tiny scarlet tongues hanging out over blond lower lips, downed in a light wool, and the dogs no more ferocious or on the scent than any good animal who adheres to his master through the seven cycles of change." Barnes was in fact lavishing her attention on the very garment that Joyce considered one of his significant legacies from his father: "I got from him his portraits, a waistcoat, a good tenor voice, and an extravagant licentious disposition. . ." (L I, 312). She recalls, "He saw my admiration and he smiled, 'Made by the hand of my grandmother for the first hunt of the season.' " No one else, before or since, seems to have communed so with Joyce over this fine article, weighted with family significance and faded grandeur, a garment that eventually went to an artistic son, Samuel Beckett.

As a recorder of the physical Joyce, Barnes captures him anew: "He raised his eyes. There was something unfocused in them,—the same paleness seen in plants long hidden from the sun,—and sometimes a little jeer that goes with a lift and rounding of the upper lip." "If I were asked what seemed to be the most characteristic pose of James Joyce I should say that of the head; turned farther away than disgust and not so far as death, for the turn of displeasure is not so complete, yet the only thing at all like it, is the look in the throat of a stricken animal.[110] "A quiet man, this Joyce, with the back head of an African idol, long and flat. The back head of a man who had done away with the vulgar necessity of brain-room.[111]

Joyce shared with Barnes many of the same literary opinions he offered to Arthur Power, or much earlier to his schoolfellows in Dublin. Yeats was "a good boy and a fine poet, but too proud in his clothes, and too fond of the aesthetic—as for the rest of them - - - Irish stew! They don't even know that Gaelic is not the tongue of Dublin!!" Synge was "a great lump of a man who could not be argued with." *Riders to the Sea* was "as good as any one-act-play can be" but one-act plays could not offer "knock-down argument."[112] Great talkers including Oscar Wilde speak the language of "Sterne, Swift and the Restoration." "Hamlet is a great play written from the standpoint of the ghost . . ." Strindberg offers "no drama behind the hysterical raving."[113] Unlike Powers's accounts, Barnes's do not record her own, perhaps divergent opinions, whether or not she dared to differ with him in person. Robert McAlmon's description of her in Joyce's presence would seem to indicate that she looked the part of a worshipper,[114] though this may have merely reflected his perceptions.

Barnes hints at her method, suited to Joyce's interpersonal style, when she says, "Because one may not ask him questions, one must know him." By following the stream of his discourse, Barnes encountered many subjects of interest, not all of them reported by Joyce's other acquaintances of the era:

We have talked of rivers and of religion, of the instinctive genius of the church which chose, for the singing of its hymns, the voice without "overtones"—the voice of the eunuch. We have talked of women, about women he seems a bit disinterested. Were I vain I should say he is afraid of them, but I am certain he is only a little skeptical of their existence. . . .

We have talked of death, of rats, of horses, the sea; languages, climates and offerings. Of artists and Ireland.[115]

In the remark on women, one senses that Barnes has responded only internally, but with the sardonic attitude of non-acceptance that colors much of her writing. The remark on the "eunuch" voice of the church may have unique significance, offered to a woman, when we recall the attention Joyce lavishes upon Aunt Julia's exclusion from the choir, in favor of a boy, in "The Dead." The subject of Joyce as a "singer" seems to have been particularly useful to Barnes in summarizing the man. "Joyce must indeed have begun life as a singer, and a very tender singer, and because no voice can hold out over the brutalities of life without breaking—he turned to quill and paper, for so he could arrange, in the necessary silence, the abundant inadequacies of life, as a laying out of jewels—jewels with a will to decay."[116]

Publication of the article "James Joyce" was timed so that it provided publicity for *Ulysses* when it was just off the press. Although it is more personal than critical, Barnes's piece does offer some critical responses. Beneath a drawing of Joyce by Mina Loy, it describes *Chamber Music* as a "frail volume of verse [which] contains lyrics, subdued in tone, but of irreproachable loveliness." A *Portrait* "brought to the novel an interest in form, selection and style, more French than English." *Ulysses* "represents, in form, a following and elaboration of that method which Joyce first made apparent in the 'Portrait.' It is a question in many minds whether Joyce, in this new volume, has not pursued his theory too far for coherence and common understanding."[117] The last opinion is not necessarily Barnes', and may be offered as a sort of challenge to a potential reading audience. She reports early in the article her reading of *Dubliners* over her coffee during the war, and serving on theatrical committees "long enough to suggest the production of *Exiles*. Thus, she has noticed the earlier works, but it is *Ulysses* that arrests her with the sense of Joyce, the singer.[118] Elsewhere, she is reported to have said, after reading *Ulysses*, "I'll never write another line . . . Who has the nerve to after that?"[119] In response to those who have called Joyce "eccentric, mad, incoherent, unintelligible, yes and futuristic," she "wonders why, thinking what a fine lyric beginning that great Rabelaisian flower *Ulysses* had, with impartial adenda for foliage,—the thin sweet lyricism of *Chamber Music*, the casual inevitability of *Dubliners*." She equates Joyce with Stephen's vow in *A Portrait*: to go alone, not serving what he no longer believed, "to express myself in my art as freely as I can . . . using for my only defense . . . silence, exile and cunning."[120]

Djuna Barnes was more than an acute observer of Joyce. To some extent she adopted the Dedalus personal approach to life for herself. Furthermore, she may have extended Joyce into female-centered literature in her fanciful *Ladies Almanac* and her serious linguistic experiments in the novel *Ryder*, both published in 1928. Like Joyce, she stayed on in Paris; she contributed to Eugene Jolas's *Transition* at the same time that *Work in Progress* ran through its early installments. She fractured language and delved into the unconscious, like the tall man who had approached her out of a fog.[121]

Gisèle Freund, another young woman who shared Paris with the famous Joyce, has left an exquisite set of photographs of Joyce with his family at home, taken in 1938. One of these was most broadly circulated in Ellmann's *James Joyce*, but more are published in *James Joyce in Paris: His Final Years*. Freund's account reveals the continuing female network that surrounded and promoted Joyce in his late years. She presents a temperamental, yet considerate subject in Joyce, and a family-centered man. "Joyce, who possessed an almost mystical belief in blood ties, in the father-son relationship that pulsated through his creative work, derived a strange pleasure from posing beneath a portrait of his own father . . . 'Now everyone can see how much we look alike—four generations of Joyces,' he said."[122] The Joyce family portrait collection also features the work of a female artist, Mina Loy, who sketched both Joyce and Lucia, and provided lessons to the latter, and the brilliant photography of Berenice Abbott.

Brief mention should be made at this point of Margaret Anderson, who had founded *The Little Review* and made it an important vehicle of avant-garde art in America while still in her early twenties. Until they were stopped and prosecuted by the courts, she and Jane Heap serialized *Ulysses*. An anarchist and a solitary individual who conceived of herself as the artist, Anderson had much in common with James Joyce, especially the aspects of him represented in his persona,

Stephen Dedalus.[123] Joyce did not form a close relationship with Anderson and Heap, although they did seek him out in Paris. According to Arthur Power, Joyce's shyness and sensitivity with strangers, not the women themselves, made one early meeting awkward.[124] In later meetings at Joyce's flat, Anderson found in Joyce a gentle, kindly man, with "the same deprecating humor in the smile, the same quality of personal aristocracy" that her sympathetic father had possessed as a young man. Like many women of this era in Joyce's life, she was moved by his failing eyesight. He gave her the impression of extreme sensitivity, and of having "less escape from suffering about irremediable things than anyone else I had ever known."[125] Her memoirs also express regret that she had remained quiet and meek at her *Ulysses* trial, as instructed by the highly reputed literary lawyer, John Quinn. Anderson felt that she could have explained Joyce's "motives"—"the quality of Joyce's mind or the psychology which explains Rabelaisian tendencies" better than her supposedly learned defender.[126]

In Zurich, from the late twenties until his death, Joyce's female guardian and intellectual stimulus was Dr. Carola Giedion-Welcker. Primarily an art critic, but well-informed on the avant-garde in all genres, Giedion-Welcker wrote a brilliant article on *Ulysses* for *Neue Schweizer Rundschau* in 1928. This came to the attention of Sylvia Beach, who added it to the growing archive at Shakespeare and Company, and later that same year introduced the young Zuricher to Joyce. As is typical of her careful networking, Beach also brought Giedion-Welcker to Joyce's aid when he underwent an eye operation in Zurich the next year.

Giedion-Welcker's memoirs and articles reveal a strong intellect as well as a sensitivity to qualities of Joyce frequently missed in the memoirs and biographies offered by men. Although she failed to arouse in Joyce any deep interest in modern art, Giedion-Welcker was able to articulate analogies between James Joyce and avant-garde works in art and music. She compares Joyce and Paul Klee for their "totalization of the object" and for "linguistically humaniz[ing] the world of things and creatures."[127] In the 1929 essay on *Ulysses* she discusses the modern "work of reconstruction of" the "two great containers of reality, space and time" within the musical theory of George Antheil and the pronouncements of Gabo on pictoral art— all related to the interpenetrations achieved in Joyce's work.[128] Spatial and light metaphors and contrasts seem to occur readily to this art critic, and through them she often represents Joyce's intricate structures with clarity and perception. She distills Stephen's character, "The sharp brightness of his intellect and the half-darkness of his Irish soul produce the tragic conflicts of his being."[129] She describes Bloom's presentation: "Mr. Bloom . . . does everything in front of the reader's eye, that in our decent world is usually done behind locked doors. That means this: Mr. Bloom walks around without a facade. Since the sensual is this man's main sphere, it also takes the main place."[130] She offers a beautiful spatial reconstruction of "Proteus":

> Abstract reflection is mixed with momentary perception: the landscape is mystically Irish—pantheistically covered, in between is caustically surrealistic garbage-can smell. Not only the rhythm of the waves, horizon, distance, rocks but also washed ashore fragmentation. . . . Again and again, beside the bright splendorous side is the crumbling reverse of things.[131]

The neat aspects and divisions with which she had articulated her essay on *Ulysses* seem less appropriate to Giedion-Welcker's discussion of *Work in Progress* in 1929. While the principles of time, space, and penetration still apply, "form and contents . . . interpenetrate each other more intensely, are transposed onto a remote abstract plane."[132] In this essay, Giedion-Welcker sets up interesting complementary functions of masculine and feminine. She divides human existence into three primitive instincts—power, procreation and nutrition and assigns the principle of power to primitive man-mountain types. (Joyce had used a Chinese symbol of mountain— 凵 —for HCE.) Then she goes on to women:

> As complementary color to the massive- heroic type of virility (deep blue) a feminine fluid serpentines under numberless names and shades throughout the book. This many-headed complete phenomenon composes itself out of movement, vivacity, playfulness, garrulity, eroticism, maternity, love of clothes, fantasy, caprice, irrationality. As cosmic symbol: The River.[133]

In her memoirs, Giedion-Welcker suggests that Joyce had a greater interest in nature than has been generally supposed. She comments on his love of lakeside walks and the sound of running water. She cites his interest in the mountains, rivers and lake that formed Zurich, and the analogies that he loved to draw between that city's situation and other cities that fostered civilization.[134] Giedion-Welcker seems also to have elicited and recalled more political interest in Joyce than most of his contemporaries. She defends him against Stephen Spender's criticisms of Joyce for antisocial and arrogant attitudes, and recalls that Joyce was very interested in the modern Greek Revolution, and may have contemplated it as a subject for his next work.[135] She summarizes the attitude behind Joyce's politics and his dealing with people as a respect for individualism—the same quality that had made *A Portrait* a valid text for *The Egoist* and Miss Weaver.

Carola Giedion-Welcker, like Maria Jolas, was a mother as well as an intellectual. Her daughter recalls being somewhat timid toward Joyce, who maintained a reserved distance, perhaps hampered by his poor eyesight, while Nora played and interacted with children intimately.[136] He does seem to have shared parental concerns and insights about "the intense spiritual battles during puberty, a period of physical and psychic threats that he portrayed in his *Portrait of the Artist.*" Whether the allusion to *A Portrait* is Joyce's or Giedion-Welcker's, it is interesting to see Stephen's problems generalized to the difficulties both parents were having with their female children. In this case, Joyce gave family help, locating appropriate medical treatment for the Giedions' daughter, and also offering sympathy and reassurance.[137] In doing so, he grew out of narrowly masculine roles and into deep empathy with women.

The mature and capable women who lived through *Finnegans Wake* with Joyce repeatedly suggest that this was a man who had grown beyond the limits of Stephen Dedalus. Though he could still resurrect his earlier persona—especially with male encouragement—the mature Joyce does seem to have grown more family and friend-centered, to have learned to give as well as receive assistance in daily affairs, and to have placed a greater value upon the helping roles usually provided by women. These realizations may have come too late for Joyce to change roles in any major way—being by then incapacitated by ill health, troubled by his daughter's condition, and goaded on by an international reputation. Yet he could work these revisions in attitude into the text that slowly accrued in his final two decades.

From the start, Joyce offered something different in his art that appealed to the perceptions of intelligent women, striving for directed, conscious lives. They, in turn, saw that his difference might be conveyed to literary tradition, making it increasingly theirs.

Feminist Critics
on Joyce

6

□ The female critics we now turn to are not entirely distinct from
the intellectual, avant-garde women of chapter 5. A division at this
point marks a shift in attention to the various forms of feminist criticism, as discussed in the introduction, that have been applied to
James Joyce. As discussed earlier, a range of possibilities is accepted
in this study. Some are included as women responding to female
experience; some as self-avowed and/or publicly recognized feminists. Our purpose is not to restrict or just to record, but to detect
patterns of criticism, so as to direct the final inquiries of this study.
Harriet Shaw Weaver, Adrienne Monnier, Djuna Barnes, and Carola
Giedion-Welcker, whose "company" with Joyce led to their assignment to the previous chapter, also have their place among the figures
that follow.

Joyce's earliest women critics gave him mixed reviews, but provide
us with interesting records of women's perspectives at the end of
the first women's movement. Irish-American Mary (Molly) Colum
was not entirely an outsider. She had followed Joyce's educational
path in the National University in Dublin, heard about him from
friends, and married Padraic Colum, with whom Joyce was ac-
quainted. She claims that her review of *Ulysses* was one of the three
American reviews that Joyce liked. He couldn't have liked the whole
thing. In it Colum asserts that the latter half of *Ulysses* "ceases to
be of paramount literary interest," and takes this as a dangerous
indication that "science will oust literature altogether as a part of

human expression."[1] Later she would challenge the literary identity of *Work in Progress* in a review and in person to Joyce, claiming it was "outside literature." Joyce brooded over her remark sufficiently to send her husband back to her, days later, with the retort, "It may be outside literature now, but its future is inside literature."[2] Molly Colum was also not impressed by Molly Bloom: "The revelation of the mind of Marion Bloom in the last section would doubtless interest the laboratory, but to normal people it would seem an extraordinary exhibition of the mind of a female gorilla who has been corrupted by contact with humans."[3]

Unlike some of her contemporaries among women critics, Colum saw no harm in the "obscene" contents of *Ulysses*. Her early review also insists upon the autobiographical nature of both *A Portrait* and *Ulysses* and emphasizes the importance of Joyce's nationality and former religion. She claims, interestingly, that the death of his mother was "the great episode" of Stephen's life, claiming that death is the great emotional interest of the Irish race, but not placing particular emphasis upon the maternal role.[4]

Around 1923, the Colums began seeing the Joyces regularly. Richard Ellmann concludes that Joyce was "occasionally annoyed" by Mrs. Colum (JJ, 634); she had gained a reputation as a rather vociferous woman during her years at Columbia University, which lends credibility to Joyce's reported reaction to her. In her own remarks, Colum suggests that Joyce appreciated her repartee. She also notes, as did Sylvia Beach, Joyce's pleasure at Nora's "snappy remarks,"[5] Scholars often quote Joyce's remark to Molly Colum, "I hate women who know anything."[6] It has a significantly fuller context. Colum recalls it in the course of discussing Joyce's habit of pulling people's legs—in one case an American instructor whom he had fed tales of his indebtedness to Dujardin. Mary Colum challenged him to acknowledge his debts to the "great originators," Freud and Jung. Joyce was "evidently angry, and moving irritatedly in his chair," he said, "I hate women who know anything." But the exchange did not end there. Colum responded, " 'No, Joyce, you don't. . . . You like them.' After a few seconds of silent annoyance, a whimsical smile came over his face, and the rest of the afternoon was pleasant for all three of us."[7] The smile seems to offer the half-grudging admission that Colum had actually found him out, that he did like spirited, knowing women. Mary Colum sought and received financial aid for Joyce as early as 1919, and in 1930 proposed an anthology of his writings to Scribners, which was not accepted.[8] Colum shares some of the experiences of close friendship with the mature Joyce recorded by Jolas and Giedion-Welcker. Like the former, she assisted with Lucia, and like the latter, she felt that Joyce was not just the recipient of help from his friends; he gave assistance as well.

Another contemporary woman critic who is supposed to have annoyed Joyce is Rebecca West. West's literary career had begun at Dora Marsden's journal, *The Freewoman*. Indeed, her cutting review for that journal of H. G. Wells's novel *Marriage* led to her first meeting with Wells and their famous liaison. As subeditor of the later *New Freewoman*, West met Harriet Shaw Weaver, who impressed her with "her looks, but little else."[9] West liked Joyce's *Exiles* "tremendously," and as a young woman gave a lecture on it.[10] Her essays of the 1920s and 1930s were more mixed in reaction. Joyce focused on "The Strange Necessity," a long essay which he had read to him during one of his eye ailments. After hearing fifty pages, he felt, positively, that *Pomes Penyeach* "had in her case the intended effect of blowing up some bogey bogus personality and that she is quite delighted with the explosion" (SL, 337). But after further reading, he was "irritated profoundly. That his critic had had her illumination while about to buy some bonnets was a thing that seemed to leave a particularly bitter sting."[11] The mixing of bonnets with books is so Joycean a representation of thought processes, that one wonders at Joyce's being affronted. Joyce's supposed revenge was to allude to West throughout *Finnegans Wake* with references to bonnets. Ellmann suggests that the essay itself is mocked in the *Wake*. He adds the interesting note, supplied in a letter to him from West in 1959, that "her essay, which was in a personal and almost fictitious framework, was intended 'to show the power of James Joyce breaking into a mind unprepared for it' " (JJ, 605n). "The Strange Necessity" ranges through about two hundred pages, taking the persona through a day in Paris (as *Ulysses* takes Bloom and Dedalus through a day in Dublin). The action starts with the central female persona's purchase of Joyce's *Pomes Penyeach* at Sylvia Beach's bookshop. It follows her through the streets and into shops, where she buys a dress and hats, sees a lawyer, and has lunch at a fine house, all the while wondering about "the strange necessity" of *Ulysses*. Joyce's novel had competed against and cancelled out almost all of the other delightful stimuli of the autumn in Paris—including the bonnets that supposedly so annoyed Joyce. While innumerable bonnets do appear in *Finnegans*

Wake, it is probably a mistake to dismiss Joyce's reaction to West too easily. The *Wake* also frequently refers to her Paris environment, and to the odyssey through the city she makes while formulating the essay. "Look in the slag scuttle and you'll see the sailspread over the singing, and what do you want trippings for when you're Paris inspire your hat?" (FW, 453.23-25). Joyce never liked being compared to others and insists upon his difference in this passage. In the "Anna Livia Plurabelle" chapter, ALP wends her way as "robecca or worse" (FW, 203.4-5)—a significant association for West, whose travels and garnerings thus become embraced by the heroine of the *Wake*, represented as the river. To reinforce this, West is referred to a second time in ALP's journey from the hills: "And whitside did they droop their glows in their florry, aback to wist [Rebecca West] of affront to sea?" (FW, 204.24-25). Here West's "affront" to Joyce, the father, the sea, is suggested indirectly, and her "wit" may be admitted in "whitside."

West's essay, which rambles, free-associates, and compares *Ulysses* to art, dresses, and letters expressing love, is lyrical. It might be described as a less disciplined version of Virginia Woolf's effort to understand human contexts in *A Room of One's Own*. It is only partly about *Ulysses*; overall, it concerns the pleasure and preoccupation occasioned by great artistic work. It is filled with juxtaposed, trivial experiences and includes long passages on Pavlov's research on conditioned reflexes and Ingres' portrait of the young man in the snuff-colored coat. Much of this essay, and West's later impressions of *Finnegans Wake*, are critical, even insulting. But it is important to recall that West's criticisms are couched in overall respect for the power of Joyce's work, and this is something that could not have escaped him and may even have influenced his treatment of her in *Finnegans Wake*.

In attempting to come to terms with *Ulysses*, West's persona is frequently negative and judgmental. She asserts that Joyce had committed numerous literary offenses. The chief offense is a lack of taste, which allows him to admit sentimental shocks, obscene words, "excrementitious and sexual passages," and some unjustified incoherence of language.[12] Unlike Giedion-Welcker, West does not appreciate Bloom's lack of a facade. She considers him a travesty of the nature of man and labels him a "court jester," who "desiring to recede from life, looks back with nostalgia on the dung which he regards as the parent substance of the universe."[13] West's persona seems traditional here; she is more comfortable with the intellectual Stephen, and wishes that Joyce had remained within the classical tradition that had enabled him to write "A Painful Case" and "The Dead."

West's essay notes the importance of the family of father, mother, and son, with various incarnations of different phases of these three types. It offers a unique and interestingly sinister interpretation of the father:

> Simon Dedalus and Leopold Bloom are different phases of the Universal father, that which begets, which spills life anywhere, without care for its fate: and May Dedalus and Marion Bloom are different phases of the Universal Mother, that which conceives, which cherishes any life that is given to it, without care for anything but its physical fate; and Stephen and Rudy are different phases of the Universal son whose fate is Death.[14]

Although it is difficult to charge Bloom with indifference to his off-spring or to credit Molly with cherishing motherhood, West does seem to anticipate the role of the mother as survivor of the dying god, her son, which Joyce would develop more extensively in the *Wake*. Her perceptions of Simon and May Dedalus are also in line with current psychoanalytic criticism.[15] In a later part of the essay, West challenges the "philosophy" underlying the destruction of the son:

> It is not the philosophy which gives the book beauty. That eternally Leopold Bloom and Simon Dedalus will kill Rudy Bloom and Stephen Dedalus, but that that will be no victory, since eternally Marion Bloom and May Dedalus will raise up their enemies against them, is not a happy ending of the facts. Personally I would prefer man to draw a better design, even if it was drawn but once and was not repeated like the pattern on a wall paper.[16]

Although they are stated inconspicuously in the essay, these objections to the repetitive nature of the aesthetic of *Ulysses* and perhaps to murderous, male-centered themes are worthy of thought. West may be stating a wish for something not offered in the present culture—for a reintegration of female patterns or a new philosophical system revising male-centered, repetitive myths. Joyce made a chauvinistic remark to Frank Budgen in the early thirties which compares in attitude to his "I hate women who know anything," directed at Mary Colum. After cataloguing all the areas in science and letters that women have entered, he opined, "You have never heard of a woman who was the author of a complete philosophic system. No, and I don't think you ever will."[17] It is tempting to think that West may have been one of the women to challenge Joyce's own system of systems and possibly the very woman who prompted the remark. It is interesting to see how different West's view of nurturant mother-son dynamics is from those expressed in the Joycean criticism that was more attended to. Hers may be no more correct, but it serves as a vital complement.

West's "The Strange Necessity" does find beauty in *Ulysses*, particularly in its interweaving rhythms of characters and in its descriptions. The overall attitude toward Molly, unlike the reaction to Leopold, is positive, even superlative:

> Marian Bloom, the great mother who needs not trouble to trace her descent from the primeval age whence all things come, who lies in a bed yeasty with her warmth and sweat, and sends forth in a fountain from her strong, idealess mind thoughts of generation and recollection of sunshine . . . these are outside the sphere and beyond the power of any other writer alive or dead.[18]

"Penelope" is lauded as "one of the most tremendous summations of life that have ever been caught in the net of art."[19] Joyce's credibility is questioned in one area—the analyst finding it preposterous that, immediately after "a thoroughly satisfactory sexual encounter," Molly should be "immersed in frenzied and aggressive fantasies inexplicable save as the torments of abstinence."[20]

Joyce creates a "strange necessity" in the persona of West's essay. He speaks to her in that place and time in the universe. What overcomes her many objections is her sense that Joyce represents in *Ulysses* the "excitatory complexes of her own world" and that knowing *Ulysses* helps her to place herself in the universe.[21] This response may have been a little more individually oriented than Joyce would have wished. It also may not have singled *Ulysses* out sufficiently from other stimuli. But it was praise indeed. At the end of her life, Rebecca West still reacted with bewilderment to the "insane hostility" toward her which she found expressed in *Finnegans Wake* and in Joyce's reported conversation.[22]

Virginia Woolf's reactions to Joyce's *Ulysses* are in some ways comparable to those of her compatriot, Rebecca West. Both women recognized its great importance and displayed interest in the "life" it contained and the psychological interest it provided. Both questioned its taste. Woolf does more comparison of her style to Joyce's, giving us the sense that she is Joyce's literary rival as well as his critical admirer.

In "Modern Novels," a notebook she kept while first reading *Ulysses*, Woolf shows openness to Joyce's structural innovations, as Suzette Henke has observed.[23] Woolf admires *Ulysses* as "an attempt to get thinking into literature," and to "do away with the machinery— to extract the marrow—it's quite time of course." She compares his method to cinema. Several times, she also notes that it is "unfair" to approach Joyce merely "by way of his method."[24]

Woolf's most formal and favorable statements on Joyce follow in her landmark essay, "Modern Fiction," written in April 1919, while Woolf was in the midst of reading the installments of *Ulysses* then appearing in the *Little Review*. She notes that "Mr. James Joyce" is distinguished among young writers, whom she defines as follows:

> They attempt to come closer to life, and to preserve more sincerely and exactly what interests and moves them, even if to do so they must discard most of the conventions which are commonly observed by the novelist. Let us record the atoms as they fall upon the mind in the order in which they fall, let us trace the pattern, however disconnected and incoherent in appearance, which each sight or incident scores upon the consciousness.[25]

She goes on to praise the "Hades" chapter for reasons similar to those already cited in "Modern Novels": "The scene in the cemetery, for instance, with its brilliancy, its sordidity, its incoherence, its sudden lightning flashes of significance, does undoubtedly come so close to the quick of the mind that . . . it is difficult not to acclaim a masterpiece."[26] Joyce's lyrical recording of consciousness was comparable to Woolf's natural style, as she would realize in frustration as she was writing *Jacob's Room*: "I reflected how what I'm doing is probably being better done by Mr. Joyce."[27] In attempting the lyrical, perceptual mode, Joyce was entering an area where women writers were and are particularly successful, perhaps because their experience in this area was no more limited than that of experimental male writers of the early twentieth century.

Woolf detects a possible limitation to "Hades," which she tentatively attributes to "the comparative poverty of the writer's mind." She presses on with a series of questions: "Is it due to the method that we feel neither jovial nor magnanimous, but centered in a self which, in spite of its tremor of susceptibility, never embraces or creates what is outside itself or beyond?"[28] Her accusation resembles an early one made by AE, who had told Joyce, "you have not enough chaos in you to make a world" (JJ, 99). It was a problem Woolf would address in her diary, in cultivating her own method. Interestingly, it is the diary entries that are always harshest to Joyce: "I suppose the danger is the damned egotistical self; which ruins Joyce and Richardson to my mind: is one pliant and rich enough to provide a wall for the book from oneself without becoming as in Joyce and Richardson, narrowing and restricting?"[29] The focus on the individual consciousness is pertinent to the early solipsism of Stephen Dedalus and to Joyce's affinity to individualist journals like *Dana*, *The Egoist*, and *The Little Review*. Greater universality would be the effort of the *Wake*.

"Modern Fiction" also brings up the issue of Joyce's taste, his supposed "indecency"—something that troubled West as well, though not Weaver, Monnier, Giedion-Welcker, or Colum. "Does the emphasis laid, perhaps didactically, upon indecency, contribute to the effect of something angular or isolated?"[30] In the preparatory notebook, Woolf had returned repeatedly to "indecency," knowing she had to treat it, but wondering how, and even questioning her own reactions to it: "And then the function of indecency. Must get out of the way of thinking that indecency is more real than anything else—a dodge because of the part of reticence, but a cheap one." On another page she is at first superior in attitude, but ends on a confessional note. She observes that it "seems to be written for a set in a back street. What does this come from? Always a mark of a second rater. Indifference to public opinion—desire to shock—need of dwelling so much on indecency. Whole question of indecency a difficult one. It should be colourless: but this we can't quite manage yet." Elsewhere, she admits, it "may be time that the unconscious mind dwells on indecency."[31] Writing shortly before her own death and just after Joyce's, Woolf is still troubled by this aspect of Joyce, and more hardened in her attitude. She recalls Harriet Shaw Weaver's visit, made in an effort to have the Woolfs' Hogarth Press publish the manuscript:

> I remember Miss Weaver, in wool gloves, bringing *Ulysses* in typescript to our teatable at Hogarth House. . . . Would we devote our lives to printing it? The indecent pages looked so incongruous:

she was spinsterly, buttoned up. And the pages reeled with indecency. I put them in the drawer of the inlaid cabinet.[32]

Woolf's own gentlewomanly abhorrence of the text is expressed in
the distinguished furnishings, at first approached by the manuscript,
and then used to shut it neatly away. Harriet Weaver, despite the
somehow questionable wool gloves and spinsterly mien, is very like
Woolf in her upper middle-class background, and, as pictures of
Woolf suggest, even in buttoned-up dress. One may infer that the
book is just as incongruous to Woolf as Weaver. Like Lady Gregory,
who had confided to Yeats that young Joyce was not quite "out of
the top drawer," Virginia Woolf was not without class prejudices
when she assigned his book to the drawer of the inlaid cabinet.
Sarcasm radiates from the exaggerated line, "Would we devote our
lives to printing it?" Woolf seems to realize that Weaver was capable
of such devotion, and to declare that she had her own literature to
produce. The Woolfs had in fact also feared prosecution and also felt
that the size of the manuscript was too great for their slow hand
press (the reason for rejection given to Miss Weaver).[33]
     A persistent advocate of *Ulysses* to Virginia Woolf was T. S. Eliot,
to whom she confided that she felt Joyce "was virile—a he-goat."
Eliot agreed and added that "he left out many things that were
important."[34] Perhaps here Woolf again makes her charge of egotistical narrowness. But perhaps she suggests a male-centered limitation as well. An animal maleness was foreign and distasteful to
Woolf—something primitive and potentially brutal that she never
came to terms with. In her late diary entry on Joyce she recalls
reading *Ulysses* "with spasms of wonder, of discovery, and then again,
with long lapses of intense boredom. This goes back to a prehistoric
world."[35] Clearly, Joyce offered exciting, even frightening, territory
that she valued and wished to explore herself. But what he explored
was not enough and sometimes produced tedium. Like West, Woolf
sought to reintegrate more into fictional experience.
     We move now from the early 1940s to the 1960s, the decade that
brought the second women's movement and its impact upon literary
criticism. The woman critics we survey are mostly American academics and no longer are concentrated in the higher strata of society.
They are reacting not to a puzzling new figure in literature, but to
a member of the canon, and a god of the critical establishment. Some
deliberately attach themselves to feminist ideology; some casually

inform their study of Joyce with the feminist conditioning that has entered their everyday lives.

Florence Howe's ideological feminist activities include her founding of the Modern Language Association's Women's Caucus and her establishment of the Feminist Press. Howe selects Joyce to make a negative point about the established literary canon. She discovered, upon returning to Joyce, that he bored her; her discontent, she notes, differs from Woolf's, whose charges of vulgarity she links to class differences she does not share:

> Except for *Dubliners*, I remember feeling bored by his books, though I regret never having the courage until recently to admit my views. I regret also that I assumed the boredom to be a failure of taste— after all, who was I, a mere woman student, to judge the god Joyce? I could not even argue his vulgarity, as Virginia Woolf had, for my origins were as lower-class as his.[36]

Howe examines the bird-girl passage of *A Portrait* and Stephen's resulting vow to become the artist. She finds that Stephen "takes the measure of maleness" against a "land-bound," "earth-mother" woman, and discovers himself to be a powerful active, master and artist in comparison. This fits with the ideological feminist detection of woman as "other" in male-centered literary tradition. Howe allows for the cultural influences of church, class, and nation upon Stephen's ability to react to the girl as a real being, and for the reaction that Joyce was representing social reality as he knew it. But while realistic content may have allowed her to appreciate *Dubliners*, it does not satisfy her in *A Portrait*. Howe concludes that"Joyce's vision of reality is specifically male centered" and that "Joyce was neither reformer nor visionary."[37] Howe's boredom would seem to proceed from her unwillingness to accept the girl, as creatively transformed by Stephen, and her inability to accept Stephen as a universal representative of the budding artist. It could be noted that many women readers, unable to find excitement or challenge in the roles generally offered women in fiction, quite early adopt the habit of identifying with male characters, in this case becoming artist instead of "bird"! Howe was perhaps the first to express the lasting feminist desire to see women depicted as artist or intellectual in Joyce and to protest the stereotype of woman as limited "other" or muse.

Carolyn Heilbrun in her "Afterword" to *Women in Joyce* wonders whether Joyce shouldn't be called a "misogynist, a man who hates women for becoming what he has determined they should be." She finds him unable to "imagine a woman whom convention did not offer him" or to see "woman as a paradigm of humanity." She makes these observations despite the more positive views of Joyce offered in the collection by other feminist critics.[38]

Another feminist of the sixties who comments on James Joyce repeatedly is Mary Ellmann, author of *Thinking about Women*. Ellmann's very approach to writing criticism has been described as "feminine" by Patricia Meyer Spacks because of its function of "witty (i.e. intellectual) logic and rhetoric—a style whose resource and limitation is its evasiveness."[39] But even if the approach is a light one, Ellmann's agile and penetrating definitions do mock male stereotypes of women. Ellmann criticizes several "feminine stereotypes" indulged in by Joyce. She selects an obvious example: "In Molly Bloom's soliloquy . . . thinking and menstruating are similar and concomitant processes. She can no more govern the first, by sentence structure or punctuation, than she can the second."[40] With a typical touch of evasive sarcasm, Ellmann reacts to Molly's thought as "all warmth and sympathy: one could no more disapprove of [her] liquidity than disapprove of warm baths."[41] As far as the structure of her own mind goes, Ellmann warns her interviewer, "Connect my crabbed little mind with water now, flowing streams and all that. Go ahead. Do me a Molly Bloom. I dare you."[42] She thus joins Molly Colum as a depreciator of Molly Bloom as representative of the female intellect. Ellmann also uses Joyce at his own expense to head her section on a second feminine stereotype, "irrationality." The quotation used is from *Giacomo Joyce*: "My words in her mind: cold polished stones sinking through a quagmire."[43] Elsewhere, she catches Joyce in typical examples of false female sexual analogy. In the first instance, he employs maternal insult in the celebrated representation of Ireland as the "old sow that eats her farrow."[44] In the second from *A Portrait* he employs the womb-imagination: "O! In the virgin womb of the imagination, the word is made flesh."[45] Ellmann's work has generally been recognized for its startling insights and it still provides the lead for studies of women in language. Contemporary discussions of Joyce's concept of creativity still point to the physical-mental fallacy of Stephen's and Joyce's metaphors.[46] Ellmann notes that, though Joyce repeated "hackneyed criticisms of women "in conversation," he "reclaims them by affection, subtlety and wit" in his written words.[47]

Mary Ellmann balances her account of Joyce's supposed offenses with perceptions of his fundamentally positive disposition toward writing about women. She notes his personal use in Dublin of " 'silence, exile and cunning,' all conventional attributes of the defendant or the woman." She observes that Joyce and the other creators of the "introspective, or psychological, novel" (Richardson and Proust) were all "markedly indifferent to our customary heterosexual competitions in power."[48] And finally, she admires Joyce's "curiosity . . . for becoming as much as judging the other" sex.[49] Comparing him with Ernest Hemingway and Norman Mailer, Ellmann predictably finds Joyce's treatment more sympathetic or egalitarian.[50]

More radical, politically oriented feminists of the late sixties and early seventies also have some praise for Joyce. Kate Millett finds Joyce's characterization of woman as "nature," "unspoiled primeval understanding," or "the eternal feminine" more positive than what she takes to be D. H. Lawrence's identification of the New Woman as the "enemy."[51] Millett also finds Joyce preferable to Arthur Miller, since Joyce lacks the sexual hostility toward women that Millett detects in Miller.[52] Shulamith Firestone, the radical Marxist-feminist author of *The Dialectic of Sex* resembles Mary Ellmann in her appreciation of Joyce's inclination and ability to become the other sex, "imaginarily crossing the line [between male and female] at will."[53]

Marilyn French, Joyce scholar and feminist novelist, offers a fictional late sixties' feminist opinion of Joyce recorded on a lavatory wall in *The Women's Room* (published 1977). To a militant who declares "KILL ALL FASCIST PIGS!!" a Joycean writer of graffiti suggests a more subtle borrowing of "new ways . . . to kill pigs": "We must cleanse our minds of all the old shit, we must work in silence, exile, and cunning like that mcp Joyce. We must have a revolution of sensibility." This moderate view is not granted the last word. The Joycean is labeled a "FUCKING CHRISTIAN IDIOT" for her maxims and remonstrated in Marxist maxim, "THERE IS ONLY POWER! POWER TO THE PEOPLE! POWER TO THE POOR!!"[54] Even the moderate intellectual labels Joyce a "male chauvinist pig," and the militant fails to see anything useful in the tactics that Mary Ellmann has labeled as typically female.[55] The presence of Joyce in this separatist, popular fiction is mainly a curiosity, however.

Marilyn French's assessment of Joyce in *The Book as World* is more moderate and academic than even the more conservative bathroom scribe of *The Women's Room*. Like the bird-girl creation deplored by Florence Howe, Molly Bloom is not seen as a realistic woman by French. She is "other" or "symbol" and "largely a product of male imagination, male modes of vision." French is probably speaking at least in part of Joyce's own consciousness when she goes on to say that Leopold Bloom is "a symbol for the feminite (androgynous) male."[56] To many feminists in the mid-seventies, androgyny was the ideal attitude of the artist—the vision called for in particular by Carolyn Heilbrun and noted by her in Bloom.[57] French also sees Molly as "a circumference bounding the human (male) world"—a structural function that denies her reality, but also a powerful conception of the female principle; women are more stereotypically seen as confined to a small part of a man's world.[58]

Adaline Glasheen has no stated or concerted feminist approach or purpose. Yet her introduction and the initial remarks she makes on individual characters of the *Wake* in her *Third Census of Finnegans Wake* show an alerted feminist consciousness. She registers her protests to the "male-chauvinist father" at the head of a nuclear family or the incestuous designs of the father on his daughter " 'maker mates with made': This is one of those masculine concepts . . . and it makes a woman's head go round."[59] Glasheen is also aware of the presence of goddesses like Artemis, in aspect if not in name, throughout the *Wake*.[60] Many of Glasheen's suggestions merit systematic feminist critical handling.

Margot Norris's *The Decentered Universe of Finnegans Wake* displays the most coherent feminist interpretation of that work to date, though this may not seem obvious from the title or declared method. Norris implies that the central myths of the human family embodied by the *Wake* are patriarchal. The *Wake* family is a Freudian Oedipal family. The father represents law, which includes the incest taboo and assures the continuation of the male "hierarchy of authority." The sons pervasively enact symbolic parricide as a rite of self-possession.[61] Norris represents some of the female roles within this male order in negative terms, reflecting some feminist ideology. She notes that the love triangle pervades Joyce's works, starting with *Chamber Music*. With *Exiles*, she finds that Joyce shifts his "focus from the man-woman to the man-man relationship, thereby relegating the woman to a mediated position."[62] Norris is also critical of female narcissism and finds that unlike Joyce's contentious males, his placid temptresses are too primitive for human knowledge.[63] ALP is a more positive female figure to Norris. She represents "redemption: female salvage." She is the opposite of male law and possession:

> ALP's acts are essentially selfless. She steals van Hoother's children, but returns them improved and at peace. She plunders the battlefield and the dump, but uses the junk and the Letter to bring about the reconciliation and restoration of others. ALP's work stands in opposition to the lawful appropriations of father and sons because she does not seek self-possession through the capture of others. The problem of ALP's own self is not posed until her final monologue, when she reclaims it by a total repudiation of all others.[64]

Though ALP is largely a medial female in this description, she is finally allowed independent selfhood in the final vision. ALP is "the agent of freedom through communication or exchange." Her anarchic gathering has its linguistic correspondence in *Finnegans Wake* itself.[65] In a recent essay on ALP, Norris refines these observations in a more deliberately feminist approach. She explains ALP's contradictions by considering her "the fantasy projection of a male figure dreaming . . . expressions of the dreamer's highly ambivalent, guilty feelings about his wife, daughter, mother, and sister." As river, however, Norris's ALP also escapes the elderly HCE's male fantasy.[66]

Colin MacCabe in his *James Joyce and the Revolution of the Word* attends throughout to discourse as it relates to women. MacCabe shows feminist awareness even in his own discourse, which carefully refers to the reader as "he or she." A post-structuralist working in the psychoanalytic tradition of Jacques Lacan, MacCabe calls attention to Freudian theories of family romance fantasies and fetishism, but views them with an eye to the limited interpretations available to our phallo-centric society.[67] This represents a significant advance, from the standpoint of feminist critical method.

According to MacCabe, Joyce gradually works away from classic realism's final, privileged discourse or meta-language, with its one-to-one symbolic correspondences, and its smoothing over of incoherence. Interestingly, he sees Emma Clery in *Stephen Hero* as an early threat to Stephen's "self-sufficient identity" and notes Joyce's inability to allow central mother figures like Mrs. Mooney and Mrs. Kearney in *Dubliners* to speak for themselves, or to escape dominant meta-language. With "The Dead," Joyce breaks with his need to identify with the father and authoritatively fix the meaning of the mother.[68] In *A Portrait*, he goes on to "let the desire of the mother speak":

> In so far as the text refuses narrative and the father, it can inves-
> tigate the world of the mother that lies buried in a patriarchal
> society, but in so far as the text figures an omnipotent father, in
> so far as it still tells a story, then women will still figure as baga-
> telles, the mere means of exchange between men.[69]

MacCabe detects in Gerty MacDowell and the barmaids of "Sirens" the "female denial of female sexuality" that encourages male phallic narcissism, even in Leopold Bloom. Molly slays the suitors and the corresponding fetishism of the penis.[70] "Penelope" is "simply the movement of [*Ulysses*] all over again, the movement to writing and the speaking of female desire through a male pen."[71] *Finnegans Wake* continues Joyce's liberation from the male principle of dominance in writing and his openness to a principle of desire that attends to differences and absences and is identified with the female, ALP.[72] MacCabe sees in Issy Joyce's attempt to investigate language de-velopment in young girls, to whom "gramma's grammar" is uniquely available *via* her relationship to her mother. He suggests, however, that Issy's voice was beyond Joyce, who scattered it in her footnotes to the "Lessons" chapter.[73] In summary, MacCabe sees a male-fe-male complement in roles and language potentials:

> On the one hand you have the story-telling father, promising iden-
> tity and position and on the other you have the mother dividing
> language into its constituent parts to let desire speak. Into the
> oppositions male and female, position and desire *Finnegans Wake*
> introduces writing: desire in position and position in desire, an
> ineradicable and inexhaustible bisexuality, a constant process, "The
> seim anew."[74]

Post-structuralists like MacCabe, Philippe Sollers, and Julia Kris-teva have worked to rebalance psychoanalysis so that pre-Oedipal, pre-paternal qualities are re-emphasized. Kristeva suggests that Joyce has importance for his reversal of the rejection of the mother, ini-tiated in the Renaissance, and in the "reinstatement of maternal territory in language":[75]

> It was not until the end of the nineteenth century and Joyce, even
> more than Freud, that this repression of the mother and incest was
> affirmed as risky and unsettling to one's very flesh and sex. Not

until then did it, by means of a language that "musicates through letters," resume within discourse the rhythms, intonations and echolalias of the mother-infant symbiosis—intense, pre-Oedipal, predating the father. . . .[76]

Kristeva finds evidence of this in Joyce's "joyous and insane incestuous plunge summed up in Molly's jouissance"[77] and in "the paternal baby talk in *Finnegans Wake*," a work which she heralds elsewhere as possessing the "one language" that "grows more and more contemporary."[78]

Finnegans Wake is also very compatible with current searches for lost goddesses and other pre-patriarchal feminine images. A notable work in this vein is Nor Hall's *The Moon and the Virgin*. Hall identifies herself as an "archaeologist of the mind" who "digs up myths and stories, the foundation of human meaning." She cites as a special tool "etymology, the study of word origins, which James Joyce called 'etym-smashing.' "[79] A psychoanalyst, Hall is apt to refer to the dreams of her clients alongside folk-tales and myths. She extends Freud and Jung and uses the classification system of Toni Wolff (the intimate associate of Jung) to establish four basic feminine character types: the mother, the Amazon, the Hetaira or companion, and the medial feminine—the sibyl or wise woman. *Finnegans Wake* provides her with examples of the rituals and concerns of all four types. The Great Mother's egg of creation she finds in Joyce's "Hatch as Hatch can" and in "a certain tap-tapping running through *Finnegans Wake* as a constant tip (or clue) to the world's renew-all."[80] In Nuvoletta's fall and her cries to ALP, she finds the same mother-daughter relationship that she studies in detail *via* the Demeter-Persephone myth. An important function of the Amazonian or Artemis-Hecate type, according to Hall, is to give women back to themselves, a function she finds summarized in Joyce's phrase "making sound sense kin again," though one that she finds no Joycean characters to represent. Hetaira as companion, returning to the father, she locates in the conclusion of *Finnegans Wake*, as the river runs out to sea to meet the father. The washerwomen at the ford with their gossip, or "god-speaking," and ALP represent the medial feminine, with her powers of magical transformation and mediation between the visible and the invisible.[81] ALP is compared to the Norse "alp," a feminine elf that visits and seizes one in the dark, and a version of the medial feminine as old wise woman. As the Liffey she " 'leafy speafs' or speaks like the sibyl. . . . She is water nymph, matronly river, delightfully pure and filthy as a hag. She is the shameless barmaid and the proper and generous widow . . . . But above all, she is the 'spae-wife,' the cackling Mother Goose, or the earth-pecking hen, Biddy, who scratches the torn scraps of a gossipacious letter filled with the secrets of a woman's heart out of a dung heap." Hall takes special note that Joyce located the "manifesto or mamafesta" of the book in the Hen's scratchings, an implication that history is passed on in the old wives' tale."[82]

Additional feminist verdicts on Joyce could and, in other studies, should be assembled. Relevant criticism is cited in conjunction with Emma Clery, Molly Bloom, and Issy in chapters 7-9. Some patterns do emerge, however, from our investigations so far. Probably as a reflection of sexual and class attitudes in the early century, "decency" or "vulgarity" is an issue with early feminists, and Joyce offends some, but by no means all, of them. Feminists of the 1970s bring feminist ideological issues more to the fore. Joyce is charged with "chauvinism," sometimes (as in French's novel) for unstated offenses, most convincingly for his predominant use of male perceivers and female "others," or "companion" women. Virginia Woolf's charges of egotism, and her perception of him as a "he-goat" are related. Feminists from the start have appreciated, with a light suggestion of discomfort, Joyce's depiction of human or female nature—the latter of a culturally induced, stereotypical sort. What they value most in him is not his baffling intricacies, but his mythic, otherworldly, lyrical voice, in which woman transcends her stereotypes. This is readily identified with an alternate female order, which counters male authority and language and predates the father figure that has proved so dominant in twentieth-century society.

Emma

7

☐ Out of all of Joyce's early woman characters, why should Emma Clery be selected for close attention? She was, after all, cast into the fire by Joyce with the rest of the *Stephen Hero* manuscript and resurrected only in a few references in *A Portrait* and in fewer still in *Ulysses*. One good reason is that she offers us what cannot be found elsewhere—a central, sustained, individualized portrait of a modern, urban, intelligent young woman who is permitted to some extent to speak her mind and direct her affairs. Joyce's realistic flower girls, peasant women, nursemaids, prostitutes, and college girls are usually met briefly at a party, passed on the street, spotted on a beach, or glimpsed in a dream or vision. The development of Emma Clery's relationship with Stephen Daedalus appears prominently in half of the surviving chapters of the manuscript; it culminates three of them and arrives at a form of closure when Emma breaks with Stephen following his surprising and unexpected suggestion that they "live one night together" (SH, 198). Though Stephen is put off by Emma's supposed "loud, forced manners," (SH, 66), readers may find her engaging as she dispenses with ceremony in their first meeting and tries to involve the aloof artist in her concerns, teasing his ideas from him and insisting on his relation to the rest of humanity. Joyce typically filters identities of his early women characters through the self-sufficient identity and biased point of view of a central male character like Mr. Duffy, Gabriel Conroy, or Stephen Dedalus. He tempers this with ironic control, but without granting the reader the

133

benefit of female perceptions. In this text, Emma gives her perceptions of Stephen and reveals some of the errors of his assumptions
about women. But it remains also a study of Stephen, and its narrative
is frequently clotted with his evaluations of those who differ from
him over politics, religion, or sexual mores—Emma included.

As I noted in the previous chapter, Colin MacCabe finds in *Stephen
Hero* evidence of a "profound mutation" in Joyce's style, moving
away from a single judgmental position associated with the father,
toward a mother language.[1] MacCabe suggests further that Joyce
could not finish *Stephen Hero* because moments of it resisted the
structuring of the father's point of knowledge, the meta-language of
classic realism. Emma Clery figures importantly in these troubling
moments.[2]

Although Joyce may have undergone a sort of women's liberation
of narrative style when he moved on to *A Portrait*, he failed to produce an equally engaging woman character in the later version. As
Theodore Spencer puts it, he converts a "living personality" to an
"anonymous girl" usually known only by her initials.[3] Bernard Benstock finds this "overly refined extension" of *Stephen Hero's* Emma
"at best a failed heroine: her timidity of spirit and conventional
demeanor disqualify her as a person,"[4] with Stephen Daedalus doing
much of the disqualifying through his restrictive, symbolic interpretation of Emma's "demeanor" in thought and poetry. Charles
Rossman has considered some of the probable causes for Stephen's
reduced vision of Emma. He feels that, as a symptom of Stephen's
alienation from his physical being, the young man subjects the potentially warm relationship with Emma to his "spiritual-heroic refrigerating apparatus."[5] Paradoxically, Stephen also transforms the
real Emma into an ideal "masculine erotic fantasy" in his "Villanelle"
and an earlier poem. These symptoms of his discomfort with external
reality are very much out of keeping with Stephen's supposedly life-
centered aesthetic.[6] Stephen may be able to assign an identity to the
bird-girl that cultivates his own artistic ego (an act that Florence
Howe objects to, as we have seen).[7] But he can never completely
dismiss or control Emma. In *A Portrait*, Stephen still watches her
conversation with Father Moran jealously and feels betrayed by her
salute to Cranly. He and readers alike are made to feel curious about
the secrets of her quiet, gay conversations with other young women.
Even in *Ulysses* when Stephen spots her in the library (one of her
typical student haunts, as well as his), he is far from indifferent: "Is

that? . . . Blueribboned hat . . . Idly writing . . . What? Looked . . .
(U, 215). Stephen is slightly critical of her "idle" manner, and curious about what she is doing and whether she has seen him. At the
end of *Stephen Hero*, Lynch is skeptical, with good reason, about
Stephen's assertion that "she is nothing to me now . . ." (SH, 234).
Others who resemble Emma—Dilly purchasing her French primer
or the pert little flower girl he encounters *en route* to the University—
require quick passage. He does not want to be deflected by guilt, in
the case of his needy sister, nor does he wish to hear the flower girl's
attentions turned to the next man who passes. Emma merits our
attention in the present study because she offers a field of resistances
in style, character, and the critical interpretations she has received,
richer and broader than that for most of Joyce's woman characters,
and one worth our careful cultivation.

Seeing Emma Clery in her own right and understanding the complexities of her relationship to Stephen and Joyce are complicated
by many factors, among them some we have already discussed—the
lack of background studies on women of Emma's period, the ele-
vation of categories like virgin and whore to the neglect of other
aspects, like women in society or women in nature, and our unconscious acceptance of double standards for human behavior. The *Stephen Hero* text also creates problems with its male-centered point
of view, its often belabored narrative, and its being incomplete.

In seeking an education, Emma Clery was participating in a genteel
fashion in the feminist revolution discussed earlier (chapter 3). She
was ahead of such important contemporaries of Joyce as Virginia
Woolf and Harriet Shaw Weaver, who had to rely upon tutors at
home and their own reading for education and who always regretted
their not having been permitted to go to university. In Emma's time
undergraduate education aimed at Catholic middle-class women had
been available for only twenty years in Dublin and was still very
unequal to that provided to Protestants and men of all faiths. It was
still the accepted pattern for a young woman to attend a convent
school for a few years, learning some Latin and French, music, dancing and needlework, and then to retire to marriage and motherhood.
This was the course followed by Mrs. Dedalus, who can play the
sailor's hornpipe on the piano for baby tuckoo's dancing (P, 7), but
set aside her reading and her interest in "all kinds of new plays"
when her husband has different, more masculine interests like ath-
letics (SH, 85). Although her interests are similar to his, Mrs. Dae-

dalus' intellect goes unsuspected by her solipsistic son, who reads his aesthetic essay to her out of a need for sympathy and without much hope for comprehension. The passages in which Stephen reflects on his mother's capacity to see "beauty" as "more than a convention of the drawing-room" and suspects that she considers it a "synonym for licentious ways" are vulgar in their haughty condescension and clearly ironic (SH, 84).

Stephen's sister Isabel, like his mother, is following a typical pattern. She has been sent to a convent, probably as a student, but it is clear that her father is more interested in the financial advantage of having the nuns support her than eager to educate his daughter (SH, 109). Stephen feels estranged from Isabel "on account of the way in which she had been brought up," by which he means that she has accepted the female norms of her culture: "She had acquiesced in the religion of her mother; she had accepted everything that had been proposed to her. If she lived she had exactly the temper for a Catholic wife of limited intelligence and of pious docility and if she died she was supposed to have earned for herself a place in the eternal heaven of Christians. . ." (SH, 126). Yet he is grieved by her death, finding in her life a futility at least partially occasioned by sexual conditioning: Her spirit "had literally never dared to live and had not learned anything by an abstention it had not willed for itself." When he says he "would have done many things for her," Stephen seems to wish that he could have encouraged her to assert herself, to demand that she be recognized as a person in her own right, not just an adjunct to her brothers (SH, 165). Such autonomy is a goal worthy of a feminist. But Stephen thinks these things too late and never expresses them aloud, not even to the feminist McCann. After Isabel's agonizing death, Stephen and McCann exchange senseless *non sequiturs*, most of them demeaning to Isabel, in death, as in life:

> —I was sorry to hear of the death of your sister . . . sorry we didn't know in time . . . to have been at the funeral.
> Stephen raised his hand gradually and said:
> —O, she was very young . . . a girl.
> McCann raised his hand at the same rate of release, and said
> —Still . . . it hurts. (SH, 169)

Educated, professional women in turn-of-the-century Dublin risked a fate then considered by many only slightly better than death—

spinsterhood. Unmarried women in Joyce's works include the Morkhan sisters and their niece Mary Jane of "The Dead." As music teachers they fall into one of the few genteel professions available to
women of their era, and they participate in the accepted educational
plan of instructing young women in musical accomplishments. Their
own highly cultivated talents are not rewarded by high pay or es-
teem, however. Aunt Julia has been replaced by choirboys in the
church choir, by Papal order, to the mortification of Aunt Kate (D,
194). Many of the people in Mary Jane's audience fail to heed her
intricate performance (D, 187). Aunt Julia sings a song that reinforces
our awareness of her unmarried, implicitly unfulfilled, life, "Arrayed
for the Bridal." "The Dead" offers a much more blossoming and
professionally successful single woman in Miss Ivors. Her career has
paralleled Gabriel Conroy's, by his own admission. She comes and
goes as she pleases, unaccompanied and confident. She is attractive
and her celibate status is not made to appear pitiable. Joyce seems
to recognize that the new cultural norm for a woman of her type
was not to marry.[8] Like Emma Clery, Molly Ivors is involved in the
Celtic revival and urges her commitment and her active mode of life
on others, including the contemplative Gabriel, who is, not surprisingly, baffled and resentful. Beatrice of *Exiles* is another educated
woman, but a less fulfilled one. She seems to have strived and lost
in all but the intellectual dimensions of her relationship with Richard
Rowan. The earthy Bertha and the politically active Molly Ivors thrive
in Joyce's conceptions, but the intellectual woman sickens and is
reduced to the same piano-teaching profession that sustained the
Morkhans.

As suggested by these cases and backgrounds, by pursuing a college
education, even at an institution operated by nuns, Emma Clery was
departing from the norm for young women, and perhaps jeopardizing
any future as a wife and/or mother. *Stephen Hero* is sprinkled with
evidence of male students' discomfort with female academic competition, especially during examinations, when women sometimes
surpassed them. The rest of the time women students were usually
"other" entities, "the subject of sniggers and jokes" (SH, 130-131).
Stephen, though he feels unthreatened academically, is not an advocate of women's education. This he leaves to McCann. He also
fails to display any great interest in educating the young women he
meets socially at the Daniels' home. When one of the daughters
seems to him to be "impressed by a possible vastness of the unknown,

complimented to confer with one who conferred directly with the exceptional," Stephen vows that he has seen enough of the household. Although he finds Ibsen inadequately understood in the circle, he does nothing to advance the playwright's understanding by young women. The attitude may result from his sense of personal or class-related rejection.[9] Though praised as "exceptional" and called by his first name, Stephen (like Joyce) is not a part of the marriage game that he detects and counters with aloofness.

Emma Clery enters the Daniels' parlor immediately after Stephen's decision to eschew the place and succeeds in changing his plans. To Stephen's distress, she does not limit her attentions to him, but she does initiate their discourse and seems eager to share academic life and interests with him. The topics she introduces include theatre, dancing, the Irish language, nationalism, feminism, aesthetics, and the manners of other students. Early in their relationship, she questions Stephen about his interests and suggests that he try hers—Irish language and dancing. In later interviews, she is a mock accuser, who teases him about his reputation as "a woman-hater" (SH, 153) and a possessor of "dreadful ideas" like a disbelief in God (SH, 188). Her approach can now be seen as a fairly typical female strategy to engage and draw upon the intellect of a young man without appearing too overwhelming in her own opinions and knowledge. Stephen's responses are often confusing since they are usually ironic, evasive, or insincere. Stephen's ingenuousness is apparent to the reader when he troops off to Irish lessons merely to be closer to Emma, and when he replies that he "liked a good clown" when Emma asks for his preferences in the pantomime (SH, 16). Emma detects a lack of commitment to female education when he replies to her appeal for assistance, "Oh, I am very liberal—like Father Dillon" (SH, 153). Dillon, as college president, was denying co-education to women at the time. Despite the fact that Emma is naive, less educated, and less discriminating in her aesthetic tastes, her spontaneity and energy make her far more likeable than Stephen in their attempts at serious discussion. The excuse for Stephen's failure to initiate similar topics or to respond to Emma's cannot be disinterest, since he debates many of the same subjects with his male friends, Madden, McCann, Lynch, and Cranly.[10]

Stephen does not cooperate in these discussions for two reasons. For one, he may feel that Emma's education at the University, where he is now only a cynical participant, will only make her resemble the commonplace male students he finds so banal and futile. Their culture (the club that has reacted with hostility to his paper), and even their revolutionary movements (personified in McCann and his icons) are inadequate to the deeper human needs he perceives. Stephen's second problem is that he is in love with Emma as a "woman" and thus not eager to treat her as a "female fellow," or a compensation for the sister he had failed to educate.

If Stephen is going to love Emma, it cannot be in a conventional way, prepared by courtship and recognized in the lifelong commitment of marriage. His harshest judgments of Emma come when he suspects her (often wrongly) of acquiescence in empty cultural norms. He detects her and her companions affecting expressions "of studied purpose" (SH, 46), or "tender significance"(SH, 66-67), when little is being said or felt. He mentally berates her for "pertness and middle-class affectations" (SH, 67):

> Her loud forced manners shocked him at first until his mind had thoroughly mastered the stupidity of hers. She criticised the Miss Daniels very sharply, assuming, much to Stephen's discomfort, an identical temper in him. She coquetted with knowledge, asking Stephen could he not persuade the President of his College to admit women to the college. Stephen told her to apply to McCann who was the champion of women. She laughed at this and said with «genuine dismay» "Well, honestly, isn't he a dreadful-looking artist? She treated femininely everything that young men are supposed to regard as serious but she made polite exception for Stephen himself and for the Gaelic Revival. . . . Her eyes had begun to «imitate the expression» of Father Moran's—an expression of tender «significance» when the conversation was at the lowest level of banality. (SH 66-67)

It is interesting that Stephen is most critical of qualities in Emma that he himself has displayed. She has "loud forced manners"; he sometimes breaks into a loud fit of laughter (SH, 52) and is a master of aloof manners. She criticizes the Miss Daniels "very sharply" and passes McCann off as a "dreadful-looking artist." She is correct in "assuming . . . an identical temper" or at least a similar assessment of both the Daniels circle and McCann in him (SH, 43-46). Stephen himself trivializes "everything that young men are supposed to regard as serious." His use of "treated femininely" to mean trivialize betrays an anti-feminine bias in his language itself. Stephen is sharpness personified in his cynical handling of his mother's deep concern about his "faith."[11] Stephen's mastery of the "stupidity" of Emma's

mind is highly suspect. It classifies her with the dull mass of conventional male students and the Daniels daughters, whom he scorns.
Yet this does not prove a disqualification of Emma as a love object,
betraying a bias toward matter, not mind, in his tastes for woman.
It may suggest a wish to dominate her. Emma largely controls their
discussions and the terms of their meetings, and Stephen may have
unconsciously needed to compensate for this by declaring mental
superiority. Stephen is overhasty in assessing Emma's motivations,
and his conclusions are questionable. How does he know that she is
only coquetting with knowledge when she asks his help with female
admission to his college? In their first meeting, he assumes that "She
seemed . . . to include him in the «general scheme of her nationalising
charm: and when he helped her into her jacket she allowed his hands
to rest for a moment against the warm flesh of her shoulders»" (SH,
46-47). Not only does he assign nationalism to her as her primary
motivation, but he also links it to physical gratification offered to
himself and projects a temptress image upon her. Had we been given
Emma's point of view, we might have learned that she found him a
bit clumsy with her coat.

In a later interview, Emma penetrates Stephen's playful iconoclasm. He has tried to shock her by asking her to come to confession
to him, so that he may hear her sins. She offers a twofold surprise:

> Stephen had expected that she would blush but her cheek main-
> tained its innocence and her eyes grew brighter and brighter.
> —You'd get tired of that too.
> —Do you think so? said Stephen making an effort not to be
> surprised at such an intelligent remark.
> —You'd be a dreadful flirt, I'm sure. You get tired of everything
> so quickly . . . (SH, 154)

His posing as priest is as much flirtation as anything Emma does in
their meetings, and she is right in saying that he is not very good at
it. Her detection of his impetuousness may show that she has a better
grasp of his mind than he has of hers. Soon after this exchange,
Stephen allows himself to hope for the depths of understanding in
their relationship, even finding an explanation for her troubling manners: "Now she seemed to offer him rest. He wondered did she
understand him or sympathise with him and was the vulgarity of her
manners only a condescension of one who was consciously playing
the game" (SH, 158).

Stephen's playing at confessor with Emma was a game that Joyce invoked with Nora as well, and in both cases it can be seen as an attempt to draw the chosen woman away from a powerful allegiance to the Catholic Church, personified in the priest and his office of confession. It offers not freedom, but a new patriarchal allegiance, of course, but this was not apt to trouble the self-centered youth. Stephen's expectations of female subjection to the church have been shaped by Isabel's pious, purposeless life and his mother's irritating allegiance to the church, which impels her to betray Stephen's deeds to her confessor and to nag him about making his Easter Duty. He assumes that Emma will have similar priorities. One conversation begins with Emma's teasing that she has heard of his "dreadful ideas," such as his disbelief in God. She is momentarily shocked by his calling God "the middle-aged gentleman with the aviary" and he bitterly agrees, "Very good, Emma. I see you are afraid you will lose the faith. But you needn't be afraid of my influence" (SH, 188). In that moment, he has given up on her conversion; he half participates in the rest of the conversation and turns his attention from "the warmth of her body" that "seemed to flow into his" to the cold coins in his pocket. As if to confirm his suspicion of Emma's values, he detects "the same expression of tender solicitude . . . in her eyes" (SH, 189). "Same," used with "solicitude" here suggests a connection to Stephen's mother, who earlier used "a discreet motherly solicitude" to check up on the essayist's current study habits, the least reassuring ones pertaining to the Church (SH, 84). The fear over loss of "faith" expressed by Mrs. Daedalus is also projected upon Emma by Stephen. Emma's rebuffs to Stephen's heresies are rather light compared to Stephen's reaction. She is no longer his hope. He immediately shifts his attention to a passing woman of the night, the woman in the black straw hat.

Both Emma and Stephen have been taught, in the tradition of Aristotle, Aquinas, and St. Paul, that male as well as female chastity is essential to virtuous conduct. Society, enforcing the double standard, made chastity the *sine qua non* of Catholic maidenhood in Emma's era. But Stephen resents the control of church and society over human lives. He wants to assert that sensuality is not sinful, but instinctual. "Pride of the flesh" is Stephen's phrase for sexual drive and appeal, and it is something that he detects both in Emma and in his supposed rival for her attentions, Father Moran: "Father Moran's eyes were so clear and tender-looking, Emma stood to his gaze

in such a poise of bold careless «pride of the flesh» that Stephen
longed to precipitate the two into each other's arms . . ." (SH, 66).
Stephen is outraged by what he deems "Irish ineffectualness," or
the religious and cultural inhibitions of both the young woman and
the priest.[12] Elsewhere, Stephen criticizes "the Roman Catholic notion that a man should be unswervingly continent from his boyhood
and then be permitted to achieve his male nature, having first satisfied the Church as to his orthodoxy, financial condition, [and] prospects and general intentions . . ." (SH, 203-204). In A Portrait, Stephen idealizes a young peasant woman who demonstrates a natural
inclination for a chance sexual encounter with his nationalist friend,
Davin. Unencumbered by urban or Catholic morality, she answers
the door "half undressed . . . her breast and shoulders . . . bare,"
brings Davin a big mug of milk, detains him, and asks him twice to
stay the night (P, 182-183). Her guileless invitation of the stranger
to her bed (as Stephen interprets it) makes her closer to the pagan
peasants of John Millington Synge's plays and to the Celtic earth
goddess than to Davin, with his "dullwitted" loyalty to Roman Catholicism (P, 181).[13]

Stephen feels certain that Emma is appealing to him sensually,
particularly with her bright eyes and warm body. However, he also
thinks he detects "a point of defiant illwill" which lies "in the center
of her attitude towards him" (SH, 67). Expressions of ill will on
Emma's part are not evident in the text, so we must attribute Stephen's assessment to intuition or projection. In its second appearance, the concept of "illwill" is elaborated into a more meaningful
tension: "again in the centre of her amiableness he discerned a [cen-
ter] point of illwill and he suspected that by her code of honor she
was obliged to insist on the forbearance of the male and to despise
him for forbearing" (SH, 68). By this interpretation, Emma is di-
verted from instinct by code, and the real victim is Stephen, who
must receive the brunt of her supposed frustrations, her "illwill."
According to him the true fault lies with the codes, not with his
advances. Stephen never discusses this theory with Emma, but he
does have a related conversation with Lynch, much of which seems
derived from Stanislaus Joyce's diary.[14] Jesus never condemned adul-
tery, he goes on to explain, "If I see a woman inclined for oracle I
go to her: but if she has no inclination I stay away." Lynch puts in,
"But that girl has an inclination for oracle." Once again, Stephen
perceives himself as the one who has been put upon, this time ap-

parently deliberately by Emma, seen as a temptress. "That's the tantalizing part of it. I know she has. It's very unfair of her to tantalize me. I must go where I am sure of my ground" (SH, 191). For this man-to-man talk, Stephen invokes the patriarchal authority of Christ, despite his disavowal of the Christian religion. "Oracle" aggrandizes Stephen and gives him mystical appeal, a value perhaps derived from his recent reading of Yeats's short story, "The Adoration of the Magi." The pose is apparently a habitual one, since Emma taunts him as a "mystic" (SH, 188), and Madden suspects this same quality (SH, 81). Mark Shechner considers Emma Clery the first of a long line of "virginal villains," a negative assessment even more severe than that of Stephen and Lynch, and more reflective of male fears than actual female behaviors, as seen in Emma. Shechner describes the virginal villain as "provoking, exhibitionistic, and ultimately cold and malicious," and includes such unlikely women as the bird girl of A Portrait and Beatrice Justice on his list.[15]

Although Emma has many extended appearances and a good proportion of dialogue in Stephen Hero, her value to Stephen is located in brief, earthy or visionary moments, experiences in keeping with his epiphany theory. Her arrival at the Daniels' is perceived as an "advent" (SH, 46). Despite her efforts to engage him in teasing, activities, and the exchange of ideas, Stephen arrests Emma's "warm ample body" in moments of beauty and silence: "He had swept the moment into his memory, the figure and the landscape into his treasureroom and conjuring with all three had brought forth some pages of «sorry verse»" (SH, 67). In his "monstrous dissatisfaction" with Dublin life, Emma's beauty offers repose, a role which befits the Virgin Mary. But he goes on to fantasize his apocalyptic assumption to Emma in the image of a non-Christian deity or goddess:

> The spirits of the tame sodalists, unsullied and undeserving, he would petrify amid a ring of Jesuits in the circle of foolish and grotesque virginities and ascend above them to where his Emma, with no detail of her earthly form or vesture abated invoked him from a Mohammedan paradise. (SH, 159).

Of all the paradises Stephen could have conjured up, the Mohammedan one would offer the least to woman, casting her in a role of service and physical withdrawal from all but her husband. One afternoon Stephen falls into contemplation in "the long lofty dusty drawing-room ... «while the sunless dusk enwrapped him»" and decay

of house and leaves lie abut him. He rejects typically male forms of
hope—"egoism which proceeded bravely before men to be fright-
ened by the least challenge of conscience, freedom which would
dress the world anew in [the] vestments and usages begotten of en-
slavement, mastery of an art understood by few which owed its very
delicacy to a physical decrepitude. . . ." Emma, though away in the
Aran Islands, is "the one bright insistent star of joy trembling at her
wane" in his soul. His vision of the surrounding decay, of "congenital
lives, shuffling onwards amid yawn and howl" of "evil, in the simi-
litude of distorted ritual" is to interpret it as a call to his soul "to
commit fornication with her" (SH, 162). The decayed surroundings,
the perceiver's subjection to a mood, the reference to ritual, and
the female figure of hope and desire are all comparable to the conditions of worship in which the young boy of "Araby" immerses
himself, his ideal being Mangan's sister. Although both women have
been appropriately associated with the Catholic Virgin Mary, these
ceremonies of waning starlight and decay also partake of pre-Christian and ancient Middle Eastern worship of the moon goddesses whose
functions included death and decay as complements to fertility and
whose dark aspect represented instinct.[16] As such, the woman offers
an alternate to the rational, urban, male establishment, crumbling
around Stephen. Stephen's perfect images of Emma also pose her
against trees, another natural aspect associated with virgin and moon
goddesses, long before Freud declared them merely sexual symbols.
The association of the beloved with the moon is very evident in Poem
XII from *Chamber Music*, whether inspired by Mary Sheehy, or Mary
Elizabeth Clery as prototypes of Emma. It begins:

> What counsel has the hooded moon
> Put in thy heart, my shyly sweet
> Of love in ancient plenilune
> Glory and stars beneath his feet

Stephen associates even himself with the moon when reacting to
human futility: "he was drifting amid life like the barren shell of the
moon." The attitude reminds him of Shelley's lines:

> Art thou pale for weariness
> Of climbing heaven and gazing on earth,
> Wandering companionless. (P, 96)

When he finally discovers his poetic vocation, the moon provides a
more hopeful phase as symbol: "He climbed to the crest of the sand-

hill and gazed about him. Evening had fallen. A rim of the young moon cleft the pale waste of sky like the rim of a silver hoop embedded in grey sand. . ." (P, 173). Here Stephen takes on an aspect of the goddess, having, like her, observed the world apart, and now climbing the hill and preparing a new phase. Joyce would feature the moon with a female child in the poem "Simples" from *Pomes Penyeach*, where

> The moon a web of silence weaves
> In the still garden where a child
> Gathers the simple salad leaves.

The moon, dark rain, and mold are featured in another female-centered poem, "She Weeps over Rahoon."[17]

Although Stephen renounces Emma repeatedly, to both himself and his counselor, Lynch, he still runs to her to propose the lovemaking that he has fantasized. He has again seen her at a perfect moment: "The air was webbed with water vapours and all the flowerbeds and walks confronted the grey of the sky with a truculent sodden brown" (SH, 195). Moisture instead of decay pervades the scene, but this too is an image of fertility and an aspect of the goddess. The color brown and penetrating rain had been parts of the provocative condition in "Araby" too. The *Stephen Hero* scene offers flowers as well—like the field from which Persephone was abducted to Hades. Stephen offers a few preliminary explanations. He speaks of his life "without help or sympathy from anyone"—a form of support he had hoped for in his earlier thinking about her. He classifies her as a "human creature" and thus above the category of "vegetables" to which he generally assigns people in the college (SH, 197). Emma had failed, understandably, to see the distinction of being "alive and human" in the earlier religious discussion, after which Stephen had bitterly renounced her (SH, 188). In this, his most ardent and open approach to Emma, Stephen is more persistent, taking hold of her arm and not readily releasing it, speaking close to her face, and offering abundant, if disjointed, proposals, giving her a second chance by repeating and elaborating his plan. He tries to tell her that it is her "pride of the flesh" that distinguishes her and that they should act out their desire instead of following her tendency to be "sensible."[18]

If we're young we feel happy. We feel full of desire.

—Desire?

—Do you know when I saw you . . .

—Yes, how did you know me?

—I knew the stride.

—Stride!

Do you know, Emma, even from my window I could see your hips moving inside your waterproof? I saw a young woman walking proudly through the decayed city. Yes, that's the way you walk: you're proud of being young and proud of being a woman. Do you know when I caught sight of you from my window—do you know what I felt? . . .

—I felt that I longed to hold you in my arms—your body. I longed for you to take me in your arms. That's all . . . Then I thought I would run after you and say that to you . . . Just to live one night together, Emma, and then to say goodbye in the morning and never to see each other again! There is no such thing as love in the world: only people are young. . . . (SH, 197-198)

Stephen adds that "I wanted to say that to you for my own sake," and supposes that she thinks him mad "because I do not bargain with you or say I love you or swear to you." He also declares, "It is no insult . . . for a man to ask a woman what I have asked you. You are annoyed at something else not at that" (SH, 198-199). Stephen is apparently unaware of the logical leap which he takes between the male intention, expressed in the penultimate sentence, and the assumptions about a female reaction, in the last. These statements resemble his theories about Emma's point of "illwill," which he has already blamed on social and religious codes. Reluctance to declare love for a woman also characterized Joyce's early letters to Nora, as Ellmann has noted (JJ, 159). Joyce was also suspicious of the value of the form of love he thought women offered, telling Stanislaus in November 1906, "A woman's love is always maternal and egoistic. A man, on the contrary, side by side with his extraordinary cerebral sexualism and bodily fervour (from which women are normally free) possess a fund of genuine affection for the 'beloved' or 'once beloved' object" (L II, 192). Stephen betrays this same superior attitude toward women in Stephen Hero, without ever declaring Emma a "beloved object."

What Stephen proposes is a ritual, not a commitment to an individual, and it is understandably outside of Emma's ken. Stephen could offer no models for it from his own society. But as an initiation ritual for the "young"—a quality emphasized as strongly as "desire"—Stephen's proposal does have ancient precedents. The institution of sacred marriage or *hieros gamos*, which was part of the ritual of the virgin goddess, demanded in some cultures that every woman prostitute herself in the temple once in her lifetime. As interpreted by the Jungian analyst, M. Esther Harding, this religious ceremony was a response to inner needs which are relevant to ones perceived by Stephen. "The ancients felt it to be essential that every woman should once in her life give herself, not to one particular man, for love of him, that is for personal reasons, but to the goddess, to her own instinct, to the Eros principle within herself."[19] Since he knows Emma, Stephen does not qualify as the stranger who is supposed to be the virgin's sexual partner. Harding suggests that "men in need of strengthening" rather than especially virile men would have frequented the Temples of Ishtar and Aphrodite, and this might characterize Stephen, or even Joyce. Stephen has envisioned Emma as a power that will raise him above "congenital lives" (SH, 162) and told her that he made his proposal "for my own sake" (SH, 198). In his earliest thoughts about the proposal, Stephen had admitted that,

> He knew that it was not for such an image that he had constructed a theory of art and life and a garland of verses and yet if he could have been sure of her he would have held his art and verses lightly enough. The longing for a night of love came upon him, a desperate willingness to cast his soul away, his life and his art, and to bury them all with her under fathoms of «lust-laden» sleep." (SH, 158)

Although Emma is also his Muse, here she offers escape from art as well as banal life. She also conveys him into the unconscious recesses of sexuality and sleep, which Joyce would explore in later works, and again in the company of a curative goddess. Although Joyce's acquaintances feared that he planned only a brief love encounter with Nora Barnacle, what evolved was surprisingly sustained. In his erotic love letters of 1909, which characterize Nora as a chance encounter and propose imaginative nights of love, Joyce may have been fantasizing a compromise *hieros gamos*. The rites do seem to have had a rejuvenating effect.

Although Emma has been excoriated for tempting and denying Stephen, it would have been extraordinary if she had agreed. She is deeply affected by the situation:

> —You are mad, I think, she said, brushing past him without taking any notice of his salute. She did not go quickly enough, how-

ever, to hide the tears that were in her eyes and he, surprised to
see them and wondering at their cause, forgot to say the goodby
that was on his lips. (SH, 199)

Stephen may be adept with his own visions, but he is inept in attracting a partner to them. Readers are better prepared than Emma,
since they have shared Stephen's developing thoughts. Although she
uses "dreadful" repeatedly to describe his unconventional ideas, she
rarely takes them seriously and is certainly unprepared for his proposal that she act out his rebellion against conventions with him.
Emma is "sensible" and also has a life of her own—both obstacles
to Stephen's impulsive, revolutionary, and ill-expressed ideas. Nora
Barnacle offered no comparably distracting interests to challenge
Joyce.

Even if no "insult" was intended in Stephen's dramatic approach
to Emma, he acts with dubious taste when he shares the experience,
now masculinely tagged an "adventure," with Lynch.[20] He doesn't
tell others, but for selfish reasons. Stephen cannot expect sympathy
from Cranly, and he has a patriarchal wish to remain "successful"
in the eyes of his younger brother (SH, 203). The discussion with
Lynch has a new emphasis, marriage, a topic which, strangely enough,
Stephen and Emma have barely discussed.[21] When thoughts of lust
with Emma occurred to Stephen earlier, he was motivated by a desire
to escape "the decayed city" and not by a mission to reform marital
customs. Stephen has been aware of the game of courtship and has
sensed the attributes of the marriage trap at the Daniels' house, even
down to the detail of the picture of the Sacred Heart that adorns
the wall (SH, 44). Perhaps still reacting to Emma's charge that he is
"mad," Stephen declares that a sane man would not "swear to love,
honor and obey" until his dying day. This reluctance to make a long-
term commitment is compatible with his preference for mute and
momentary visions of Emma, rather than sustained, banal dialogues.
With the pomposity that typically overtakes him in male debate,
Stephen roughly articulates a theory of marriage as "simony." He
admits to himself that "the economic aspect of the affair did not
present itself to him very vividly, and, indeed, was only vivid enough
to make him deplore the fact that the solution of moral problems
should be so hopelessly entangled with merely material considerations"(SH, 203). The exposition to Lynch uses the religious definition
of simony as rationale for Stephen's desire that woman give of herself,
her spirit, without compensation. He draws a perplexing and ironic

distinction between her body and spirit, however. Woman's body is not her own, but "a corporal asset of the State: «if she traffic with it she must sell it either as a harlot or as a married woman or as a working celibate or as a mistress." Somehow this is separate from woman as human being (the distinction he has given Emma over her peers). "But woman is (incidentally) a human being: and a human being's love and freedom is not a spiritual asset of the State . . . . A human being can exert freedom to produce or to accept, to love or to procreate or to satisfy. Love gives and freedom takes»'' (SH, 202-203). The theory is indeed rough. The suggestion that the state owns woman's body has a germ of legal truth, especially when legal issues of marriage, abortion, divorce, and inheritance are considered. The references to the " State" and to "freedom to produce" betray Stephen's attempt to bring Marxist perspectives to women's problems in society, as he also does with discussions of nationalism. But Stephen's rational categorizing, inherited from the Jesuits, Aristotle, and Aquinas, are jarring to our sense of the whole woman. Stephen also maintains his solipsistic tendency in his assignment of two qualities of the spirit. Woman is love, and must give. Man is freedom, and takes.

Joyce's letters of this period contain objections to the institution of marriage that are like Stephen's. Similar objections are restated in *Exiles*, where Richard Rowan has not married Bertha, though he has stayed with her into middle age. Here, Richard extends freedom to the female, but probably for selfish reasons. The experiment offers him vicarious participation in the violation of a norm (his own commonlaw marriage) and in freedom itself. It also offers treasured, momentary perfection in the poses and gestures of the woman he still needs to feel excited about. The element of excitement to Richard is doubt. Joyce would celebrate the similar quality of "incertitude" in the poem, "Flood." This tribute to a great sea mother (which Bertha is as well) ends in the verse:

> Uplift and sway, O golden vine
> Your clustered fruits to love's full flood
> Lambent and vast and ruthless is thine
> Incertitude.[22]

Stephen and Lynch both assume that Emma wants to be bought in marriage. Stephen complicates his exposition further when he draws a distinction between Emma and "the woman in the black straw hat." In a chance encounter, this woman had emerged from the shadows, giving off "an odor of ancient sweats" at the close of the religious discussion that had left Stephen deeply embittered with Emma (SH, 189). Although he never spoke a word to her, Stephen expresses the opinion that "the woman in the black straw hat gave something before she sold her body to the State. Emma will sell herself to the State but give nothing" (SH, 203). All that this probable fugitive from nighttown gave Stephen in actuality was the soliciting greeting, "Good night, love" and the request that he come for a little walk. Stephen had responded by giving her the coins that he had begun to finger in Emma's presence. By this juxtaposition, the episode itself contains the suggestion that Emma is to be bought. But instead of buying her in marriage, or even buying the body of the woman in the black straw hat, Stephen gives his precious coins away, as if in protest against both forms of barter. The coins become "benedictions" or a tribute to qualities he intuits in this strange woman. Again there is an approximation to the sacred marriage of the ancient goddess. Money derived from sacred prostitution belonged to the goddess, not the prostitute, as a form of tribute. Stephen and the woman in the black straw hat also are strangers to one another, a prerequisite of the ritual that had not been satified by the partnership of Stephen and Emma. Stephen hums the chant of the passion throughout his encounter with this strange woman, never speaking or giving his full attention to her. Yet this incidental meeting transforms the narrative into a deeply psychological passage that plunges into the first person, and into the flow of Stephen's mind. Here, he transforms the woman in the black straw hat into a kindred soul, an emblem of his revolt against religion, the cultural establishment, and the values of women in that culture. He assumes that she would share his opinions of Jesus, wonders how she would like "the story of Yasodhara's kissing Buddha after his illumination and penance," and is carried back to her image in the black straw hat when he uses the word "sweat," already associated with her appearance. He also makes a theological point of her rather conventional "Good night, love": "The greatest lover of all time could not say more than that" (SH, 190).

Stanislaus Joyce's diary describes his brother's acquaintance with the whore called Nellie, who may have provided the model for the woman in the black straw hat, as well as the positively portrayed whores of "Circe." A "Nelly" is featured in Cissy Caffrey's song

in Paris.[24] Stephen's literary tastes are like those of the three old men. Although he had no conscious quest for a wise old woman or prophetess, Stephen was committed to establishing a new order. At one point the old men are advised "to travel over Ireland continually, and upon foot and at night, that they might live close to the stones and the trees and at the hours when the immortals are awake."[25] Stones and trees are forms into which goddesses like Daphne and Artemis transform themselves. Stephen encounters his mystery woman under conditions of darkness and in natural surroundings comparable to those in the Yeats story. The three witnesses of Yeats's story are told that the secret names can be "perfectly spoken only when the mind is steeped in certain colours, sounds, and odours."[26] Stephen is impressed by the "odour of ancient sweats" of his woman. Both heroines seem impoverished but dignified—Joyce's maintaining "decorum" with only a summer hat for warmth. Finally, extensive sensual experiences are imagined for both. The old men of "Adoration" are told that the immortals "have chosen as their priestess, this woman in whose heart all follies have gathered, and in whose body all desires have been awakened."[27] They find her in an unsavory neighborhood that resembles Joyce's own nighttown. The woman in the black straw hat wears that hat "rakishly" and propositions Stephen. She is easily transformed into the prostitute in A Portrait, who detains Stephen as he stands in the middle of the roadway, gazes into his face and says "gaily, 'Good night, Willie dear!' " (P, 100). The "slumber of centuries" that Stephen awakes from in A Portrait (P, 100) may also owe an indirect debt to the ancient aura of "Adoration." The framework narrator of Yeats's story and the three witnesses all fear that they are being spoken to by devils, though the spiritual quality of the "priestess" comes through quite strongly in the story. Joyce too brings up the devil in closing his musings: "Mustn't the devil be annoyed to hear her described as an evil creature?" (SH, 190). Both Yeats and Joyce would seem to aver that society has false criteria for measuring moral worth. The vessel of this new age is not a Virgin Mary, but a sensual, experienced woman. It is notable that after reflecting upon the woman in the black straw hat as his only resource, Stephen vows never to see "the virgin" again. He could have said Emma; his word choice permits a double dismissal.

Stephen's insertion of his new priestess into musings on Jesus and Buddha also suggests revisions of religion, and culture. Throughout *Stephen Hero*, the young artist is highly skeptical about Jesus' supposed chastity, citing the fact that he continually surrounded himself with "loose women" (SH, 141), Magdalenes like the woman in the black straw hat and Yeats's heroine. Women like Mary Magdalene were accused by the patriarchs of having devils, yet, as Renan reminds us, they tended Jesus throughout his ordeal.[28] Stephen also turns to Buddhism for a more sensual and peaceful form of religion than he had been offered in Irish Catholicism.[29]

The woman in the black straw hat, unlike Emma, cooperates with Stephen in every way. She has no connection to the patriarchal institutions of marriage, religion, and education that he recoils from. She does not and cannot hold him accountable for his actions, his beliefs, or his image of her. He sees her for only an instant, in dark, watery surroundings which, like several instants with Emma, befit his treasury of moments. While Emma was too vigorous and too frequently in Stephen's presence to hold her poses, the woman in the black straw hat retains decorum and mystery by virtue of the brevity of Stephen's contact with her. After the woman in the black straw hat, Stephen would find other cooperative, briefly glimpsed women. A Portrait yields the girl on the beach, who was readily transformed into an emblematic bird, and Davin's report of the peasant woman at the cottage door, who bears the dark, sensuous soul of her race, in Stephen's imagination. As noted earlier, the few words of the woman in the black straw hat are reassigned to the prostitute in the road in A Portrait. She makes a dramatic reappearance in Ulysses: "a frowsy whore with black sailor hat askew came glazily in the day along the quay towards Mr. Bloom." But Bloom avoids her because she "knew Molly," and thus was "too dear too near to home sweet home" (U, 290)—statements which link her type to Molly herself. The Maggies and ALP can be counted as her descendants in Finnegans Wake.

After Stephen and Emma part for what she has declared to be the last time, Stephen observed, "As he watched her walk onward swiftly with her head slightly bowed he seemed to feel her soul and his falling asunder swiftly and forever after an instant of all but union" (SH, 199). Stephen's soul and its capacity to fall remain persistent themes in the later Portrait. His soul must fall in order for him to become an artist, an exile, a revolutionary. But in Stephen Hero, two souls fall asunder; a young man and a young woman must each and separately fall—Stephen to attempt an artistic, moral revolution and Emma to become herself, intellectually as well as physically. That any "union" or "all but union" is achieved is questionable, unless it existed only in Stephen's fantasies or as a fleeting recognition of differing aims. They manage some accommodation in a few conversations, but they cannot supply each other's basic intellectual and emotional needs; they depart in mutual bewilderment. No sacred marriage has been performed. Yet there has been a form of initiation. When Stephen does fall, it is into the influence of decay and instinctual life, properties of the goddess that he detected in both Emma and the woman in the black straw hat. By the end of A Portrait, Stephen may glimpse a new mode of relationship with Emma which is more compatible with her self-perceptions. He *likes* her. He questions, furthermore, whether he has thought and felt about her appropriately in the past. The problem of revising his view of her finally overwhelms him, however:

> Yes, I liked her today. A little or much? Don't know. I liked her
> and it seems a new feeling to me. Then, in that case, all the rest,
> all I thought I thought and all I felt I felt, all the rest before now,
> in fact . . . O, give it up, old chap! Sleep it off! (P, 252)

It seems likely that the Emma-Stephen relationship was something that Joyce, like Stephen, was not prepared to handle in his youth. In rewriting, Joyce's easier path was to focus on the character closest to his own identity, to internalize his conflicts, and to concentrate on his artistic processes. For this new emphasis, it was advisable to make E__ C__ a faint, peripheral image instead of a lively, interfering, and admirable foil. After making this decision, Joyce needed only to follow one adolescent through momentous choices in life. And, like a wise parent, he postponed (and indeed never treated) Stephen's serious union with a woman, insisting that Stephen first establish his aesthetic vocation and life values; quick glances at a number of women were easier to handle. And Stephen's talents and causes probably interested him more than did Emma's. Joyce later discovered alternate and more powerful figures to offer as objects of Stephen's revolution. Rebellion against religion and country would be focused upon the horrid and phantasmagoric figures of his mother's ghost and Gummy Granny in "Circe" (U, 582, 595, 600). These women are neither as affirmative nor as easily handled as the woman in the black straw hat. They demand Stephen's life in service, but their death wishes also provide epiphany and engender life and action. For all his talk about the father's ghost in *Hamlet*, it is the mother's ghost who allows Stephen to ruin space, as he knows it, and begin again. Bloom has a comparable discovery offered by the nymph, who proves to be not goddess, but nun, and a key to the ungodly corruption of Greece and, especially, Rome (U, 544-554). But Joyce came to these phantom villainesses only by first attempting to project their demands upon a more natural young woman, and it was an effort which did not succeed. His father had made the mistake of lashing out against a real woman to compensate for his frustrations; Joyce learned to reassign the responsibility to creatures of the imagination, some in female form.

As a realistic character, Emma Clery of *Stephen Hero* compares favorably with her male counterpart, Stephen, especially when we make allowances for the inequalities of her education, the country's treatment of women, and the novel's emphasis on the male point of view. Emma is far less knowledgeable than Stephen, but Joyce ended by mocking mere facts in *Finnegans Wake*, and even in *Stephen Hero*, he treated Stephen's intellectual superiority ironically. Stephen is inhumane. He makes his female acquaintance the victim as well as the subject of his art. Stephen has achieved little at this point in his career; though his analytical powers and artistic direction offer promise, his intellectual pride and his artistic manipulations are inappropriate. Emma may be overly enthusiastic about the Celtic revival, but she does not jump to conclusions about people or lose touch with reality the way Stephen does. If she has not fully cultivated "pride of the flesh," she does have control over intellectual pride. Her self-confidence in undertaking a relationship with this difficult young man is admirable. Even if she does fall short of understanding Stephen, she has a far greater respect for the individual than he does.

The creation of Emma Clery was a noble experiment, an effort in part to provide a female counterpart to Stephen. But Joyce apparently felt incapable of sustaining the portrait at this early stage and then passed beyond a similar conception in his later works. The character in the later works who is most like Emma is Issy in *Finnegans Wake*, whom I discuss in chapter 9. Though Emma is immature intellectually and emotionally and present only in the remnant of a book about someone else, she still presents a challenge to real women. She resists a young man's stereotypes and bold manipulations. She calls for understanding of her individuality. She may even suggest an equal union of man and woman, an ideal too rarely found, even in the world of her great-grandchildren.

Molly

$$8$$

□ A book on Joyce and feminism would be unthinkable without "a Molly in" it (U, 756). Joyce declared the "monologue (female)"[1] of the "Penelope" chapter to be the "indispensable countersign" to *Ulysses* (L I, 160), his most indispensable work. Yet this chapter occasions greater critical anxiety than all the rest. Penelope's web has hopelessly entwined a great number of academics since its first appearance in 1922. Molly's own musings give no indication that she will give a woman or a feminist critic easier passage. Still, this study can hope to ask different questions about her, to encounter other resistances from her text, and to reveal some sources for the critical problems of earlier colleagues.

Although "Proteus" is the title attributed to the "monologue (male)"[2] of the rather inflexible Stephen Dedalus, it is Molly's protean nature that has entangled critics with both herself and each other. As we shall see, Molly can be identified with numerous figures from Homer—Penelope (in both "faithful" and "unfaithful" versions), Calypso, Nausicaä and Circe—with Goethe's eternal feminine, with the Blessed Virgin Mary, and with the *Gea Tellus*. She also represents Jewish, Moorish, Spanish and Irish womanhood, mothers, wives, independent career women, and whores. Molly varies what she says about a number of people and subjects and is appropriately interested in "metempsychosis," defined in differing levels of abstraction and with a variety of examples by her husband, Leopold Bloom, in the "Calypso" chapter. Molly uses the appropriate plural pronoun, "us," referring to herself in this same conversation (U, 64-65).

For the critics, there has been, first, the dilemma of whether to assign Molly to a realistic or a symbolic category, and then the decision of whether to exalt or denigrate her. Mark Shechner offered a useful summary of the critical history through the 1960s when he quipped, "Most of her interpreters have staked out positions in either of two opposed camps: the "earth mother" camp and the more modern and ever-more-popular "satanic mistress" or "thirty-shilling whore" camp.[3]

The symbolic, earth-mother camp is decidedly the older; it is supported by the "Ithaca" chapter, where Molly is represented in bed "reclined . . . in the attitude of Gea Tellus, fulfilled, recumbent, big with seed" (U, 737), and in Joyce's correspondence. Joyce's accounts of Molly to his contemporaries are many and various, a fact that invites divergent critical interpretations. Harriet Weaver received a cosmic, desexualized, archetypal explanation that can be explained as a limited response to Weaver's own interpretation of the "Penelope" chapter, and as a suitable emphasis for Miss Weaver's temperate personality. It can also be seen as an aspect of Molly most suited for the appreciation of an intellectual woman:

> Your description of it ["Penelope," which she described as "prehuman"] also coincides with my intention—if the epithet "posthuman" were added. I have rejected the usual interpretation of her as a human apparition—that aspect being better represented by Calypso, Nausikaa and Circe, to say nothing of pseudo Homeric figures. In conception and technique I tried to depict the earth which is prehuman and presumably posthuman. (L I, 180)

Budgen received a much more elaborate, fleshy version, with Molly's cardinal points laid out in a vocabulary of mortal female anatomy. This description has been attractive to male critics, who have toured Molly's sensual geography for various analytical purposes ever since.[4] Molly is less cosmic in the Budgen explanation. She is assigned a supposed female word (yes) and attitudes that some might attribute to real women. The generalizations Joyce makes to Budgen are male conceptions of the female that might not have got past Miss Weaver:

> ["Penelope"] begins and ends with the female word *yes*. It turns like a huge earth ball slowly surely and evenly round and round spinning, its four cardinal points being the female breasts, arse,

womb and cunt expressed by the words *because, bottom* (in all
senses bottom button, bottom of the class, bottom of the sea, bottom of his heart), *woman*, yes. Though probably more obscene
than any preceding episode it seems to me to be perfectly sane
full amoral fertilisable untrustworthy engaging shrewd limited pru-
dent indifferent *Weib. Ich bin der* [sic] *Fleisch der stets bejaht.* (SL,
285; printed in L I, 170 without "cunt")

Joyce's final line, as Ellmann notes, paraphrases and reverses for
Molly Mephistopheles' line from Goethe's *Faust I*: "I am the spirit
that always denies" becomes "I am the flesh that always affirms"
(SL, 285n). Joyce's use of *Weib*, however, may suggest to some scholars Goethe's *Ewig-Weibliche*, from the conclusion of *Faust II*. Goethe's
great work also has an affirmative, female-centered coda. It is remarkable, however, that Joyce uses *Weib*, not *Weibliche* in his explanation, and that Molly is an eternal principle of flesh, not a spir-
itually inspiring *Mater Gloriosa*, the redeeming figure of *Faust II*.
Joyce's rejection of this Virgin Mary type of ideal after *A Portrait* is
compensated with Molly and her precursor, Bertha of *Exiles*.[5]

Stuart Gilbert, with Joyce's collaboration, promoted the "earth
mother" interpretation of Molly Bloom, which was subscribed to by
such eminent figures as Edmund Wilson, Harry Levin, and William
York Tindall.[6] It is notable that *Gea Tellus* (a figure combining *Gaea*,
the Greek, and *Tellus*, the Roman, names for the earth goddess) in
these early interpretations was narrowly defined as representing the
function of procreation—a reduction and oversimplification inappropriate to both Molly and the goddesses, whose fuller stature has been
suggested in chapter 2. Gilbert noted and excused Molly's supposed
"vulgarity." He also glossed over her opinions, rather loosely calling
her "classic grievances" against her husband "the eternal feminine."[7] This was the beginning of the attempt to reweave Goethe's
spiritual and metaphysical *Ewig-Weiblicht* on Molly's mortal loom.
"Eternal feminine" has since become an almost meaningless gen-
erality in the hands of twentieth-century critics. From the start, Molly
inspired lyrical appreciations of her symbolic identity, which is especially evident in the poetic, affirmative ending of her monologue.
Ulysses was completed, and the first critical appreciations of it were
written in an era when the avant-garde flourished, when writers and
critics alike were especially interested in myth, in Carl Jung's theories, and in James Frazer's *The Golden Bough*. It was a time when
women were enjoying greater freedom and economic power than

they had had for centuries, and in England and the U. S., they had recently won suffrage. These conditions would not be repeated until the late nineteen sixties, with the advent of the second women's movement, and a return to mythic criticism, inspired by Claude Lévi-Strauss and others.

Interpreted as a realistic being, Molly has been found offensive repeatedly. Shechner considers Hugh Kenner, in his *Dublin's Joyce* (published 1956), the first of the anti-Molly revisionists. She is the "satanic Mistress" whose " 'Yes' of consent . . . kills the soul that has darkened the intellect and blunted the moral sense of all Dublin."[8] Molly's welcoming womb has become an agent of death, her body a threat to many male critics. Kenner's important early work actually devotes very little space to Molly; it is centered in the male structures of the first seventeen chapters of *Ulysses*. In the 1980s, Kenner continues to see not only a female threat in Molly and other women in Joyce but even a conspiracy between Molly and the Blooms' fifteen-year-old daughter, Milly.[9] Other critics working in the late fifties searched the text for evidence that Molly was far from a *Gea Tellus*; she was found wanting in fertility and further indicted for her lack of marital fidelity.[10] As James Card has noted, at least one of these searches erred in its selectivity, ignoring the ever-present contradictions of Molly's monologue where they did not suit the new, iconoclastic thesis.[11] The critics were also limited by the male-biased social sciences of their era. Edwin Steinberg measures Molly's infidelities (and goes for the long list given on U, 731) against Helene Deutsch's concepts of "the normal woman in our society," who "can gratify both sexuality and motherhood through the mediation of one man," and "whose love for her child is normally greater than her self-love."[12] J. Mitchell Morse follows Freud, placing primacy on the now discredited notion of the vaginal orgasm and citing as proof of Molly's sexual inadequacy that she "can achieve orgasm only by masturbation or by the friction of her partner's finger."[13]

In the 1960s, Darcy O'Brien offered a shriller denunciation, which Shechner appropriately calls "evangelical," but "patriarchal" and "puritanical" are equally apt. O'Brien both leads us out of temptation and hurls derogatory epithets: "For all Molly's attractive vitality, for all of her fleshly charms and engaging bravado she is at heart a thirty-shilling whore."[14] In the critical assault during the fifties and sixties on Molly Bloom, Shechner has detected "the hardening of sensibility in postwar America."[15] More important from the viewpoint of this

study is the extension into literary criticism of the postwar social
ethos that glorified woman's devotion to home, husband, and a passive, virtuous "feminine mystique" (Betty Friedan's summary of the
age), and produced the baby boom. These were offices that Molly
did not serve. As these norms changed in the late 1960s, so did much
of the critical opinion.

Specialized critical approaches, including Shechner's, have enriched studies done in the 1970s. Shechner's psychoanalytical in-
vestigation of *Ulysses* has the typical Freudian limitation of phallic
concentration. It finds the fetishistic Joyce incessantly adorning the
female with imitation penises, and it uses the word "phallic" to characterize Molly herself. Like the first wave of scholars, Shechner sees
Molly as a symbol rather than a real woman, but this symbol is rather
negative. Instead of *Gea Tellus*, she is "phallic mother," or "petticoat
government incarnate." The effect of this power on Bloom, however,
is seen as negative, as serving his supposed oral, infantile regres-
sion.[16] Shechner also offers the more useful judgment that Molly's
psychological portrayal is not a deep view of a female mind and that
the "wise feminine passiveness" or "impersonal *Weiblichkeit*" of her
final paean to love and nature, is a devotional, not a psychological
exercise.[17]

Commenting upon his colleagues' critical responses to Molly Bloom,
Shechner remains the psychoanalyst and focuses upon male sexuality.
He takes "the case of Molly Bloom as evidence that critics may still
be men." Being "men" seems to permit only two responses, the
"courtship" of the earliest appreciators, or the "masculine protest"
of the critics of the fifties and sixties. In summary, male critics use
"tactics of seduction" or "flattery and assault."[18] This is a courageous
statement that men in academe are not as solidly objective and rational as established standards would dictate, but it seems to be ut-
tered with the tones of a slightly threatened male who wants men
to be men, with the emphasis more on the "macho" than the genteel
model.

Shechner ignores the less accessible early critical responses by
women, as cited in chapters 5 and 6. As we have seen, early reactions
by women were divided on Molly. Rebecca West resembles the early
male critics in celebrating Molly as a "great mother," and mentioning
her "thoughts of generation." But she also makes Molly a counter-
principle to male values in *Ulysses*. She celebrates Molly as a "sum-
mation of life," pointing to experiential phenomena like the "sun-

shine" contained in Molly's final coda. Both West and Harriet Shaw Weaver see Molly's ancient qualities and embrace them. Molly Colum, however, had earthly standards and will not accept a "female gorilla" for literature, even from Joyce.[19]

Molly has been given additional symbolic significances in recent criticism by both women and men. Attention has gone to the consciousness expressed in Molly's syntax, which Suzette Henke has described as "a pre-intellectual, poetic consciousness that delights in naming."[20] Colin MacCabe celebrates this as a revolutionary form of the word.[21] Critics like Henke and MacCabe, working in the school of Jacques Lacan, connect Molly to a different female principle of "desire," which has intrinsic creative potential. It substitutes for the earlier symbolic interpretation of *Gea Tellus* as "procreation," and other qualities commonly suggested as "feminine principles"; these might include "passivity," which is frequently attributed to Molly. "Desire" is a counter to male-associated principles like "authority." Yet desire has its own limits within the scope of human possibility, and may not deserve the kind of pre-eminence given to earlier female principles, any more than they did.[22] Many critics now see Molly as an "other," a male attempt at the female, her interests framed to complement the interests expressed by males in the preceding pages of *Ulysses*. She is "a female projection of the male psyche"[23] or anima; she is "a circumference bounding the human (male) world."[24]

There has also been a return to Molly as mimetic or real character. The 1970s generated some gossip-type criticism—a panel named "What Blazes did to Molly," and several efforts to enumerate and discuss Molly's potential and actual lovers. A realistic Molly is better served in recent textual study of notesheets and sources for *Ulysses*. These enrich our awareness of planned inconsistencies in Molly's monologue, and of the complicated Jewish-Spanish-Gibraltar backgrounds that affect Molly's validity as a mimetic character.[25] The most thorough feminist-realist treatment of Molly to date is by Elaine Unkeless. She measures Molly against the feminine stereotypes offered by such feminists as Simone de Beauvoir and Mary Ellmann, and finds a troubling correspondence. In traits assigned by Joyce, such as lethargy, passivity, narcissism, and irrationality, Molly embodies "conventional notions of the way a woman acts and thinks."[26]

In this chapter, Molly will be allowed the full scope of the ambiguity and contradictory nature that has been detected in her. She will be considered, not just as the extremes of realistic individual and archetypal goddess, as has been the practice, but also as conglomerate spokeswoman, a middle ground between the two. Molly cannot qualify as feminist advocate or superwoman, but, as with Emma Clery, she can be seen in the female contexts of her era and her several cultures, and her attitudes toward woman-centered issues can be assessed. Recent reinvestigations of myth and oral culture also have given us expanded archetypal contexts, where woman has new functions as goddess and earth.

Molly Bloom, the realistic character and individual, takes on the values, limits, and possibilities of mature, married woman, mother, artiste, Jewess, Irishwoman, Dubliner, and exile of Gibraltar in 1904. But she is more evasive than even these varied identities. Complicating circumstances include her mixed parentage, her cuckolding of Leopold Bloom, the loss and departure of her children, the low fortunes of her singing endeavors, and the variations in time afforded by her memories and fantasies of the future. Her habit of contradicting herself is not merely a female foible, but a useful representation of how an individual's attitude is affected by time and mental association. Molly's ability to play so many roles, and to range in attitude from conventional matron to liberal feminist makes her a useful representative of the spectrum of female types. At the same time, Molly is intensely female, a factor that makes her relevant to real women only if she is taken as a concentration of specific elements that, in any real woman, would be mixed with asexual and male identity elements. Both Frank Budgen and William York Tindall recognized this extreme femaleness in their early considerations of Molly.[27] Another aspect of Molly's situation in the novel should be kept in mind. These are Molly's thoughts at two in the morning, as sleep first evades and then enfolds her. Fatigue may release inhibitions, but it also may shift one's thoughts toward memory, or body, or subjects immediately associated with one's bed. Molly may not be an ideal representative of woman, but her nocturnal thinking may not be an ideally representative expression of her. It is what Joyce chose to show, however, and what we must deal with.

Molly's lack of accomplishment as a professional and an intellectual seems undeniable from "Penelope." Yet this is essential to her character and even provides an element of social criticism, whether intended or not. Like Gabriel Conroy, Molly Bloom is one aspect of what Joyce might have become, had he remained in Dublin—in her case a not too successful singer. She is the veteran of scattered engagements, but has no real career, and spends more time in her home than on the concert stage. Molly missed at least one important engagement, "the Greystones concert" because of pregnancy (U, 89). As a female performer, Molly relies upon male managers, still a typical arrangement.[28] "Poldy," as she calls her husband, has managed some of her concerts (U, 748)—a solution to the management problem that avoids gossip. But both he and Professor Goodwin, another manager, have "botched" some opportunities (U, 745, 748). As her latest manager, Blazes Boylan has arranged sexual as well as choral engagements. Male performers (especially successful ones) could also elicit sexual favors from attractive young female artistes, as shown by Bartell d'Arcy's kissing Molly on the stairs after one concert. For Molly, these encounters do not seem to constitute an unwelcome problem. She retains an ability to criticize both men, and still to assert woman's right to sexual freedom. In the case of d'Arcy, she sneers at his "tinny" voice and his presumption, but sees the incident as reassuring proof that she can have secrets from Bloom (U, 745). Molly does not advance the feminist battle against sexual harassment, although she does allow us to glimpse the conditions in which it flourishes. Joyce had viewed the problems of two other women within the male-dominated world of the music hall in "A Mother." Kathleen Kearney, like Molly, suffers from poor family management—in her case the management of her mother. Although Mrs. Kearney can be viewed, and usually is, as a meddlesome woman, she can also be interpreted as an intelligent, enterprising, just person, deprived of her rightful scope by a coterie of inept and corrupt males.

Although conditions have not always been favorable to Molly Bloom, the worst impediments to her singing career are probably her socialized or intrinsic lack of drive and professional concentration. As is now widely recognized, these are qualities encouraged in little boys but rarely cultivated in little girls, especially in Molly's day and in Ireland. Only occasionally does Molly make a case for the natural virtues of her voice, and she never recalls or plans efforts to cultivate it or to polish her technique for specific pieces. As reflected in her accommodation of d'Arcy and Boylan, Molly's thoughts concern men and sensual experience much more than singing. Elaine Unkeless has noted that music is nearly always linked to sex in Molly's memories.[29] Rivalry with other women performers ranks next in her musical musings. Molly claims superiority to two other artistes, the same Kathleen Kearney who appeared in "A Mother," whose career seems to

be progressing despite its rough beginning, and Molly's faded contemporary Mrs. M'Coy:

> Kathleen Kearney and her lot of squealers Miss This Miss That
> Miss Theother lot of sparrowfarts skittering around talking about
> politics they know as much about as my backside anything in the
> world to make themselves someway interesting. . . . theyd lie down
> dead of their feet if ever they got a chance of walking down the
> Alameda on an officers arm like me on the bandnight my eyes flash
> my bust that they havent passion God help their poor head I knew
> more about men and life when I was 15 than theyll know at 50.
> . . . (U, 762)

Her glorious past with the officers in Gibraltar does not hide the fact
that Molly has been out of the footlights for over a year, while the
more active Kearney and company have been in them. Their nationalist numbers are also more popular than Molly's Anglo-Boer War
selections, as Molly realizes. Her unpolitic selection may have some
inspiration from her upbringing in the British garrison at Gibraltar,
but a more likely association is her affair with the British officer, Lt.
Gardner; again love outweighs career. Molly also bases her claim to
musical fame on the questionable criteria of bust size, passion and
experience with men. Molly is feeling competition from the younger,
small-busted style of woman, whose interest in politics smacks of the
"New Woman." Her earlier observation, "thin ones not so popular
now," is probably a wish that this type will go away (U, 750). Although Molly has planned a costume for the Belfast concert "to show
off my bubs," she scorns Mrs. M'Coy's similar stratagem, again as-
serting her physical supremacy: "trying to sing my songs shed want
to be born all over again and her old green dress with the lowneck
as she cant attract them any other way" (U, 773). Mrs. M'Coy is a
troubling reminder of the defects of her own wardrobe and of her
own aging process. It strikes Molly elsewhere that "as for being a
woman as soon as youre old they might as well throw you out in the
bottom of the ash pit" (U, 758), and she counts (incorrectly) the
"years left up to 35," apparently her view of the terminal year for
female attractiveness. Molly exposes the cultural bias against the
aging (especially females), which has been the subject of recent feminist attention, but she still clings precariously to the youth that the
dominant society celebrates in the media, and preserves with potions
like the lotion she uses.

Intellectual achievement seems never to have been a central concern of Molly, and what shreds of intellectual interest she displays
are often related to sexual allure. She acknowledges that Mrs. Riordan was "welleducated," but scorns her "chat," as well as Leopold
Bloom's unrewarded attentions to her. Molly expresses an interest
in "the body and the insides," which she has satisfied so far only by
asking Poldy questions. The interest is closely related to her emphasis
on sensual matters, and it is improbable that she will do anything to
actively pursue it (U, 743). She also asks Poldy for definitions of
words like "metempsychosis," but mocks his abstract answers with
her eyes, demanding, "O rocks . . . Tell us in plain words." This
turns Bloom to amorous memories of "the same young eyes. The
first night after charades. Dolphins barn" (U, 64). The diversion from
learning to love is typical of Molly. Privately in "Penelope," she
makes fun of Bloom's learned answers, "if I asked him hed say its
from the Greek leave us as wise as we were before" (U, 744).[30] One
of Molly's fleeting plans for self-improvement is to educate herself
for Stephen Dedalus, and then exchange additional lessons, her offerings being in Spanish and sexuality, his being Italian. Red slippers
are a desirable, if distracting, component of the fantasy (U, 779). "Ill
read and study all I can find or learn a bit off by heart if I knew who
he likes so he wont think me stupid if he thinks all women are the
same" (U, 776). Molly's "the same" seems a troubling dismissal of
most women to the ranks of stupidity (where her culture placed
them). Her intended research methods are comic in their unlikeli-
hood of impressing the young man who has scorned Emma Clery's
college learning. Hitherto, Molly has retained nothing from Byron's
verses, given to her by Poldy, and relies exclusively on the products
of popular culture for reading material.[31] Molly thinks of poets, "they
all write about some woman" (U, 755), and she is willing to become
the subject, or perhaps an erotic version of the muses for Stephen's
art.

Molly's plans for the future of her daughter, Milly, provide an
opportunity for us to consider the educational and vocational history
of mother and daughter, as well as the options open to young women
in 1904. At fifteen, Milly is no longer in school and no one has urged
her toward the university. The letter she sends home to her father,
unlike her mother's monologue and many of the letters by Joyce's
female family, has abundant stops. The first half resembles Lucia
Joyce's letters—Milly expresses thanks for things received for her

birthday and gives considerable news of her work and social plans in Mullingar, where she has recently been sent to work as an assistant in a photographic shop. Only in the letter's most intimate news do the sentences run together. The effect is to associate her boyfriend, Bannon, with Molly's Boylan, and to confuse and combine men, as Molly does in her monologue (U, 66). Molly's idea for Milly would have been to send her to a technical school, probably to learn secretarial skills: "Sherry's academy where shed have to learn not like me getting all at school" (U, 766). Though the phrasing is ambiguous, Molly seems to be admitting to little school education and to be expressing the wish that Milly be forced to get more. Phillip Herring notes that Molly was not sent to England for education, as was the norm with the children of British officers at Gibraltar.[32] No recollections of the alternate garrison school appear in her monologue. Molly's loose grammar is evident twice in her interview with Poldy in "Calypso," where she sniffs "a smell of burn" (U, 65), and observes that the book "must have fell." This lapse does not go unnoiced—Bloom mentally substitutes "must have slid down." The narrator also, in effect, corrects her: "The book, fallen, sprawled against the bulge of the orange-keyed chamberpot"—a resting place not unsuited to the contents of *Ruby: the Pride of the Ring* (U, 64).

Molly's possible reasons for wanting to send Milly to secretarial school merit some scrutiny. She seems to have been experiencing difficulty in controlling her daughter's comings and goings, some of them with young men. She may also prefer to remain the family expert in the school of life and men. Secretarial training was conventionally respectable by 1904, women having entered the previously all-male office ranks in considerable numbers. Joyce planned for his sister Eva to take lessons in typing and shorthand when she came to live with the family in Trieste in 1909 (L II, 247). As demonstrated in "Counterparts," women office workers were not necessarily at the bottom of the office hierarchy; they were certainly above the Farringtons, who scratched away with their pens while bright young women manipulated their new typing machines. Unmarried female office workers would tend to remain in their parents' homes, supplementing the family income (to which Molly has a constant eye) and retaining pin money for clothes and cosmetics (which have gained Molly's and Gerty's attention *via* the media). There were some chances of harassment or adventure. One secretary we meet in *Ulysses*, Miss Dunne, is the object of flirtation by her boss, the

ubiquitous Blazes Boylan; Martha Clifford (probably another secretary) has the freedom of a clandestine correspondence with Bloom.
Still, Molly may feel that secretarial training will get her daughter
out into the world just far enough to attract a husband, her progress
carefully monitored by Mother. It is the same stratagem attempted
by Mrs. Mooney with Polly in "The Boarding House," before she
resorted to more physical and domestic tactics at home.

Leopold Bloom, interestingly, has bolder ideas for his daughter,
which he has implemented: "such an idea for him to send the girl
down there to take photographs on account of his grandfather" (U,
766), thinks Molly. Bloom's apprenticing Milly to a photographer's
shop is unusual in that day. He is also encouraging her to fulfill a
personal taste and go into a field that he associates with his male
progenitors. He recalls "poor papa's daguerreotype atelier he told
me of. Hereditary taste" (U,155) and in "Ithaca" brings out the
daguerreotype of his father and grandfather. It would be a mistake
to claim that Bloom has carefully planned a non-traditional career
for Milly, or that the girl has sought one. Bloom has never had a
proper career for himself. Overall, Bloom gives far more attention
to Milly's sexual awakening than to her intellect, education, or money-
making potential—a penchant he shares with Stephen Dedalus of *A
Portrait*. Bloom exhibits "troubled affection" over Milly's letter about
her boyfriend Bannon and suspects that this, rather than photography, is her "destiny" (U, 66). Though hardly a Mrs. Mooney, Bloom
seems prepared to take conventional measures if Milly's distance
from home and new involvement should get her into trouble. She is
not without supervision. A Mrs. as well as a Mr. Coghlan is reported
to be at the photo shop in her letter (U, 66).

The Blooms' plans for Milly and Molly's history of courtship, marriage and early middle age have surprisingly conventional elements,
considering the rebelliousness of many of Molly's remarks. Biology
remains an important component of woman's destiny, though in *Ulysses* this includes enjoyable sexuality, not just the Victorian ideal of
frigid forbearance for the purpose of procreation. Marriage is probably still woman's most important aspiration. Molly denigrates Miss
Stack for her "old maids voice," identifies Boylan's sisters as "old
maids" (U, 745), and notes Mrs. Riordan's incessant mentioning of
"Mr Riordan," despite his desertion (U, 738). Molly feels that "women
walk on you because they know youve no man" (U, 751). Molly's
era of courtship, with its love letters and initiation to male sexuality,

is a pleasurable memory for her. Molly has practiced pre-marital and extra-marital sex. But she carefully calculated the limits and timing of her sexual activities with Mulvey and Bloom, with a view toward future marriage (U, 743, 761). She uses her marriage date of 1888 as the temporal point from which she estimates the dates of other happenings, suggesting the experiential impact of wedlock.

Molly also differs from the Victorian norm of motherhood. Her number of confinements and devotion to children (who like her) are relatively modest, but not so inconsequential as the 1950's critics argued. Motherhood is an important, if subordinate, part of her identity. She is proud of her firstborn, Milly, and still deeply grieved over the loss of her baby son, Rudy. As befits a Penelope, as well as a mother, she participated in the maternal rite of knitting little things, and tearfully buried Rudy in the precious garment. Leopold Bloom has been an atypically active father and has fonder memories of caring for Milly than Molly does. Yet Molly's recollections of wet-nursing and tending the girl's mumps and worms and buttons suggest thorough involvement, and probably sole responsibility for most of the unpleasant aspects of childrearing. Molly thinks about the essential role of mothers in men's lives, and registers a quick regret of her own lack of a mother: "They dont know what it is to be a woman and a mother how could they where would they all of them be if they hadnt a mother to look after them what I never had. . ."(U, 778). Molly likes to recall the time and conditions of her conceptions of both children, and has not totally given up the idea of having another baby by Poldy. The "darling" and attractive Milly seems likely to carry on the maternal line for the Blooms, even if the male line (more strongly emphasized in *Ulysses*, as in life) should end.

Apart from conception, Molly's sexuality is a driving force in her life. Even mental admission of this in 1904 seems most unusual. Denied full sexuality in marriage ("a woman needs to be embraced" [U, 777]), she sought it first with Lt. Gardner, and on June 16, 1904, with Blazes Boylan. She has creative fantasies of many other embraces—a nice young boy (U, 740), a priest in vestments (U, 741), or a sailor or gypsy, no matter what the consequences to health or safety (U, 777). She envies men for their greater freedom of sexual selection (U, 777). Molly's sexual concentration has both a liberating force and a severely limiting quality, especially in the confines of her culture. It is more manageable in a figure of male fantasy, or a goddess, neither of which is real. Molly Bloom's failure as a model of female achievement, and her alternate concentration on sexual relationships are both propensities that befit *Ulysses*. It is a work in which nobody achieves much, and usual judgments of success are rejected. The first seventeen chapters of *Ulysses* address the sexual poverty of the culture Joyce had known, and Molly is a deliberate part of the recompensating process.

Alongside Molly's conventional values, and her appeals to male sexuality, Molly makes shocking statements that work like the "clicks" of recognition recorded in popular ideological feminist publications of the 1970s. She topples the masonry of sentimental, proper, polite interpretations of women's lives. Throughout her monologue there runs a questioning refrain which asks, who made life the way it is for women? Her attitude is that of someone who feels greatly imposed upon, who questions the authority of the framers of her circumstances, and even her body. These agents range from the humble, well-intentioned Poldy to the creator, who is once identified as a "He" (U, 780). Rather than discount Molly's most revolutionary statements because they are sometimes contradicted, we must understand their weight, both in her discourse, and as the final word on life in *Ulysses*.

Within the first three pages of "Penelope," Molly sounds the rebellion against two of the most widely practiced roles for women: tending the sick and housekeeping. "I hate bandaging and dosing," she exclaims amid impatient memories of old Mrs. Riordan "telling me all her ailments" and thoughts of Poldy's past and potential ills, both real and imagined (U, 738). She also resists the "damn cooking and throwing out the dirt" (U, 740). The impositions here are a cleaning woman who is too old and a house that is ill-equipped, poorly arranged, and vulnerable to burglary. Poldy is implicated in all of this. He shouldn't have wasted his time on Mrs. Riordan. He couldn't avoid the temptations of a younger servant, hence (one infers) the ancient Mrs. Fleming. Molly also implies that Bloom's checkered employment history has not permitted her to live in the style she expected. She has needed to help Poldy secure and maintain employment; had sex roles been different, Molly might have been the better breadwinner. Although Bloom has projected vast improvements for the rest of Dublin throughout the day, he has not yet supplied his own home with a bathtub. Molly declares that he should "get a leather medal with a putty rim for all the plans he invents then leaving us here all day" (U, 765).

Molly's protests are far from absolute, even if they are pervasive and accompanied by a casual response to domestic duties. She is as preoccupied with personal and even household cleanliness as Poldy is with feces. Molly thinks of sending Poldy to the hospital for an illness for cleanliness sake. She criticizes male carelessness in genital hygiene and carefully maintains her own. Molly assists Mrs. Fleming when the old cleaning woman arrives at eleven (U, 87, 93). She has fished out "a rotten old smelly dishcloth" from behind a dresser (U, 768), moved the coats from the hall and burned old newspapers (U, 755). As with her singing, Molly becomes inspired in her house-keeping when it serves her need for sexual relationships. She plans with some interest to prepare Poldy's breakfast, in the context of renewed sexual relations (U, 780); she considers adorning the house with flowers for Stephen's benefit (U, 781); she has moved the parlor furniture on the day of Boylan's visit. Molly is aware of prices and where quality goods can be obtained. Like many other people, Molly finds housekeeping for its own sake unchallenging, inconclusive, and unrewarding; many would conclude that she gives it about what it is worth. At #7 Eccles Street, boredom is as big a problem for Molly as it had been in the male garrison at Gibraltar. Molly is happiest with thoughts of walking in the outdoors, not of sitting at a window, or lying in a bed within the confines of a house. The house is exciting only if it encompasses human relationship, not if it isolates and cre-ates loneliness. Despite her disappointments, Molly copes on her own level. Her drinking of stout and consuming of pulp fiction are age-old solutions, and at least she has avoided the addiction to alcohol that blighted Mrs. Sinico of "A Painful Case," and made Mrs. Cun-ningham a family problem referred to in "Grace" (D, 157). Molly also has more common sense than another avid reader, Flaubert's Mme. Bovary, to whom she is sometimes compared.

Molly utters a mild protest against the dress of her day, which she justifiably finds physically confining, and even dangerous: "clothes we have to wear whoever invented them expecting you to walk up Killiney hill then for example at that picnic all stayzed up you cant do a blessed thing in them in a crowd run or jump out of the way" (U, 755). Molly's "whoever invented them" is her usual refrain, a questioning of qualifications with a suspicion that the inventor never wore the fashions. Molly also resents the torments of shopping for clothes. She is particularly irritated with the "insolent" attitude of a hat shop girl (U, 752), whose demeanor matches that of the cake shop attendant who deals impatiently with Maria in "Clay." As with the housekeeping, Molly bows to convention, however. She thinks of buying one of the "kidfitting corsets" she had seen advertised and of doing fad exercises (U, 750). Molly is far from indifferent to the attracting powers of clothing. She bought one "rubbishy dress" because Poldy liked it (U, 752), and tends to recall what she wore on occasions of success with the men in her life. She has apparently compensated for Poldy's limited earnings by running a costume business in the past (U, 774). Molly's present discontent with her wardrobe (U, 751) is another indication of reduced resources, and a less than satisfying life. Molly is not capable of Stephen's absolute *non serviam*, directed at the institutions he protests. Even in things she dislikes, there are momentary pleasures. She limits her revolt to a mental registry of complaints, and a lazy fulfillment of expectations.

Molly joins Stephen in one protest—her condemnation of overly religious women like Mrs. Riordan and Mrs. Rubio, the servant in her father's house. She also questions the role and authority of priests in the confession. Why did a priest have to draw her out about where a young man had touched her when she went to confession, and why should she have to confess "to the priest when Id already confessed it to God"? When speaking to the priest as "father," Molly always thinks "of the real father" (U, 741). Molly as goddess would seem to have a more direct channel to God. She also hopes God will "send sense" to a bishop who is currently preaching "about woman's higher functions and girls now riding the bicycle" (U, 761). Joyce continues to think of the "bisexycle" as a vehicle of sexual freedom in *Finnegans Wake* (FW, 116.16). Molly has worried about Milly's freedom on a boy's bicycle, but has the sense not to combine this with "higher functions." Molly does have some use for religion, however. Her fear of thunder is eased by saying Hail Mary's, and she lights candles in the chapel for good luck (U, 741).[33] Molly will not accept intellectual men's denial or replace mentof the deity. She reveres a God as the only creator (U, 782).

In discussions of sexual anatomy, Molly is at her boldest. She questions the wisdom of the creator of female anatomy, as she does others whose creations she has inherited: "Whats the idea of making us like that with a big hole" (U, 742). When her menstrual period arrives three quarters of the way into the chapter, she recapitulates her protests, using the typical refrain: "Whoever suggested that business for women that between clothes and cooking and children this damned old bed too jingling like the dickens. . ." (U, 769). Menstruation is "this mischance of a thing I hope theyll have something better for us in the other world" (U, 772). Interestingly, no stigma other than nuisance is placed upon the menstruating woman in *Ulysses*—a rather remarkable state of affairs considering the Hebrew attribution of uncleanness. Molly may be thinking of Poldy when she notes that some men like it (U, 769). Early in their relationship, Poldy had sent her a dirty letter (reminiscent of Joyce's to Nora), declaring "everything underlined that comes from it [her "glorious Body"] is a thing of beauty" (U, 771). Joyce's notes for "Penelope" also contain the positive association, "roses-menses," working menstruation into Molly's reflections on nature, which focus upon flowers, and into possible associaton with a standard symbol of the Virgin Mary.[34] Molly's description of vaginal orgasm (U, 754) and her admiration of Boylan's organ for making her feel "full up" (U, 742) are questionable as female perceptions of coitus, though they reflect male and Freudian fallacies, uncorrected in an era preceding Masters and Johnson.[35]

Though Molly criticizes vaginal structure and is annoyed by the "pooh" of menstruation (U, 769), she is usually very positive about the external female body. She so admires women's thighs that she quips, "I wouldnt mind being a man and get up on a lovely woman" (U, 770). She cultivates her breasts for firmness and fatness, but as with her housekeeping and dressing, this effort has a male orientation; breasts are an important asset with men, as shown in classical art. Molly thinks about the male ideal expressed in female nude statues, "theyre supposed to represent beauty . . . are they so beautiful of course compared with what a man looks like with his two bags full and his other thing hanging down out of him or sticking up at you like a hatrack no wonder they hide it with a cabbage leaf" (U, 753). Molly's defaulting description of male genitals was unmatched in literature until Esther Greenwood of Sylvia Plath's *The Bell Jar* likened them to a turkey neck and gizzards. Plath was a reader of Joyce, and in the novel, Esther is contemplating a senior thesis on *Finnegans Wake*, so Molly's description may have inspired Esther's.[36] In general, Molly finds women's bodies more beautiful than men's. She makes one exception. Perhaps encouraged by Stephen's visit, she discovers "real beauty and poetry" in the statue of a young male, with "his lovely young cock" (U, 775-776). Rather than seeing this as another of Molly's contradictions, we should perhaps see Molly's admiration of this nude as part of an ongoing effort in the monologue to create a female ideal of male beauty. This would match the many male ideals of female beauty that flood Molly's culture. Poldy visits his favorite nudes at the Museum on this very day, and has apparently led Molly throught the same territory. Although her effort is not concerted, in searching for a female aesthetic, Molly has an endeavor in common with contemporary utopian feminists.

Molly frequently thinks about penises, but on balance, she is more fascinated than envious,[37] and despite her unromantic description of male genitals, she shows no castration impulse. Molly's childhood attempts to urinate, male fashion, are typical experiments, and probably should not be taken as evidence of a desire to be male. Molly scoffs at male exhibitionists, of whom she has encountered several (U, 753). She recognizes the prodigious size of Boylan's organ. She recalls that with Mulvey she "loved rousing that dog in the hotel," (U, 760), this being her first experience with arousing a male. Elsewhere, Molly comments on the magical, transforming nature of the penis, "swelling up upon you so hard and at the same time so soft when you touch it" (U, 776). But one thing that the female discovers in early sexual encounters is her own power to arouse "that dog." She also admits that each sexual encounter is not the same. She favors the initial experience (U, 740). She realizes that, perceived one way, the male's participation in the sexual act is violent: Boylan's penis is a "brute" and his eyes have a "vicious look" (U, 742). This may be her countersign or female equivalent to Poldy's fear of losing sight of his penis in sexual intercourse.

Molly's selection of words relating to coitus and sexual anatomy is naive and often euphemistic. Coitus is usually an indefinite "it," though "blocking" is also admissible, and Molly fantasizes yelling "fuck." The penis is a "thing": the vagina, a "hole"; the buttocks, my "bottom."[38] Molly condemns a male gynecologist's use of the word "vagina." When this dried-up, odd-spoken doctor sits down to write, however, Molly suddenly likes him. His pen is a form of authority with Molly, suggesting that she has less than total control of what happens to her body. His technical language, of course, works the same way over her in society. It is interesting that the notesheets contained "new woman surgeon" for "Penelope." It was a note that Joyce apparently never put to use. Did Joyce contemplate having Molly consult a female doctor or even just reflect upon a female member of the medical profession? Perhaps the phenomenon of the new woman surgeon was just too new for inclusion. Joyce had shown interest in a young woman doctor he encountered in Locarno while he was writing *Ulysses*, and this could have inspired the note.[39]

Molly Bloom repeatedly generalizes about "men," a "them" who are obviously different from her and other women. She usually finds women superior to men, though she criticizes her own sex as well. There are aspects of personality: "they havent half the character a woman has" (U, 761); "all their 20 pockets arent enough for their lies" (U, 772). Men are hypochondriacs, while women make light of their illnesses to save others trouble (U, 738). She finds "man tyrant as ever" with his whimsical demands about sexual practices (U, 773). Molly is not keen on marriage, despite her youthful aspiration: "why cant you kiss a man without going and marrying him first . . . theres nothing like a kiss long and hot down to your soul" (U, 744). Men's writing and art also fail female experience. Molly doesn't like books "with a Molly in them" (U, 756), perhaps trusting her being more. She questions the reality of the pornographic novels Poldy brings her: "I hate that pretending of all things with the old blackguards face on him anybody can see its not true and that Ruby and Fair Tyrants he brought me that twice I remember when I came to page 50 the part about where she hangs him up out of a hook with a cord flagellate sure theres nothing for a woman in that all invention made up about he drinking the champagne out of her slipper after the ball was over like the infant Jesus in the crib at Inchicore . . . sure no woman could have a child that big taken out of her " (U, 752). One of Molly's most quoted statements puts intellectual men in their place: "I wouldnt give a snap of my two fingers for all their learning why dont they go and create something" (U, 782). The only creation Molly exalts is that of God the creator. She is not interested in the womb as a metaphor for artistic creation (as was Stephen/Joyce), nor does she dwell upon the natural generative function of the womb, her own, or anyone else's. That seems to be a locus for male worship. Molly is generally opposed to politics and violence, implying that she leaves war and political disputation to men. Interestingly, the mild-mannered, womanly Poldy is the subject of her disdain for early political posturings (U, 742-743). Has she perhaps discouraged this in him over the years, thus contributing to his womanly or andro-gynous makeup? She scorns the political discussions of the Kathleen Kearney types (U, 762). She is interested in a story of female do-mestic violence (such pieces were common in contemporary newspapers): "that Mrs Maybrick that poisoned her husband," but Molly generally believes women to be more peaceful and orderly than men. "Theyre not brutes enough to go and hang a woman surely are they" (U, 744). The "they" who are brutes enough to hang anyone are clearly men. "I dont care what anybody says itd be much better for the world to be governed by the women in it you wouldnt see women going and killing one another and slaughtering when do you ever see a woman rolling around drunk like they do or gambling every penny they have or losing it on horses yes because a woman whatever she does she knows where to stop" (U, 778).

Despite her general wisdom about women and her claims of female superiority, Molly has little to do with women herself, a factor which may detract from her reliability as an evaluator of female experience. Molly's remoteness from other women may have been encouraged initially by a male-centered upbringing in what Herring describes as the "man's world" of Gibraltar. Like the highly independent and revolutionary Maud Gonne, Molly was raised by a single male parent, in a British army setting. The supervision of Mrs. Rubio "with all her religion domineering" (U, 759) only encouraged her into the embraces of Mulvey. Her mother was a mystery, not a companion or advisor, and Lunita Laredo's reputation may have limited Molly's exposure to respectable young women, just as it reduced her marital prospects. Herring has suggested that, as the child of an Irishman from the British garrison and a Jewess from the town, Molly would have been both a cultural anomaly, and an outcast of both societies. Lunita Laredo's liaison with a Christian would have been unforgivable to her patriarchal society. It is likely that a marriage never took place and that the mother was left to wander or die. Herring suggests that Molly has oddly suppressed much of what could be expected as her background. The Laredo family is in fact a remarkable clan that had fled religious persecution in Spain by moving to Morocco in the middle ages.[40] Molly seems to have had a rather dull existence at Gibraltar, but aside from her relative lack of companions, does not record any social ostracism.

Molly recalls some female friendships from her younger days (Esther Stanhope in Gibraltar and Floey Dillon and Josie Powell in Dublin) but has fewer close friends after years of marriage—a pattern which is not unusual in women's friendships today (U, 758). Bloom's courtship had turned Josie into a rival. Over the years the Blooms had done less socializing as a couple, thus increasing Molly's isolation, and their Jewish identity could be expected to contribute additional separateness. Molly has discussed intimate matters like copulatory postures with Mrs. Mastiansky (U, 749), but now avoids discussing husbands with Josie Powell Breen, and considers answering letters from Mrs. Dwenn and Floey Dillon a bother (U, 758). At some level, Molly longs for female friendship and discussion: "they have friends they can talk to weve none" (U, 778). Molly isn't so sure about male friendship either. She questions the depth and altruism of the male friends who attend Dignam's funeral with Poldy: "they call that friendship killing and then burying one another" (U, 773). Male friendships seem to depend on rounds of drinks, purchased from family funds; Molly worries about Poldy in their "clutches," and realizes that he is more responsible about his family than most.

Molly's most pessimistic, but perhaps most interesting comment on women suggests that they too have dangerous clutches, but goes on to explore the female pressures that produce regrettable behavior: "its some woman ready to stick her knife in you I hate that in women no wonder they treat us the way they do we are a dreadful lot of bitches I suppose its all the troubles we have makes us so snappy im not like that" (U, 778-779). The statement comes at a particularly low moment for Molly, just after she has been thinking herself "into the glooms" over Rudy's death. Though she disclaims, "Im not like that," throughout her monologue, Molly does what is termed "bitching" in our male-generated lexicon. Molly's explanation for female snappiness is "all the troubles we have," and her "we" clearly includes herself. This observation fits well with Molly's memory of boxing Milly's ears—an act which she regrets and tries to understand by thinking over what she has eaten and what pressures she has been under (U, 768). Molly can be perceived as a woman well provided for by Poldy, from the breakfast he brings in "Calypso," to the accounts he keeps in "Ithaca." She has had the shattering loss of Rudy. But, personal considerations aside, Molly has feelings of loss and desire that she finds reflected in the lives of other women she has observed. Described as "troubles," these problems take on political and Irish dimensions as well. We sense that Molly is actually snapping away at norms of power that are far more general than her individual case, or even that of womankind.

The Blooms' troubled marriage should probably be taken as a general as well as an individual problem. Molly Bloom's feelings about

Poldy fluctuate as much as her feelings about men and women do. If he has suspicions about her extramarital affairs, she too has suspicions. She anticipates current observations on "male menopause" with her comment, "all men get a bit like that at his age especially getting on to forty" (U, 739). At times, Poldy represents the worst aspects of male tyranny and pride, but, on balancing things, Molly sees his unusual qualities and considers him superior to mankind in general, a judgment that has been expressed in feminist Joyce criticism.[41] Leopold has fewer harsh thoughts about Molly than she has about him, but he also thinks about her less. He sets about getting the lotion Molly has requested but fails to retrieve it (U,84-85, 440, 735 etc.). Compared to Molly, who perceives herself as being left home alone all day, Leopold's day is more varied in geography traversed, people encountered, and subjects contemplated. Although Poldy is "womanly" in his attitudes toward people and love, he has interests in science and technology and a rational cast of mind that are culturally associated with men, and to which Molly offers her "countersign" (L I, 160). When he does think or talk about Molly, Bloom is nearly as inconsistent as Molly herself. He seems defensive and unhappy about her appointment with Boylan, but it is unclear whether cuckolding or possible loss of her affections troubles him more. Their present incomplete sexual relationship seems to have been more his doing than hers. Somewhat boldly, considering the era and his benevolence, Bloom has contemplated divorce (U, 277, 773). Still, he displays Molly's picture to Stephen with pride, and happily assumes his place beside her in their well-used bed.

Ulysses is in part the study of a sixteen-year-old marriage, of husband and wife entering what is now termed the mid-life crisis. Concern over the quality of a marriage or relationship affects both man and woman, but has been considered more woman's responsibility. *Ulysses*, with its womanly man as husband makes the concern intense on both sides. The Blooms' marriage has twice lost aspects of completeness. First, the marriage was shaken by Rudy's death, an event that terminated the couple's practice of "complete sexual intercourse" after only five years. A second event involving the children— Milly's puberty, achieved nine months previous—has received less critical attention, and is indeed less evident in *Ulysses*. In "Ithaca" the consequences of Milly's development are phrased similarly to the impact of Rudy's death: they supposedly terminated the Blooms' "complete mental intercourse." This announcement has incestuous as well as conspiratorial possibilities. But the "Ithaca" voice is a male one, perhaps reflecting only male speculation, and thus remains suspect in this chapter on Molly.

Critics have exchanged their reasons for why Milly is in Mullingar.[42] Clearly her job is secondary. Quite possibly, the preservation of the Blooms' marriage is the major reason that Poldy has sent her away. James Joyce cautioned Nora that their children must never come between them in their relationship (L II, 242). But Joyce's admonishment came when his children were babies, not adolescents on the brink of going out into the world, like Milly. As far as we can tell, Milly never came before Poldy in Molly's scheme of priorities. Molly's present diversion clearly is Boylan, not her daughter. There is no evidence in "Penelope" of the female alliance to control Bloom, suggested in "Ithaca": "a preestablished natural comprehension in incomprehension between the consummated females" which served lately to circumscribe Bloom's "complete corporal liberty of action" (U, 736). It also seems unlikely that Poldy has sent Milly away to protect her from any kind of incestuous impulses on his part or hers, though in the *Wake* and even "Eveline," Joyce evokes this problem. The primary effect of Milly's maturing seems to have been to remind her parents of their own aging. Bloom has been replaced by Bannon as a courter of young women; Molly sees that her daughter's breasts are bouncing and budding as hers did when she was first meeting young men. Molly detects evidence of age in her contemporary, Mrs. M'Coy, and Leopold buries a friend.

As an individual and as a representative and observer of many women, Molly Bloom offers a picture of the female, more acted upon than acting. She can make small efforts toward a life that is exciting, or even just comfortable and clean. She can also ask who is responsible, thus questioning the very norms that envelop and characterize her. In her countersign, we also note many parallels. Women suspect men of many of the defects men suspect in women—vanity (though in differing forms), infidelity, and deceit. Women and men need each other sexually, and find features to admire in the other's physical nature. Women and men generalize about their own sex, and seem to criticize it, but ultimately to prefer it. In this book of memories, both of the Blooms seek energy, direction and relationship for the future. For most of the day, the search is separate, and best conducted without the one child of past love present. Toward morning, Molly and Poldy come together, having merged to foster the lost son, Stephen. This is not a new parenthood, however. It joins them in service to artistic creation. There is also a merger into an eternal scheme of life, celebrated at the end of both the male ("Ithaca") and the female ("Penelope") closings of *Ulysses*.

The eternal man and woman is an aspect of "Penelope" best served by Molly Bloom's super-human, goddess aspect. Early archetypal interpretations, and criticisms of them, considered the goddess narrowly, in her procreative role. Molly is like her in more ways than this, and takes on aspects of the goddess that have been ignored until recently, the enriched view inspired largely by feminist criticism. The richness intended in the chapter is suggested by the entry in Joyce's notesheets, "old gods slumber in her brain," which is plural and male or bisexual in its "gods" reference.[43]

Like mythical female deities, Molly has a shadowy beginning. The male source is fairly certain in Major Tweedy, who like mythical fathers is a warrior, in service to the king (actually Queen Victoria, and the authenticity of his credentials is suitably dubious to offer Joycean irony). Mystery, if not miracle, surrounds her mother, Lunita Laredo. Her first name connects her to the moon, the orb originally associated with mother goddesses, later attached to the Blessed Virgin Mary, and also connected to a female ideal by poets like Shelley and Goethe. The Laredo surname is Spanish, for Joyce an identity associated with Galway in the primitive west of Ireland, and also linked with the early Celtic race of Milesians. Like the moon, the mother goddess Demeter, and the Jew, Lunita has wandered on. She has left Molly with many goddess-like aspects of her own. In Ithaca, the "mystery" of Molly is represented by her light in the window, above Bloom and Stephen, as they water the earth. Bloom has been thinking about "special affinities" that "appeared to exist between the moon and woman." Not all of the shared qualities listed by Bloom suggest the goddess. One inappropriate aspect is "satellitic dependence." But many of the qualities he detects are powerful and worthy of a female deity: "antiquity in preceding and surviving successive tellurian generations," "potency over effluent and refluent waters," and "omens of tempest and calm" (U, 702). Molly's aloofness from other women, coinciding with sympathy for their troubles, is also appropriate to the goddess. As with the goddesses and many conceptions of the female (including Dora Marsden's scheme of female space and masculine time), Molly is associated with place or space; this is a suitable accompaniment to Bloom's preoccupation with time.[44]

She presides over #7 Eccles Street, receiving Boylan, Bloom and (in effect) Stephen there in succession. She also mentally associates herself with the places where significant events in her life history occurred. The two most significant are pap-like eminences, like the geographic features frequently named for goddesses (Anu and Medb in Ireland): the Moorish Wall in Gibraltar, where she stroked Mulvey, and the Hill ow Howth, north of Dublin, where she first made love with Bloom. Molly's emphasis on space is a countersign to Bloom's preoccupation with time, visible throughout the preceding seventeen chapters, but irrelevant to "Penelope," and constantly violated by Molly's freedom in memory and association. Robert Boyle has suggested that Molly represents the Holy Spirit—the completing third part of the trinity.[45] This is compatible with the triple aspect usually assigned to the moon goddess, though it is notable that her pre-Christian three is all female.

Celtic myth shared the unrestrained attitude of Molly Bloom toward human functions of elimination and sexuality.[46] Medb was one of the first women whose menstruation was treated in myth. Molly restores this commonplace of female experience to literature, with lusty indelicacy worthy of the Celts. Her menstruation is further evidence of continuing fertility and new possibilities for procreation. The recollected flow of milk from Molly's breasts also bears heroic suggestiveness. Molly has been reproached for her limited number of children, but this aspect belongs to her realistic, not her symbolic self. Goddesses, unlike real women, can give birth freely without ever becoming encumbered by the rearing of their children. Irish goddesses give birth in the course of strenuous athletic activity. Medb effortlessly produced nine sons, all of whom she gave the same name, and many of whom perished in the course of The Táin. Molly's limited motherhood, and her grieving over Rudy, relate to the Egyptian mother goddess, Isis, who loses and regains her son-husband as part of the annual cycle.

One of the most memorable pronouncements of Medb was, "I never had one man without another waiting in his shadow."[47] Molly has also had her series of men, though Bloom's own longer list of her liaisons increases the mythical dimensions of this achievement. Molly has outlived Gardner, lost track of Mulvey (and almost lost memory of his first name), and mentally dismissed many of the lovers on Bloom's list. She sometimes mingles memories of her men indiscriminately. Medb offers her "friendly thighs" as an enticement in her dealings with men, and Molly places a premium on this female asset, as we have noted. It probably does not stretch the analogy to Medb too badly to suggest that the "pillowtalk" which occurs between Medb and Aillil in *The Táin* is echoed in the two bed conferences between Molly and Poldy in *Ulysses*. As in ancient Irish custom, Molly has contributed her marriage goods—the jingling bed, its humble origins deliberately shrouded in mystery. The morning tea Poldy brings her can be taken as an offering to the goddess, a seasonal rite enacted by the king in hope of winning her favor, her endorsement of his sovereignty, the flourishing of her earth. She radiates appropriate moist morning warmth from her earthy bed. Molly asks other tributes, another book and bottle of lotion for her eternal youth. In the night, Molly seems to agree to Poldy's nebulous request for eggs, served to him in bed, where he will be "sitting up like the king of the county" (U, 764). It is the fulfillment of the chieftain's wish for fruition (eggs) from the goddess, as her seedcake had been at the start of their relationship. Molly's consideration of women's bodies as flowers, and the Blooms' very name are in keeping with this flourishing of the earth. Bloom's worship of "the plump mellow smellow mellons of [Molly's] rump in the final pages of "Ithaca" (U, 734-735), also have mythical precedents. Fergus regrets having followed "the misguided rump of a woman," Medb, toward the end of the *The Táin*. Dublin tradition also suggests that a pagan Irish king resisted the Christian incursion of Christ Church, Dublin, by having his queen sit upon the altar. This eminence given to a female bottom is appropriate to Bloom's worshipping at the altar of Molly's mellons; it also serves Joyce's replacement of Christian rites, especially the Blessed Virgin Mary, as adored object. The "chilly bombom" of the pagan queen makes a more definite appearance in *Finnegans Wake* (FW, 552). Molly is a much more versatile and powerful creature than Homer's Penelope. She also prevails over Circe and Nausicaä. Unlike the dangerous nymph, suggested in Gerty and the *Tit-Bits* reproduction over the Blooms' bed, Molly has no self-destructive secrets. She survives with Bloom, orbiting into sleep and eternity (U, 737).

Like the women of the ancients, Molly creates her own poetry, and with her Tarot cards, she tells the future. Her biting, satiric tongue also has precedent in Celtic woman satirists and prophetesses—Fedelm, prophetess of *The Táin*, and Leborcham, the old satirist who turned nurse and protectress of the beautiful young

Deirdre. Molly's voice is revolutionary—it takes us back, before literature, and even before the traditions of Homer.

The explanation of "Penelope" that Joyce gave to Frank Budgen has been used to support the *Gea Tellus* interpretation of Molly. Some of its details deserve our reconsideration in this feminist reinterpretation. Joyce's powerful analogy , "It turns like the huge earth ball slowly surely evenly round and round," and his stress on what he identifies as the "female word *yes*" are particularly in need of clarification. Joyce had also written "MB = spinning Earth" in his notesheets,[48] and he further elaborated the female "yes" for Louis Gillet:

> I had sought to end with the least forceful word I could possibly find. I had found the word "yes," which is barely pronounced, which denotes acquiescence, self-abandon, relaxation, the end of all resistance. (JJ, 712n)

To the first wave of feminist criticism, the "yes" seemed an imposed stereotype of feminine passivity by Joyce, a cop-out by Molly.[49] It is well to remember, however, that Joyce discussed "Penelope" as "prehuman" and "posthuman" with Harriet Weaver. He does not label "yes" as feminine, but uses a noncultural sexual identification, "female." Joyce's "least forceful" is in opposition to "force," a quality which Joyce resisted but found inevitable in society, even in his youthful essay, "Force" (CW, 17-24). The Molly of the close of "Penelope" is no longer the protester against society. She never acquiesces or abandons herself to society. What she yields to are larger principles, human fatigue, and the cycles of being on which *Ulysses* itself closes. Perhaps acquiescence even to these forces is to be resisted. Woman's right to individuality has been one of the major concerns of the current women's movement, and individuality is certainly yielded up to eternity. Julia Kristeva finds Molly's monologue, like two Beckett works (*First Love* and *Not I*) "haloed, in all their nonsense, with a paternal aura, ironically but obstinately raising her toward that third-person-God—and filling her with a strange joy in the face of nothingness."[50] Kristeva seems unconvinced that Joyce fully escaped Christian patriarchal frameworks, despite his rejection of religion. But while the male voice of "Ithaca" orbits Molly and Poldy off into oblivion, in "Penelope," Molly closes by remembering themselves in an earthly embrace. The sexual and sovereign energy of that moment, described with the force of the quiet, breathy, female word, and not the void or the patriarchal deity, powers the close of *Ulysses*.

Molly Bloom, the prehuman, posthuman, spinning earth, takes much of her dynamics from real and mythic women. The initial sentence of 2500 words, the chapter with sentences numbering just 8 (the sign for eternity on its side, like Molly) are in a syntax derived from the flowing, pre-literary letters of Joyce's female family, and infused with their contradictory but still valid wisdom about human relationships. The sharp tongue of the ancient Celtic prophetess or the modern Irish ones Joyce knew in Aunt Josephine and Nora Barnacle are also apart from male governance, and also contributory to Molly.

Molly should be seen as more than a principle of fertility, or desire. She is desired, but not just as mother; she is sought as an alternate to structures that have been granted undue sovereignty. Molly's language answers Robert Graves's quest for the lost, magical language of poetic myth in *The White Goddess*.[51] It can be interpreted, as Colin MacCabe does, as a shattering of phallic male modes of discourse, including their systems of rational authority and linear patterning of knowledge.[52] Although Molly Bloom is not a common individual woman, a feminist woman, or a goddess, she serves all three. Although still an overconcentrated, male-projected entity, Joyce's female voice has changed literature and aroused criticism. Perhaps it may still serve a return to woman's self-ordered place in literature and life. "Penelope" as "coda" or "countersign" was not intended as a central part of *Ulysses*. From the evidence of the notesheets and correspondence, it does not seem to have been particularly difficult for Joyce to write. Perhaps this was so because Joyce was already in a highly experimental mode by the time he got to the end of this revolutionary work. Or perhaps the elements of "Penelope" were an ancient, positive, always present, though denied part of his humanity. "Penelope" is certainly not the last word on female consciousness, nor are its extensions in *Finnegans Wake*. However, both works tentatively reorder a male-centered, rational world, and make a female "other" an immediate, insistent presence.

Issy

$$9$$

□ Though she confidently proclaims, "Is is," (FW, 620.32) critics have so far been perplexed as to *what* is "Is," "Isobel," or "Issy," as she is now popularly named. Consensus has been reached on a few identifications as well as the notion that we need not limit ourselves to one. She is the young woman (or women) of *Finnegans Wake*, the daughter (or daughters) of the ALP-HCE family, the sister of Shem and Shaun. But she is also one or both of the Iseults of the Tristan and Iseult legend, the Irish heroines Grainne, Deirdre, and Arrah na Pogue, the two young friends of Jonathan Swift (Stella and Vanessa), Lewis Carroll's Alice, both fictional and in life (Alice Liddell and Isa Bowman), any girl who is loved by any prurient old man, or incestuously by her father or brother(s). As a babe in her "april cot" in III.4, she is associated with the fleeting goddess, Daphne, and her forest setting, which includes the mystical hawthorn blossoms, usually associated with goddesses: "Isobel, she is so pretty, truth to tell, wildwood's eyes and primarose hair, quietly, all the woods so wild, in mauves of moss and daphne dews, how all so still she lay, neath the whitethorn, child of tree, some losthappy leaf, like blowing flower stilled . . ." (FW, 556.16-20). Issy has her most important roles in II.1 ("The Mime of Mick, Nick and the Maggies"), where she provides Glugg with clues to her name, while his brother Chuff is more generally admired by seven rainbow girls, and in II.2 ("The Lessons"), where she writes the footnotes. Issy also writes and talks about letters (FW, 143-148, 279n.1, 457-461). The first part

Joyce wrote for her (Isolde with Tristan on board King Mark's ship in II.4), and her brief appearances as Nuvolette (FW, 157) are less notable, but confirm remarkable patterns.

Issy has also won from her critics a number of dubious distinctions. It is not the intention of this study to dismiss these out of hand, but to ask if cultural biases might have encouraged their early discovery, and to invite new and fuller perceptions of Issy. It seems obvious that Issy is modeled to some extent upon Joyce's own daughter, Lucia. Indeed, the "april cot" passage, with its white flower and the child's "wild" eyes is reminiscent of Joyce's poem "A Flower Given to My Daughter," cited in the consideration of Lucia in chapter 4. Issy's dancing also suggests Lucia. Yet it does not necessarily follow that she must share Lucia's schizophrenia or what Hélène Cixous takes to be Lucia's "tragically violent jealousy" over her parents' mutual companionship.[1] Adaline Glasheen was one of Issy's first analyzers, and her assessments that Issy is "mad" and "a triumph of female imbecility and sexual attraction" still stand in her *Third Census of Finnegans Wake*.[2] Many find Issy not just attractive, but a veritable temptress, and draw the perennial critical dichotomy of virgin vs. whore to describe the aspects of her personality. Issy's frequent use of the looking glass has won her the label "narcissistic."[3] None of these attributes suggest that Joyce has created a character worthy of feminists' admiration or enhanced the range of literary conceptions of woman in this key late character.

Women and madness seem to go together, both in psychological and literary research of the last decade.[4] Issy's supposed madness is widely accepted, based upon contradictory attitudes displayed and dialogues held with her mirror companion, both readily located in the text. Glasheen discovered Joyce's borrowing for Issy of the letters and behaviors of Sally Beauchamp, one of the personalities of a young woman from Boston, whose case was described in *The Dissociation of a Personality*, by her psychiatrist, Morton Prince.[5] Though he acknowledges the structural importance of Prince's report, James Atherton notes that "all characters split into parts at some place in the book."[6] Shari Benstock notes that the fragmentation of Issy may exist only in the mind of the presumably male dreamer.[7] Our task will be to look for undetected reasons for Joyce's creating these divisions in Issy.

Issy presents one of the most obvious explanations for her mirror self in a dialogue to that image: "I call her Sosy because she's sosiety

for me. . . ." The mirror image is a "linking class girl" (FW 459.4),
perhaps connecting her to women as a "class" or even a lower class
of humans—a notion that accords with some modern feminist theories
on women in society. Elsewhere Issy is described as "Isolade, Liv's
lonely daughter"—isolated and lonely (FW 289.29-30). In another
appearance as the nubile Nuvoletta, "She was alone" and was also
ignored by the Mookse and the Gripes, who were involved in their
own convocation (FW 157.13, .24-29). The ALP-HCE family offers
same-sex companions to the boys, but no sister for Issy. It represents,
in miniature, the special loneliness of women, noted by such an authority as Molly Bloom (U, 778). As a second alternate to the path-
ological explanation, we can refer to the childhood propensity for
creating imaginary friends, who frequently serve as scapegoats in
small children's explanations of who did a sinful deed. Issy, as youngest child, could be best expected to create such a fantasy.

Looking-glass gazing has been given a bad name for both moral
and psychological reasons. Conventional moralists consider it an act
of vanity. We are told repeatedly of Issy's beauty, of her striking
and fashionable clothes, and occasionally of her use of hygiene and
cosmetics. All of these she knows how to turn to the purpose of
allurement. Her "firstclass pair of bedroom eyes of most unhomey
blue" (FW 396.11-12) and "her ensemble of maidenna blue with
an overdress of net, tickled with goldies" (FW, 384.30-31), seemingly good examples, are reported by one of the four old, lecherous
chroniclers, however, not Issy. Though she does array and display
herself, her appearance is more the preoccupation of men than the
dominant aspect of her own thinking. We have already learned to
distrust Stephen's limitations of another young woman, Emma Clery,
and the same caution must be applied to *Finnegans Wake*. Issy is in
one aspect Venus, a goddess of love, who holds the looking-glass as
a positive symbol of beauty. Venus' glass has become the symbol of
woman for feminists as well as astronomers and biologists. Issy's glass
can also be seen as the medium of vision and communication: "while
m'm'ry's leaves are falling deeply on my Jungfraud's Messongebook
I will dream telepath posts dulcets on this isinglass stream" (FW
460.19-21). Issy reenacts woman's ancient role as seer and prophetess, communicating her message to the hero. Recall that in *Stephen
Hero*, as discussed in chapter 7, it was the male who played "oracle"
(SH, 191). The "Mime" chapter, in which she plays a large role, is
filled with references to magic, witchcraft, and the occult.[8] Though

he satirized them as a popular movement, Joyce may have found in theosophy and witchcraft a useful counter element to established political and religious powers of his era. Issy with her mirror serves momentarily as their priestess.

Psychological analyses of Issy's mirror are more complex to contend with. They may be set beneficially in a Joycean context. While Issy contemplates herself, she does not relate to other beings. Like Stephen Dedalus of *A Portrait* (who shunned only a cracked looking glass), she is solipsistic—one of the most frequently damned traits in late twentieth-century criticism. But she is also contemplative, silent, peaceful. She does battle with herself instead of others, and she only occasionally plays tricks on her alter-ego (a favorite practice of Sally Beauchamp). In the positive mode, for example, she addresses her substitute: "Understudy of my understandings, Sostituda, and meek thine complinement gymnufleshed" (FW 271.n4). There is ambiguity in this. The reflection is instructed to be meek, genuflect, and compliment, perhaps. But the common endeavor is understanding, and the effect is to detect "line" and be new-fleshed. Issy does not spend an inordinate amount of time before the mirror. She reacts to all her family. Furthermore, the two images may be more a matter of psychological actuality than illness. The demand that personality must be unwavering, that doubts and differences should be masked and not communicated, is a dominant value of a society still founded on eighteenth-century rationalism. Issy's second, sexual self is not a possessing devil, to be rooted out as witches were for several centuries, but a denied part of humanity, which both Freud and Joyce wished to summon forth from the glass.

Adaline Glasheen's straightforward proclamation of Issy's "imbecility" seems itself a criticism of acculturated values of young girls. The charge is readily documented in *Finnegans Wake*. Her own mother, ALP, regrets "If only she had more matacher's wit" (FW 620.29). Yet it is usually Issy among her frequent complements of seven or twenty-eight other young girls, or as one of the Maggies who is ment allydeficient. "And how war your maggies? . . .they hate thinking" (FW, 142.31-33). The "twentynine hedge daughters out of Benent Saint Berched's national nightschool" greet Jaun with "that chorus of praise of goodwill girls on their best beehiviour who all they were girls all rushing sowarmly for the post as buzzy as sie could bie to read his kisshands, kittering all about, rushing and making a tremendous girls fuss over him pellmele" (FW 430.1-2,.18-

22). It is Issy's chorus, the rainbow girls, who twice render their adoration of Chuff in the "Mime" and listen devotedly to Jaun's sermon.

Even the buzzy enthusiasm of Issy's companions is mixed with attitudes that require explanation. The second of their demonstrations to Chuff is tinged with a good measure of feminist independence:

> Hightime is ups be it down into outs according! When there shall be foods for vermin as full as feeds for the fett, eat on earth as there's hots in oven. When every Klitty of a scolderymeid shall hold every yardscullion's right to stimm her uprecht for whomsoevrer, whether on priveates, whether in publics. And when all us romance catholeens shall have ones for all amanseparated. And the world is maidfree. (FW, 239.16-22)

Fritz Senn has detected the rich ambiguities and ambivalences of these political statements,[9] ranging among militant, separatist feminism, sexual freedom, and domestic, kitcheny submissiveness. They echo Marx ("foods for vermin. . ."), The Lord's Prayer ("eat on earth as there's hots in oven"), and Daniel O'Connell ("romance catholeens shall have onesk for all amanseparated"). Its combination of the women's movement with other popular movements like socialism and Irish nationalism is appropriate to the mode of social reform in the late nineteenth century.

The style of the rainbow girls' oration suggests an intriguing irony. The feminist movement, which is political in nature, employs the same rhetoric and style as the politically established male, Shaun, who offers only the most conservative and restrictive advice for young women of St. Brides school in III.2. It is equally ironic that another feminist outburst occurs in Shaun's narrative style in I.5: "Lead kindly foul! They always did: ask the ages. What bird has done today man may do next year, be it moult, be it hatch, be it agreement in the nest. For her socioscientific sense is sound as a bell. . . . Yes, before all this has time to end the golden age must return with its vengeance. Man will become dirigible. Ague will be rejuvenated, woman with her ridiculous white burden will reach by one step sublime incubation. . ." (FW, 112.9-21).[10] This vision is further clouded by the ambiguities of its puns—man becoming "dirigible," and woman assuming the historically reprehensible, "ridiculous" white man's burden. The four evangelist-historians, whose habits of leering at Isolde suggest that they are hardly of the feminist persuasion, seem also to bear a feminist message. They recall much of history as "gynecollege histories" (FW 389.9), substituting women's names for men's names (Mrs Dana O'Connell) and even for addresses (Fitzmarry Round) (FW 386.15-393.3). Implicit in all of this is the suggestion that women will never be liberated by following the model of Shaun or the male academic establishment. Although he failed to express it adequately, this same caution may have been in Stephen's mind when he failed to show any enthusiasm for Emma's education at University College during their arguments in *Stephen Hero*.

Joyce's vision for the future of women may lie with Issy alone, rather than Issy as a group or movement. Issy's flighty, flirtatious behavior is often an assumed pose—a woman's typical ploy for power that can be considered demeaning or smart, depending on the circumstances. She cynically labels female preening "The law of the jungerl" (FW, 268 n.3) and speaks of the "strangle for love and the sowiveall [so wive all] of the prettiest" (FW, 145.26-27). Courtship in general is "a nastilow, disigraible game" (FW, 301, n.4). She thinks of woman's supposed delicacy and asks the probing question, "With her poodle feinting to be let off and feeling dead in herself. Is love worse living?" (FW, 269 n.1). As will be shown later, Issy often delivers scathing criticisms to Glugg or to her Pepette lover (both male writers) in the petting, flattering style of a young girl schooled to please men. Here the tension between manners and thoughts is extreme, but it is also a very real part of female experience. Issy has considerable hostility toward "my all menkind of every desception" (FW, 270 n.4). "Improper frictions is maledictions and mens uration makes me mad" (FW, 269 n.3). Here Issy rebels, or is perhaps driven mad, by men's orations and their fictions, some undoubtedly concerning woman. This outcry also protests menstruation. Perhaps it is only the contempt for its "pooh" stated by Molly Bloom, a woman with an equally candid attitude about her body (U, 769, 772). The ancient connection of menstruation with madness is a subject we will return to. Issy's overall view of the career of male-female relationships is another echo of Molly's pessimism about aging women (U, 751,758): "To be slipped on, to be slept by, to be conned to, to be kept up. And when you're done push the chain" (FW, 278 n.5).

Issy is also not so singularly devoted to Shaun-Chuff as early explicators have suggested. The stage directions of the "Mime" tell us that Izod "having jilted Glugg, is being fatally fascinated by CHUFF"

(FW 220.10-11). Issy's color, heliotrope, suggests that she is a fol-
lower of the sun god Chuff, instead of the dark devil character, Glugg.
But Issy is repeatedly identified with cloud and moon, both symbols
with aspects of darkness. As Nuvolette she wears a "light" dress
which is also a "night" dress. She refers to "lethemuse" in one of
her notes, suggesting familiarity with the river of forgetfulness in
Hades, perhaps becoming its muse (FW, 272 n.3). Though she hints
of her romantic attachment to Father Michael (comparable to E. C.'s
flirtation with Father Moran), and though Father Michael would seem
to be identified with Mick-Chuff-St. Kevin-Shaun, the very thought
of loving a priest is counter to the church. In intelligence, attitude
and siglum, Issy is at least as close to Shem-Chuff-Nick as to Shaun-
Glugg-Mick. Her $\perp$ is closer in shape to Shem's $\sqsubset$ than to Shaun's
$\wedge$. In her loneliness, she also resembles Shem. The cynicism and
iconoclasm of her footnotes in the "Lessons" chapter are much closer
to Shem's satirical comments than to Shaun's Latinate labels.[11] While
the rainbow girls echo Shaun's enthusiasm for patriarchal religion
and nationalism, Issy, like Shem, is apt to trivialize them. Take, for
example, this questionable attitude toward Tara (Ireland's ancient
capital, frequently idealized in romantic songs and poems) and Mt.
Ararat (resting place of Noah's patriarchal ark): "All abunk for Tar-
ararat! Look slipper, sopppyhat, we've a doss in the manger" (FW
267 n.6). On top of the other debasements, Issy's manger houses a
dog and an ass, not Christ. Similar satire is visible in numerous other
notes, including 260 n.2, 264 n.3, 266 n.1, 267 n.1, 268 n.2, 274
n.1, 276 n.5, 277 n.3, 5, 281 n.4, 303 n.2 and 308 n.1. In this same
spirit, Issy offers her agreement with the Edgar Quinet sequence,
used with numerous variations in *Finnegans Wake*. She annotates "les
ruines du Numance" as "the nasal foss of our natal folkfarthers so
so much now for Valsinggiddy rex and his grand arks day triump."
(FW, 281.6-7, n.1). The message of the sequence is, of course, that
the flowers (identified always with women's rites in the *Wake*) disport
themselves as ever, while cities have changed masters and names,
and civilizations have clashed and disappeared. The giddy king, and
the ark, have a day's triumph, according to Issy.

The "Mime" chapter enacts a timeless courtship ritual in which
the suitor who must answer the riddles is Shem,[12] and the witty, not
unwilling maiden is Issy. Shem as devil repeats Stephen's impish role
in courting E. C. in *Stephen Hero*, where he is suspected of disbe-
lieving in God and shocks Emma by calling God "the middle-aged

gentleman with the aviary" (SH, 188). If anyone is afflicted by madness in the "Mime," it is not Issy, but Glugg, whose reactions to his
three incorrect guesses rival the enraged dances of Cuchulain in Irish
legend. Issy takes the initiative in meeting Glugg and giving him
riddles and clues. She has criticisms of the learned Glugg that could
also apply to the earlier artist-wooer, Stephen Daedalus, suggesting
he is "lost to lurning" (FW 222.25) and that he might do better "if
he's lonely talk instead of only gawk" (FW 225.18). These resemble
some of her charges against her Pepette lover, which suggest that
he is cold and patronizing—like Stephen:

> Of course I know, pettest, you're so lerningful and considerate
> in yourself, so friend of vegetables, so long cold cat you! Please
> by acquointance! Codling, snakelet, iciclist! My diaper has more
> life to it! Who drowned you in drears, man, or are you pillale with
> ink? (FW 145.8-12)

But she is at times more positive toward Glugg than scholars have
tended to note. Upon his first failure to guess her color, she responds,
"Oh tears, who can her mater [mate-r] be" (FW 225.32). Issy's feelings for or against Glugg are given typically mixed expression near
the end of the chapter: "As for she could shake him. An oaf, no more.
Still he'd be good tutor two in his big armschair lerningstoel and she
be waxen in his hands" (FW, 251.21-24). Issy can shake him . . . no
more. Or she can take him no more. He is an oaf. He is an oaf, no
more. "Still" suggests second thoughts about him as a tutor "turning
up and fingering over the most dantellising peaches in the lingerous
longerous book of the dark." Here two pairs of old men with young
loves are suggested—Dante and Beatrice plus Daddy Browning and
Peaches. Also present is the allure of secret or forgotten texts, like
the Egyptian *Book of the Dead*, from which comes repeated references to the goddess Isis, who is evoked repeatedly with Issy in the
Wake. Recognizing that this master-female student pattern has persisted since "Headmaster Adam," she exclaims "let his be exaspir-
ated, letters be blowed! I is A femaline person. O, of provocative
gender. U unisingular case" (FW, 251.21-32). While these last lines
could be interpreted as Issy's renunciation of "letters," and more
evidence of her mindlessness, there is more to them. They are also
a repudiation of male dominance in education, a reversion of her
exaspiration to him. "Femaline" shows the same concern with her
own shape or "line" as do many of the mirror passages—a desire to

know herself. "Provocative" can make Issy a confirmed "temptress" if that is what one is looking for. Or she can be reviewed as a protester. "Unisingular case" insists on her oneness, her separation. The IOU links Issy's musings to Stephen's in the library scene of *Ulysses*, where he states "A.E.I.O.U." (U, 190). Both have a debt to the establishment, which they resent even as they acknowledge it, and insist on their separateness.

Issy, when alone, demonstrates wit as well as wiles. Clive Hart, in effect, rejects ALP's relative judgment of her wits vs. Issy's when he finds Issy's passages "excitingly perspicacious" in comparison to ALP's.[13] Issy is far from disdainful of "letters" of various sorts. The apparent repudiation contains three very important letters, the vowels I, O, and U. Like important women in Joyce's life—May Joyce, Nora Barnacle Joyce, Lucia Joyce, and most notably Harriet Weaver— Issy is a writer of letters. No other character in Joyce surpasses Issy in wordplay, a talent shared by Sylvia Beach. This propensity is demonstrated in a large proportion of the footnotes Issy writes for the "Lessons" chapter, in the three letters she writes in the course of the *Wake*, and in the "Mime" chapter. Earlier women in Joyce take an interest in language. Emma and Miss Ivors are proponents of the Gaelic revival. Even Molly Bloom takes an interest in love-letters and in words, asking the definition of metempsychosis, and constructing her own puns, based on names—Bloom, bloomers (U, 761) and Mr. de Kock, nicknamed for "going around with his tube from one woman to another" (U, 765).

At the start of the "Mime," "wordchary is atvoiced ringsoundinly" by the ensemble of girls" (FW 225.2). Being "chary" with the "word" is also witchery, and the group of girls could resemble a coven of witches, whose secret words work magic. In the "Lessons," Issy provides a reference to "Llong and Shortts Primer of Black and White Wenchcraft" (FW, 269, n.4). Joyce links the young women to ancient traditions in which women were sorceresses and diviners, and—in Ireland especially—satirists as well. Preparing to give Glugg his first set of clues, Issy can evoke esoteric letters "the airish signics of her dipandump helpabit from Father Hogum," suggesting an alphabet of sign language for the deaf and dumb, and the ogham writing of ancient Ireland (FW, 223.3-4). At the end of the "mime," she asks, "Parley vows Askinwhose? I do, Ida" (FW 276 n.4), suggesting a familiarity with Eskimo language. She also offers a footnote on "Huntler and Pumar's animal alphabites, the first in the world from aab to zoo" (FW 263 n.1), which suggests such things as biting language, eating one's words, primitive (animal) language, or language consumed by children (Huntley and Palmer's alphabet biscuits). At the end of the "Mime," "Geamatron" or the earth goddess shows the children "coneyfarm leppers" (cuneiform letters) (FW 257.5-6)— showing another female knowlegable in ancient letters. Issy has also been provided with the Greek letter gamma in the celebrated and "inbourne" "gramma's grammar" of the "Lessons" chapter (FW 268.17).

To Colin MacCabe "gramma's grammar" is a key to the differences in sexuality and language between girls and boys. The language of the grandmother "is available to girls but not to boys."[14] MacCabe extends Freud's tentative suggestions about female child development and language. According to this, in her pre-Oedipal separation from the mother, the girl suffers no fundamental wound to her narcissism, nor does the phallus occupy a central symbolic position. While the boy may take up aggressive defense of his wounded narcissism, the girl's is unchallenged. The challenge to the boy's narcissism "ensures access to language" according to MacCabe. But for the girl, the "grasp of language is not so sure, for there is no one term which takes up and stabilizes the separations."[15] MacCabe suggests that *Finnegans Wake* is produced by the impact of "this [female-identified] discourse on phallocentric male discourse."[16] One might question the valuation implied by MacCabe's suggestion that the female's grasp of language is not so "sure," since "sure" receives positive connotative value in contemporary language. Nevertheless, the theory as a whole makes Issy's letters vital to *Finnegans Wake*.

Issy's preoccupation with grammar has been more trivially handled. Roland McHugh suggests that the siglum ⊥ (Issy) is writing a guide to conversation modeled on P. Carolino's *English as She is Spoke*, an abridgement of a larger work which the editor described as "the monstrous joke of publishing a Guide to Conversation in a language of which it is only too evident that every word is utterly strange to him."[17] Gramma's grammar, as represented by Issy, is extremely opaque: "if there is a third person, mascarine, phelinine or nuder, being spoke abad it moods prosodes from a person speaking to her second which is the direct object that has been spoken to, with and at. Take the dative with his oblative 5 for even if obsolete, it is always of interest . . ." (FW, 268.17-23). If Issy is writing this error-riddled explanation of cases, she is hardly absorbed by it. Her note 5 is in her sexually aroused, iconoclastic mode: "I'd like his pink's cheek." Elsewhere she proclaims "conversation lozenges? How awful!!" (FW, 148.12).

Rather than view Issy as a young student, struggling with and misinterpreting her primers on language, and cultivating manners for courtship, it seems preferable to perceive her as a critic of language, perhaps even the purveyor of the "girlic teangue" or woman's language (like Gaelic, suppressed language) which she announces in her first footnote of the "Lessons" (FW, 260 n.1). Or, echoing Emma and Miss Ivors, she protests in a later note, "None of your cumpohlstery English here!!" (FW 271 n.3). Like Harriet Weaver, Issy also helps to write the book. She gives the author advice on at least two occasions. She suggests modifications in his rendition of the Quinet motif, as Clive Hart has noticed: "2 Translout that gaswind into turfish, Teague, that's a good bog and you, Thady, poliss it off, there's a nateswipe on your blottom pluper"(FW 281 n2). Hart interprets this as a suggestion "that the flatus of his very spiritual style be transmuted into the rather more solid matter to be found on Anna Livia's cloacal scrap of tissue." He reports that Joyce takes her advice and parodies the offending sentence five times in *Finnegans Wake*.[18] There are other occasions when Issy is less than awed by her creator: "I thought you knew all and more, ye aucthor, to explique to ones the significat of their exsystems with your nieu nivulon lead" (FW, 148.16-18). She also bids the writer of the "Lessons" text to "wipe your glosses with what you know" thereby criticizing the presentation of Nubilina as "presainted maid to majesty" (FW, 304 n.3, 304.19-22). As if given privileged information by Joyce, Issy reveals the sigla of the "Doodles family" (FW, 299 n.4). Boldly she challenges, "You'll see if I'm selfthought" (FW, 147.8-9).

Issy, like Joyce, delights in wordplay. Some of her notes that seem nonsense at first sight, yield experiments in orthography and sound when we give them a second examination. An obvious example is Issy's footnote with most individual words spelled backwards, mirror-fashion, to accord with its subject matter: "O Evol, kool in the salg and ees how Dozi pits what a drowser" (FW, 262 n.2). It achieves more than nonsense, but bears the ominous suggestions that love is evil, cool, and inducing of sleep or death. She plays with punctuation: the comma in one note (FW, 273 n.8); the apostrophe in another, "H'dk'fs' h'p'y" (FW, 265 n.3)—obscuring "handkerchiefs halfpenny"[19] or a myriad of different messages. As recalled in a note

(FW, 276 n.6), Issy lavishes a love (like ALP's) of alliterative, liquid, soothing sound upon her letter to her Pepette lover: "With my whiteness I thee woo and bind my silk breasths I thee bound! Always, Amory, amor andmore! Till always, thou lovest! Shshshsh! So long as the lucksmith. Laughs!!" (FW, 148.30-32). Much of the most childish wordplay in the letters and notes is of course reminiscent of Swift's *Journal to Stella*. But here the sexes are reversed, and the playful but patronizing lover is a young woman, not an old man. Sylvia Beach's letters to her family display a similar form of wordplay, which Joyce may have been aware of.[20]

Issy has another important dimension in *Finnegans Wake* in the intriguing parallels she is given to heroines and goddesses of story and myth. Arrah na Pogue has been accounted for as an example of Joyce's interest in brother-sister incest. Grainne, Deirdre, and Isolde of Ireland are seen as examples of young women claimed as lovers by old men—another theme that explicators have preoccupied themselves with, and one which Vladimir Nabokov develops with conscious reference to *Finnegans Wake* in *Lolita*.[21] Arrah, Grainne, Deirdre, and Isolde are more than sexual beings, however. Arrah saves a rebel brother by passing him a secret escape plan with her kiss. Thus she is herself a rebel. Lorna Reynolds has recently described the Deirdre legend as a prototype of female rebellion against patriarchy—in her case Conohor's determination at Deirdre's birth that the girl would marry him.[22] Deirdre, Grainne, and Isolde all employ their young lovers as a means of escape from the patriarch. The interpretation of these legends in the rebellious vein is entirely in keeping with the cynical remarks about patriarchal institutions sprinkled throughout Issy's footnotes, as we have seen.

Issy's relationship to a number of goddesses is also powerful and has suffered from critical inattention. When he launched his "struggle against conventions" (L II, 99), Joyce turned first to the continent, and ultimately to the ancient and primitive world for models. Here, the figure of the goddess had been worshipped as the primary deity. The goddess behaved with the kind of sexual freedom that Stephen had found so difficult to represent to Emma, or to relate to their contemporary world, though he had fantasized about her beckoning him from a Mohemmedan paradise, a goddess-like, fleshy icon to replace the "baffled" icons of his peers (SH, 159). The goddess is free from prudery, and comfortable with the profane and even the corrupt.[23] She bares her breasts and, like Issy, exposes her underthings: "my middle I ope before you, my bottom's a vulser if ever there vulsed and my whole the flower that stars the day rolly well worth your pilger's fahrt" (FW, 249.11-14). Legendary goddess-queens like Medb, as represented in *The Táin*, take pride in their powers of micturition, as do Issy, the Prankquean, and the girls in the park. Decay is also their province: "the midden heap where god is hidden."[24] The ancients had less chaste definitions even for the virgin, which meant to be "true to nature and instinct," or to "belong-to-no-man."[25]

Issy with her looking glass immediately suggests Venus or Aphrodite, whose mirror provides the emblem of woman. Perhaps intending to criticize HCE's own self-centeredness, Glasheen identifies Issy as "daughter of HCE and Anna Livia. . . , though at times the father is under the strong impression that he alone gave birth to her."[26] The passage Glasheen cites is evocative of the birth of Venus, borne up from the foam of the sea: "biguidd, for the love of goddess and perthanow as you reveres your one mothers, mitsch for matsch, and while I reveal thus my deepseep daughter which was bourne up pridely out of medsdreams unclouthed when I was pillowing my brime" (FW, 366.12-15). The "perthanow" of this passage suggests the Parthenon, temple of another Virgin conceived of the father, Athena. The conception of Venus in the sea is explained by a tale of patriarchal castration—one appropriate to the *Wake*. Chronos, at the bidding of his mother, had castrated his father and thrown his sexual members into the sea; from them sprang Venus, who retained a correspondingly masculine self-willed movement and a penchant for night-time liaisons. Nor Hall suggests that Venus seeks the father in every man she meets, and that "every girl who leaves her father is Aphrodite."[27]

Adaline Glasheen has suggested that the virgin huntress, Artemis, though rarely named, "is all over the place"[28] in various disguises in *Finnegans Wake*. Two of her disguises, the moon and the tree, are used repeatedly in Issy's contexts. Like Issy, Artemis is a shape-shifter. Both are also associated with their brothers, Artemis being the sister goddess of Apollo; brother-sister relationships for both alternate between love and hate. As patroness of childbearing, nurse, and healer, Artemis is also identified with ALP, who as the washerwomen at the ford merges with tree and stone.

The prostitute, like the virgin, was a free woman in the ancient world, which even had as a rite of female initiation a sacred form of

prostitution in the temple of the goddess, as noted in chapter 7. Issy
is Ishtar, an ancient version of Mary Magdalene, who is Issy as well.
In a ninth-century panel Ishtar was pictured like a prostitute, peering
from a window.[29] She was protectress of prostitutes, and like many
women in ancient myth, she offered an alternative to the domestic
realm of Penelope and goddesses like Hera. She submits creatively,
not to men, but to instinct. As the moon, Ishtar alternates in effect.
When present, she unites male and female in love. But she also
wanders or plunges into the dark land of the dead, and in her absence
there is no sex or singing.[30] Her exploits include prophecy of a great
deluge and the rescue of some of her children in an ark, making her
a female prototype for Noah, one of the most pervasive patriarchs
of the *Wake*.

Issy is also related to Lilith, "Lillabil Issabil maideve" (FW, 513.25).
Adam's first wife, Lilith, was cast out of Eden for refusing to submit
to his notions of her proper position in intercourse. Lilith has been
perenially slandered as a demon, a menace to children, and the devil's mate by the religious establishment. She represents the female
in protest and retreat from the male world—a role also played in
Finnegans Wake by ALP and the Prankquean.[31] The Prankquean's
kidnapping of Jarl van Hoother's sons suggests Lilith's alleged threat
to children, though in Joyce's version of the legend, the Lilith figure
works more good than harm by reforming the patriarch; she is also
not feared by other women. Even Van Hoother's daughter comes to
her aid. Nor Hall describes other behaviors of the Goddess that resemble the Prankquean's assault on van Hoother's castle:

> If [the goddess] is given space . . . she will come into consciousness
> and culture positively: healing divisions, generating warmth and
> insight. But if she is not welcomed (or worse, is devalued and kept
> outside the outer walls, she will break the doors down and come
> in to individual or cultural consciousness in a negative, devouring
> (literally "shit-eating"), stone-cold way.[32]

Issy is very frequently the Egyptian goddess Isis, who like the
Babylonian Ishtar and the Greek Artemis is a moon goddess, associated with nature in aspects of both birth and decay. Her traditions
(dating back to 3000 B.C.) are so ancient that they vary with changing beliefs over time. Joyce consulted *The Book of the Dead*, probably
E. A. Wallis Budge's Egyptian text with interlinear translation, Budge's
Osiris and the Egyptian Resurrection, and Frazer's *The Golden Bough*.[33]

He could also have been aware of Plutarch's version of Isis, which is contained in Budge. Isis is seen giving birth to the sun in some ancient drawings,[34] and worship of lunar gods and goddesses is known to have preceded reverence for solar deities. The structure of Isis's family, as offered by Plutarch, bears some resemblance to Issy's. Nut, mother of the gods, would correspond to ALP,[35] and is herself alluded to in the *Wake* (FW, 360.15, 370.15). Instead of conceiving the children of her spouse, Ra, the sun, she conceives of Seb, time, and through a stratagem worked out by Thoth, manages to evade Ra's curse that she shall not bring forth in year or month. She is more productive than ALP, bearing five deities in the five days that Thoth has added to the calendar. First is Osiris, Isis's most important sibling, worshipped for centuries as the moon, but later transformed into a sun god. Second is Horus, actually the son of Isis and Osiris, but borne in their mother's womb. Third is Set or Typhon, the representative of desert heat and unbridled lust. He plots the capture and death of Osiris. Fourth is Isis, representing nature and later the moon. The fifth is Isis's sister Nephthys, goddess of the extreme end of fertility, next to Set's desert, and hence his spouse.[36] Roland McHugh identifies Issy's mirror personality with Nephthys, and provides one of several illustrations from the *Book of the Dead* in which the two sister goddesses are twinned.[37] The three sons share the roles of Cain and Abel, Shem and Shaun, Nick and Mick. Isis' many-colored veil is comparable to Issy's Rainbow troupe. It can be interpreted as the "ever changing form of nature," as the material forms clothing and veiling the creative spirit, or as an entangling mortal net,[38] of the sort that Stephen Dedalus wished his spirit to fly by. When Osiris is killed by Set, Isis collects his body and returns it to Egypt. In some versions of the tale, she models a new phallus for his remains, and through it conceives a new cycle of their son, younger Horus. Like many goddess legends, this conception story trivializes the generative role of the male, and substitutes a mother-son duo for the masculine trinity of the Christian religion. In repeated ritual, Horus becomes Osiris, is slain again and wept over by Isis, who collects his remains, conceives a new god, and survives him as well.[39] As in many of the goddess identifications for *Finnegans Wake*, ALP shares some of the functions of the goddess with Issy, especially her capacities as scavenger and survivor. Thus the family story of Nut, Isis, Osiris, and the others contains cuckolding, incest, family violence, female resilience, and cyclic renewal, providing Joyce with reinforcement and development of basic elements of *Finnegans Wake.*

The strong presence of Isis in *Finnegans Wake* probably has some remote and ironic connections to the Dublin Theosophists, Madame Blavatsky, and her work *Isis Unveiled*, which Stephen Dedalus treats mockingly in the "Scylla and Charybdis" chapter of *Ulysses*: "Yogibogeybox in Dawson chambers. *Isis Unveiled*. Their Pali book we tried to pawn" (U, 191). Mme. Blavatsky's "Mahatma letters" are referred to repeatedly in the *Wake*, connecting her to the hen, as a recoverer of letters, and thereby to ALP.[40] Roland McHugh takes Joyce's reading of *Isis Unveiled* for *Finnegans Wake* more seriously than any of the other explicators. He suggests that $\perp$'s (Issy's) underwear becomes conflated "with the diaphane of the temple sanctuary" in FW, 249.6-20 and thus $\perp$ becomes Isis Veiled; (ALP) he identifies with Isis Unveiled, from references to the Chaldeo-Jewish cosmogony of Blavatsky's *Isis Unveiled* in the "Lessons" chapter.[41]

Although references to Isis are far more abundant, Issy is also Persephone, "pretty Perserpronette whose slit sachel spilleth peas (FW, 267.10-11)—the peas also linking Issy and Persephone back to the Prankquean. The myth of Persephone (Kore) provides a more female-centered mode of viewing Issy in *Finnegans Wake* than do the other myths we have reviewed. It is especially relevant to Issy's role in the "Mime" chapter and to her relationship with her mother. In the myth, Persephone is lured by flowers (especially a narcissus) into the soft meadow where Hades or Pluto (brother of Zeus) seizes her and abducts her to the underworld. Persephone's beautiful and powerful mother, Demeter, the bringer of seasons, hears her daughter's cry and longs to have her back again. Her actions (which resemble those of Isis, when that goddess was seeking the stolen Osiris) include a vain plea to Helios, the sun, for Persephone's return, but he can see no objection to the match. Demeter roams through the land, disguised at times as an ancient woman; she works for a time as a wet nurse. Most ominously, she works destruction on the land by denying the harvest. Eleusinian rites for some 3,000 years celebrated Demeter's loss and recovery (for nine months of the year) of Persephone. Since she had consumed three seeds (Issy's spilled peas?), Persephone was never quite the same, and could not always be in her mother's realm. The withdrawal into darkness and the triumphant reemergence of Demeter represent a female rhythm appreciated by Joyce in ALP.

There is no denying that *Finnegans Wake* centers upon ALP's loss and recovery of the father, not the daughter. But ALP, like Demeter, is a "bringer of plurabilities." ALP and the Prankquean can bring destruction to the landscape, as did Demeter, out of their desire. In the "Mime," Issy stands amid alluring flowers, admirers of the sun god. Shem is her dark seducer, enacting a courtship ritual of riddles instead of an abduction, and failing at that. But the aim is to take the daughter from her parents. In Joyce's version Zeus thunders in protest instead of favoring the match. But ALP intervenes as well. Issy would seem to be more open to seduction than the original Persephone, but her cynical remarks on Shem and patriarchal institutions suggest that she feels their otherness and has real reluctance to join them. Issy's contentment with her mirror can also be seen as an instinctual attachment to the mother:

> A girl child grows up in accord with the rhythm of the mother; the blood bond of pregnancy had a hold on the girl, who is made in the image of the mother A boy's journey is underscored by a different longing and a different adventure. His sense of being "other" makes separation from the mother more plausible. He may come back to her in every woman he meets. But a girl meets her mother in herself and in her reflections.[42]

Nor Hall suggests that, as Nuvoletta, Issy cries out to ALP when she "finds herself fallen in love . . ." *Why, why, why! Weh, Oweh! I'se so silly to be flowing but I no canna stay!!"* (FW, 159.17-18).[43]

The dances of the "Mime" are predominantly in circle fashion, suggesting the patterns typically used to re-enact Persephone's separation from the mother in Demeter rites. Their eroticism resembles the dance of Baubo for Demeter (the Baubo figure resembling the sheela-na-gigs I discussed in chapter 2). The constant citation of of nursery-rhyme gibberish is also suggestive of mysterious, lost female devotions. Like Ireland's ancient keening rituals for the dead, they can be seen as survivals of a woman-centered culture, handed down from woman to girl, independent of literature. ALP renews the husband-brother-son, but like Demeter, she also recovers the daughter at the end of the *Wake*. Here she rejoices that "she is coming. Swimming in my hindmost. Diveltaking on me tail" (FW, 627.3-4). But Issy is not identical to the ebbing mother. She has mixed with and taken from the "Divel." She is a new and old woman of Joyce's dreams, themselves a fuller collection of the female as well as the male unconscious than had ever been managed in literature.

A Joycean
Feminist Re-vision

——————— 10 ———————

□ Re-vision, the "seim anew" (FW, 215.23) that begins with a pro-
claimed "struggle against conventions" (L II, 99), and ends with
restructuring at the level of the word in *Finnegans Wake*, might well
be considered James Joyce's ultimate vocation and the ultimate challenge to his critics. His method is not one of simple, static substitution
or violent destruction of past forms. He offers a process of collection,
accretion, and recovery. He favors systems that multiply meanings,
offer contraries, and are multiply voiced. For such traits, his writing
has been acclaimed for "inexhaustible bisexuality."[1] From the young
male artist's ideal of classic Aristotelian stasis, he has moved to the
elderly sleeper's verbal flux, which retains the attitudes taken
throughout life, and is delimited by female commentary.

Joyce and Feminism began with dual challenges: to talk to and be
heard by male colleagues, as suggested by Sandra M. Gilbert, and
to "find a new language, a new way of reading that can integrate
our experience, our reason and our suffering, our skepticism and our
reason," as directed by Elaine Showalter.[2] As the description of Joyce's
method in the above paragraph should suggest, the visionary task of
Joyce and Feminism is highly compatible with Joyce's own experimental processes. This book offers initial movement toward seeing,
reading, and criticizing Joyce anew from a variety of feminist perspectives. Most simply, it offers a shift in attention by focusing deliberately upon women in the cultural history, life, and works of
Joyce. It does not invent or substitute a subject, but reclaims one

201

that was there, too little recognized and worked, from the start. As noted in the first chapter, reclamation work is one of the core definitions of feminist criticism; it needs to be done early to prepare for new visions.

Language has been a constant concern in the writing of this study, as well as a subject within the Joycean texts. If the book is to be read to its conclusion by non-feminist colleagues of both genders, its discourse must engage, not alienate them. Much misunderstanding and even anger have crystallized around terms like "feminism" and "patriarchy." There is a risk of lost audience in the use of "feminism" in the title of this book. It is a chance taken in the hope of revising attitudes toward feminism. This work should provide an experience of what feminist criticism encompasses and how it complements existing treatments of the total culture of man and woman. Joyce's critical interest in the father figure, in social institutions, in patricide and social revolution still make "patriarchy" an indispensible term. I have avoided some words familiar in early feminist discourse like "sexist." These, in my own experience, have aroused emotional responses and thus closed or impeded my communication with colleagues. Other terms are tempered by variation, accurate substitution, or careful explanation. These are measures that some of my feminist colleagues may regret, and ones which still will not satisfy the most sensitive traditional readers. The latter group may also wince at s/he, where it appears, or at the generic man, where he fails to. Enough of the women in my experience feel excluded in a generic man or a universal male pronoun that I cannot perpetuate these conventions. I feel fully supported by Joyce in such struggle against linguistic convention. As I noted in chapter 3, Joyce used "men and women" persistently in his early essays; *Finnegans Wake* just as consistently performs gender switches in language, perhaps in part to achieve a universalizing effect. While the language of this study has been chosen to attract and include readers, I hope that future feminist studies will be able to play and create more with language, moving readers more toward delight and vision.

Critical integration of female experience, called for and given the dignity of authority by Showalter, is part of the informing process of *Joyce and Feminism*. It is not easy for the scholar conventionally trained in the late sixties and early seventies to suddenly voice her own female experience as authority on Joyce. One discovery in reviewing the criticism of Joyce's women, and particularly Molly Bloom, was that Joyce criticism already offered abundant generalized male experience of the female, stated in an authoritative voice, backed by Freud or Jung or the androcentric history then available. James Joyce treats the roles of daughter, sister, sexual partner, wife, and mother that I have practiced.

With consciousness of the need to adjust to Joyce's era and locations, and to differences between individual women, I have considered the authenticity and insight of Joyce's depictions of women in the realistic range. I think that I have found ironies about Stephen's pursuit of Emma that were intended by Joyce but largely missed by scholars attentive to other things. I have not been able to find in Joyce some things that a woman may be especially prone to look for—a mother amid a brood of small children, woman in the workplace, the intellectual or creative woman. All of these existed in Joyce's time and place, but they are only hinted at in his realistic fiction. Joyce gets at my vulnerable places. I feel mocked for the feminine wiles I have occasionally practiced and the consumerist vanities I have indulged in, as did Adrienne Monnier in reading "Nausicaä." He catches me at feminist propagandizing. But I am comforted by Joyce's impartial selection of targets, most of them incorporating aspects of himself, including the authority of the pen, wielded by the male. It is a lesson in good-humored self-criticism that self-assured feminist critics, too, bring to their work. I have seen less of the temptress and devourer in Joyce's depiction of female sexuality, and more of the female's sense of her magical power to arouse and revive the male. I have questioned the preoccupation of Joyce's later women with sexuality, perhaps betraying my own concern for intellect. It is important to remember, however, that Joyce's sexual women are intended in part to serve a revolution of values that would overturn Catholic and Victorian English-inspired puritanism and help to counterbalance the male-associated emphasis on reason. It is a role that moves women in Joyce beyond realism, as does their association with the world of sleep and the primordial.

Joyce's late archetype of woman has the lusty, affirmative sexuality of the goddess, and the powers of magic, prophecy, sovereignty, and language which, until recently, critics have slighted. Archetypes relate less well than realistic portraits to real experience and authentication. Yet, the archetypal women do have resonance for me and, as I noted in chapters 7 and 9, they have served as positive examples in feminist studies of archetypes. As feminist archetypal criticism develops further, it will have a rich field in Joyce. Usually Joyce saves his female archetypes for his codas, and I question why they were not more centrally placed. That may be the immediate challenge for contemporary writers.

Along the lines of more traditional scholarship, *Joyce and Feminism* has assembled critical opinions on Joyce. Often the women's voices use female experience as a premise, Virginia Woolf meditating on her reactions to "indecency" and Rebecca West questioning Molly's post-coital fantasies. What his early female critics and patrons have said about Joyce's writing informs us about their world and allows them to enunciate their values. Their metaphors, which are often maternal, inform us about their self-perceptions. Such visions are highly valued in this study; they await more extensive and, in some instances, more innovative consideration. Women writers like Djuna Barnes and Janet Flanner deserve to be better known, Barnes especially for her stylistic resonances with Joyce and her application of many of his techniques to female-centered works. We can see somewhat belatedly that the modernist era was in an important sense a women's era. When the norms of their family life and occupations of the dominant culture failed them, women like Dora Marsden, Harriet Shaw Weaver, Sylvia Beach, and Adrienne Monnier went their own ways, and devised their own spaces, networks, publications, financial accounts and alliances with the avant-garde. We need to achieve a better understanding of women as a force in modernism. Through creative effort, the codes and visions and energy of Odéonia and *The Egoist* must be infused into culture as a resource and model for both genders.

Lucia Joyce belongs in a general study of aspiring, revisionary performers, fashion designers and artists of the twenties. She has been the subject of much psychological speculation, the commentators including Jung and Joyce himself. Recent feminist studies of mother-daughter relationships might profitably be applied to her. Lucia Joyce's case may also help us to understand the tensions that the ever-changing politics and moral norms of Europe in the early twentieth century produced in young women; the extremes were strongly represented in the shifting residences and conflicts of tradition and revolution within her family experience and within her father alone.

Biographies of Nora Joyce have begun to appear and will have an interested audience.[3] They can now be written with greater respect for and knowledge of the ancient, rural and female subcultures from which she came, origins of great importance to Joyce. Although she seems to have presented no intellectual or social challenge to him and to have offered a wealth of conventional allure, forbearance, and loyalty, Nora did not bow to male authority altogether. Her gifts of expression, her penchant for mockery, and her independent opinions seem to have been both a resource and a delight for Joyce. We must not get too analytical about this relationship, forgetting that it seems to have been inspired mainly by love. Nora may be a better subject for drama than scholarship, or may call for an innovative combination of the two.[4]

Feminist criticism should not be the preserve of women critics. Despite my proffering of first-hand female experience, I have no wish to claim an authority unapproachable by my male colleagues, especially as more and more of them enter, for substantial periods of their days and lives, the spaces and experiences that have been traditionally assigned to the female. The acculturation of scholars, as I know them, is changing, and I expect this to be expressed positively and creatively in future forms of scholarship.

The works of Joyce can be usefully studied from varied feminist approaches for years to come. *Joyce and Feminism* is heavily contextual and in its treatment of texts focuses upon a limited number of individual characters. This is a foundation. Works like *Exiles* and characters like ALP deserve their own careful attention. Studies more deliberately focused upon language and metaphor, considering and making accessible contemporary post-structuralist, deconstructionist and sociological literary theory, would constitute a useful critical progression.

In James Joyce, there is the richness of content and expression of the major writer, to which each age will bring its specialized perceptions. His temper, once defined as classical, can now be understood as political,[5] and in the future will invite other perspectives. This study reflects our age's participation in the second women's movement. It is intensified by the fact that Joyce came of age in the era that generated what we now call the first feminist movement. In time, feminist criticism itself, and feminist criticism of Joyce should be integrated with other critical schools and applied to broader cultural issues. "The Woman Question" of Joyce's era was part of a confluence of great liberal movements for social change and, it was hoped, progress. Others were socialism, internationalism, and pacifism. Coinciding with these were new theories of sexuality, race, and the unconscious plus various alternatives to established religion, including mystical, ancient cults. Joyce's love of system suggests the advisability of understanding how these varied, coinciding systems of belief can be related in his work, and a greater understanding of the feminist dimension can certainly build and prepare approaches to the others.[6]

Feminist criticism may also offer new form to literary criticism, or facilitate responses to Joyce that transcend it, moving into artistic and popular forms. I have already suggested the power of experience, the subjective verifications often contained in feminist criticism. Some contemporary feminist criticism supplants and questions singular, rational thought processes with multiply voiced discourse, a pattern verified in Joyce's own writing, especially in the contradictions of Molly Bloom and the plurabilities of ALP.[7] Revised critical form along these lines could be seen as both a Joycean and, by Joyce's own inferences in *Finnegans Wake*, an archetypal female heritage.

Unlike many books on Joyce and his own last two works, *Joyce and Feminism* cannot end with a grand, female-inspired coda. Joyce in the context of women and Joyce as the creator of female character and language is a mixed experience. He made some extremely misogynistic statements in his lifetime. He consumed great amounts of female nurturing. He created female monsters who may have fulfilled his need to feel betrayed or hounded or reconfirmed his suspicions of the pervasive power of the church. He offered few female intellectuals or artists in his works. If the critic has a mind to, s/he may collect these aspects of Joyce and present a very dark interpretation indeed. Against the negative must be poised his positive statements about women in cultural change, his cultivation of an intelligent female readership, and his undeniable attraction to the bright and enterprising women of his era and our own. His realistic works may seem at first glance to offer an image of woman as domineering; upon further scrutiny, they expose the conditions that made her that way. The later works with Molly and ALP reclaim the sovereignty and power of the goddess as an image of woman, an alternate tradition offered by ancient Irish culture. Leopold Bloom offers men a model of androgyny and male nurturing. The late works judge the male artist harshly, and they suggest the intellectual woman in Issy. They claim woman's gossip, letters, and dance as central forms of expression. As early as *Stephen Hero*, Joyce rejected the notion that the world will be remade by fitting women into traditional male roles and directing them toward goals of authority or power and behaviors of aggression and egotism. *Ulysses* and *Finnegans Wake* raise questions about the "moral nature" (L II, 99) that has held the ascendancy in culture and seem to invite a set of new critical standards as well. Largely through representations of female consciousness, Joyce demonstrates the vulnerability of rational absolutes, the truth of contradictions, the power of desire, the multiplicity of language and style. Joyce imagines an ancient, dark goddess to match the satanic young hero of his early works and life, and both are revolutionary.

The reader or critic is probably neither young male artist nor ancient goddess. Joyce does not construct neat and lasting roles or visions for us to participate in.[8] He does not offer a feminist utopia. His quest for wholeness is never restful. He fills his final works with licentious patriarchs, trivial women, violent men and women, and rising establishment males, who mix with more primal and beneficent beings and voices, identifiable with both genders, sometimes expressing androgyny, but only momentarily. The conventional, mechanical, paralytic voices nag us with the failings of ascendant culture and with the psychological weaknesses in ourselves. We are goaded and mocked, sung to and soothed, written about, but also written for. It is his language that accomplishes a troubled freedom in flux and multiplicity. We learn to be wary, but also to laugh, to see for ourselves, to multiply our vision, to be "maid free" (FW, 239.22).

Notes

1. Introduction: Feminist Frameworks for Joyce

1 Sandra M. Gilbert, "Life Studies, or, Speech after Long Silence," *College English*, 40, No. 8 (1980), 862. Gilbert and Susan Gubar are co-authors of the important study, *The Madwoman in the Attic: The Woman Writer and the Nineteenth-Century Literary Imagination* (New Haven and London: Yale University Press, 1979).

Nina Auerbach has regretted that "feminist critics seem particularly reluctant to define themselves to the uninitiated." "Feminist Criticism Reviewed," in *Gender and Literary Voice*, ed. Janet Todd (New York: Holmes & Meier, 1980), p. 258.

2 Gilbert, p. 862.

3 Annette Kolodny, "Some Notes on Defining a 'Feminist Literary Criticism,'" *Critical Inquiry*, 2, No. 1 (1975), 75. Kolodny discusses three central propositions of feminist scholarship in the more recent "Dancing through the Minefield: Some Observations on the Theory, Practice and Politics of Feminist Literary Criticism," *Feminist Studies*, 6 (Summer 1980), 1-25, an essay aimed more at feminist critics. Three other feminist critics offer correctives to Kolodny in "An Interchange on Feminist Criticism: On "Dancing through the Minefield," *Feminist Studies*, 8 (Fall 1982), 629-675.

4 See Jessie Bernard, *The Female World* (New York and London: The Free Press, 1981), and Elaine Showalter, *A Literature of Their Own: British Women Novelists from Brontë to Lessing* (Princeton, N. J.: Princeton University Press, 1977), and "Feminist Criticism in the Wilderness," *Critical Inquiry*, 8, No. 2 (1981), 179-206. Showalter's article concentrates on women writers and ends upon an anthropological model of women existing both in dominant male and less obvious or "muted" female cultures. Showalter would have feminist critics continue their concentration on the "difference" of female writers.

5 Kolodny, p. 75.

6 Ibid., p. 92.

7 See the following separate studies of women writers: Elaine Showalter, *A Literature of Their Own* (cited above); Patricia Meyer Spacks, *The Female Imagination* (New York: Knopf, 1974); Ellen Moers, *Literary Women: The Great Writers* (Garden City, N. Y.: Anchor, 1977). For a provocative comparison of critical attention given Joyce and Gertrude Stein, see Catharine R. Stimpson, "The Power to Name: Some Reflections on the Avant-Garde," in *The Prism of Sex*, ed. Julia A. Sherman and Evelyn Torton Beck (Madison: University of Wisconsin Press, 1979), pp. 55-77.

8 For a comparison of traditional scholars' resistances to post-structuralist and feminist criticisms, see Carolyn Heilbrun, "Men, Women, Theories, and Literature," *Profession 81* (1981), 25-29.

9 See Kolodny, p. 89.

10 Gilbert, p. 850.

11 Mary Ellmann's *Thinking about Women* (New York: Harcourt Brace Jovanovich, 1968) is an excellent pioneering study in this area. Recently, Judith Kegan Gardiner suggested that there are three fairly definite ideologies" to feminism—liberal, radical and socialist, and identifies favored critical strategies for each. See "An Interchange on Feminist Criticism" 629-635. All three of the ideologies suggested by Gardiner appear in *Joyce and Feminism*.

12 See Clara Thompson, "Penis 'Envy' in Women," in *Psychoanalysis and Women*, ed. Jean Baker Miller (New York: Penguin, 1973), and Karen Horney, *Feminine Psychology*, ed. Harold Kelman (New York: Norton, 1973).

13 Carolyn Heilbrun and Catharine Stimpson, "Theories of Feminist Criticism: A Dialogue," in *Feminist Literary Criticism: Explorations in Theory*, ed. Josephine Donovan (Lexington, Ky.: University Press of Kentuck y, 1975), p. 64. 14 Carolyn G. Heilbrun, *Reinventing Womanhood* (New York: W. W. Norton, 1979), 199-212.

15 Betty Friedan, *The Second Stage* (New York: Summit Books, 1981), pp. 27, 31ff., 248.

16 Heilbrun, "Men, Women, Theories, and Literature," p. 28. Heilbrun describes her re-visions of her training by Lionel Trilling briefly in this article, and more extensively in *Reinventing Womanhood*.

See Julia Kristeva, *Desire in Language: A Semiotic Approach to Literature and Art*, ed. Leon Roudiez (New York: Columbia University Press, 1980) and Jacques Derrida, "Becoming Woman," trans. Barbara Harlow, *Semiotext(e)*, 3, No. 1 (1978), cited by Heilbrun. Colin MacCabe works along these lines in *James Joyce and the Revolution of the Word* (New York: Barnes & Noble, 1979).

17 For a defense of the archetypal approach in feminist terms, see Annis Pratt, *Archetypal Patterns in Women's Fiction* (Bloomington, Indiana: Indiana University Press, 1981), pp. 5-7.

18 See *Women in Joyce*, ed. Suzette Henke and Elaine Unkeless (Urbana, Ill.: Univ. of Illinois Press, 1982). In their introduction, Unkeless and Henke note the tendency of male critics to assign Joyce's women characters to symbolic and archetypal identities. See p. xii.

19 Kolodny suggests that "the images of Nature-as-Woman or Woman-as-Muse" shouldn't necessarily be disposed of altogether. They "once held their own kinds of truths and worked forcefully within" the shared cultural psyches of men and women: "as such they will always be with us—an inheritance from our past, not to be annihilated or forgotten, but, with a new consciousness of their less attractive implications, to be transcended, superseded, or even subsumed into something else." Kolodny, pp. 90-91.

Two reinterpreters of Jungian archetypes are M. Esther Harding, *Woman's Mysteries Ancient and Modern* (New York: Harper, 1976), and Nor Hall, *The Moon and the Virgin* (New York: Harper and Row, 1980).

20 Elaine Showalter, "Towards a Feminist Poetics," in *Women Writing and Writing About Women*, ed. Mary Jacobus (London: Croom Helm in association with Oxford University Women's Studies Committee; New York: Barnes & Noble, 1979), p. 39.

2. Mythical, Historical, and Cultural Contexts for Women in Joyce

1 Joseph C. Voelker, " 'You think its the vegetables': Aristotle, Aquinas, and Molly Bloom," *Modern British Literature*, 1 (1976), 37.

2 Merlin Stone, *When God was a Woman* (New York: The Dial Press, 1976), pp. xix-xx. See also Carolyn Heilbrun, *Toward a Recognition of Androgyny* (New York: Knopf, 1973), pp. 3-8 for a discussion of early matriarchy and an introduction to J. J. Bachofen's *Das Mutterrecht*.

3 Robert Graves, *The White Goddess: A Historical Grammar of Poetic Myth* (New York: Creative Age Press, 1948), p. x.

4 Liam de Paor, "Women in Irish Legend," paper presented at the Fourteenth International Seminar of the Canadian Association for Irish Studies, March 19, 1981. See also Maire and Liam de Paor, *Early Christian Ireland* (London: Thames and Hudson, 1978).

5 Thomas Kinsella, "Introduction," *The Táin*, trans. Thomas Kinsella (London: Oxford, 1970), pp. xiv-xv.

6 *The Táin*, trans. Kinsella, pp. 52-55. Heinrich Zimmer suggested that this dialogue represented a "conflict between Celtic-Aryan father-dominance and the mother-dominance of the pre-Celtic inhabitants . . . ." Kinsella, p. xii.

7 de Paor paper. For an article that applies the myth of female sovereignty to Joyce, see Janet Grayson, " 'Do You Kiss Your Mother?': Stephen Dedalus' Sovereignty of Ireland," *JJQ*, 19, No. 2 (Winter 1982), 119-126.

8 Peter Harbison, *Guide to the National Monuments in the Republic of Ireland* (Dublin: Gill and Macmillan, 1975), p. 204.

9 Jørgen Andersen, *The Witch on the Wall: Medieval Erotic Sculpture in the British Isles* (Copenhagen: Rosenkilde and Bagger; London: Allen and Unwin, 1977), pp. 12-31.

10 Suggested by Margaret MacCurtain in conversation, 1981. I also discussed sheelas with Yvette Sencer, who is preparing a study on the subject. Another good discussion of Sheelas is contained in Helen Hickey, *Images of Stone: Figure Sculpture of the Lough Erne Basin* (Belfast: Blackstaff Press, 1976), pp. 57-58, 70.

11 For a discussion of woman's position in the societies that worshipped the Great Goddess, see Stone, pp. 30-61.

12 Donncha Ó'Curráin, "Women in Early Irish Society," in *Women in Irish Society: The Historical Dimension*, ed. Margaret MacCurtain and Donncha Ó'Curráin (Westport, Conn: Greenwood Press, 1979), pp. 1-11.

Katharine Simms, "Women in Norman Ireland," in *Women in Irish Society*, pp. 14-23.

13 Virginia Woolf, "Professions for Women," in *Collected Essays*, Vol. 2 (London: Hogarth, 1966), p. 286.

14 Margaret Cousins, *We Two Together*, by James Henry Cousins and Margaret Cousins (Madras: Ganesh, 1950), pp. 54-55.

15 Margaret MacCurtain, "Towards an Appraisal of the Religious Image of Women," *The Crane Bag*, 4, No. 1 (1980), 27-28.

16 Ibid., pp. 28-29.

17 Hanna Sheehy-Skeffington, "Women and the Nationalist Movement," typescript (1909), Ms. 22,266, The Sheehy-Skeffington Collection, National Library of Ireland, p. 1.

18 Jacqueline Van Voris, *Constance de Markievicz in the Cause of Ireland* (Amherst: University of Mass. Press, 1967), the picture referred to is on p. 18 of this volume.

19 Sean O'Casey, *Drums under the Windows: Autobiography: Book 3, 1906-1916* (London: Pan, 1973), p. 212. See also *Inishfallen Fare Thee Well: Autobiography, Book 4, 1917-1926* (London: Pan, 1973), p. 178.

20 From Yeats's poem, "Easter 1916."

21 From Yeats's poem, "Adam's Curse."

22 William Butler Yeats, *The Autobiography of William Butler Yeats* (New York: Collier, 1967), p. 242.

23 Small wagons were favorite speaking platforms for all social reformers of the era, including suffragettes. See Margaret Cousins, "Votes for Women: Ireland I," chapter 14 of *We Two Together*, p. 166.

24 See Robert Boyle, "The Woman of Chamber Music," abstract in *Joyce and Paris*, ed. J. Aubert and M. Jolas (Paris: Publications de l'Université de Lille III, 1979), p. 147.

25 Hugh Kenner, "The Look of a Queen: Women of the James Joyce Repertory Company," paper presented at the Fourteenth International Seminar of the Canadian Association for Irish Studies, March 21, 1981. Published as "The Look of a Queen" in *Woman in Irish Legend, Life and Literature*, ed. S. F. Gallagher (Gerrards Cross: Colin Smythe and Totawa: Barnes and Noble, 1983), pp. 115-124.

26 Sean O'Casey waxes malicious on the supposed rivalry of Yeats and Griffith for Maud Gonne's affections. See *Drums under the Windows*, pp. 117-119.

27 See Victory Pomeranz, "Note: Maud Gonne and M. Millevoye," *JJQ*, 2, No. 2 (1974), 169. Malcolm Brown, *The Politics of Irish Literature* (Seattle: University of Washington Press, 1972), p. 225.

28 Gonne explained that she could not receive Joyce in 1903 because of "a little cousin . . . with diphtheria." The "cousin" was probably Iseult, her daughter by Millevoye. Ellmann perpetuates another of Gonne's subterfuges, calling Iseult Maud's "niece" (JJ, 112).

29 Maud Gonne frequently used Griffith's columns to express anti-British positions. Weldon Thornton, *Allusions in Ulysses* (Chapel Hill, N. C.: University of North Carolina Press, 1968), pp. 77-78.

See Zack Bowen, "Lizzie Twigg: Gone but not Forgotten," *JJQ*, 6, No. (1969), 368-370 for a characterization of Ms. Twigg's poetry.

31 Sheehy-Skeffington, p. 2.

32 Ibid., p. 5. Sheehy-Skeffington seems to anticipate the present Irish Constitution, with its glorification of woman's role in the home and its outlawing of divorce, among other forms of patriarchal control.

33 Ibid., p. 1.

34 Hanna Sheehy-Skeffington, "Hanna Sheehy-Skeffington's Radio Interview with Dr. Charles Dixon," Ms. 24,164, National Library of Ireland.

35 Interview with Andrée Sheehy-Skeffington, June 1977. She is the widow of Owen, son of Francis and Hanna Sheehy-Skeffington. Kathleen Sheehy became the mother of the contemporary Irish politician and author Conor Cruise O'Brien.

36 *Irish Figaro*, Feb. 10, 1900, p. 85.

37 Peter Costello suggests that Joyce was infatuated with Mary Elizabeth Clery, who graduated from the Royal University at the same time as Joyce. Her surname, interest in Gaelic, and travel to the Aran Islands all make her

a convincing source for Emma Clery. *Portraits of the Artist as a Student,* exhibit at the 8th International James Joyce Symposium, June 1982, by Peter Costello and Augustine Martin.

38 Stanislaus Joyce, *The Complete Dublin Diary of Stanislaus Joyce,* ed. George H. Healey (Ithaca, N. Y.: Cornell University Press, 1971), p. 23.

39 Hanna Sheehy-Skeffington, Radio Interview, p. 4.

40 Ibid.

3. Early Encounters with Feminism

1 In 1975 an exhibition and booklet, *Votes for Women: Irish Women's Struggle for the Vote* were organized by Andrée Sheehy-Skeffington, Nancy McInerney, Rosemary Owens, and Tom Owens. Also a collection of studies on the position of women in Irish society was delivered on Radio Éireann from October to December 1975. These provided the basis of *Women in Irish Society: The Historical Dimension,* ed. Margaret MacCurtain and Donncha Ó'Corráin (Westport, Conn.: Greenwood Press; Dublin: Arlen House, 1979).

2 *Votes for Women,* p. 5.

3 Stanislaus Joyce, *The Complete Dublin Diary of Stanislaus Joyce,* ed. George H. Healey (Ithaca, N. Y.: Cornell University Press, 1971), p. 11n.

4 Owen Sheehy-Skeffington, "Francis Sheehy-Skeffington," in *1916: The Easter Rising,* ed. O. Dudley Edwards and F. Pyle (London: 1968), p. 145. The name of Sheehy-Skeffington's fictional counterpart was spelled differently in *A Portrait* (MacCann) and *Stephen Hero* (McCann), and these differences are preserved in this text, as are the variants Dedalus (P) and Daedalus (SH).

5 Hanna Sheehy-Skeffington, "Hanna Sheehy-Skeffington's Radio Interview with Dr. Charles Dixon," Ms. 24,164, National Library of Ireland.

6 Francis Sheehy-Skeffington, "My Philosophy," typescript, Ms. 22,256, National Library of Ireland.

7 "Francis Sheehy-Skeffington," *Irish Citizen,* 4, No. 38 (1916), p. 219.

8 Francis Sheehy-Skeffington, *Michael Davitt: Revolutionary Agitator and Labour Leader* (1908; rpt. London: MacGibbon and Kee, 1967), pp. 98-100, 217-218. Sheehy-Skeffington lapses repeatedly into purple prose, sarcasm, the piling of gritty details of abuses, or nationalist propaganda of the type burlesqued in *Ulysses.* Joyce did obtain a copy of this work and seems to have used it to build allusions to Davitt in *Finnegans Wake.*

9 Eugene Sheehy, *May it Please the Court* (Dublin: C. J. Fallon, 1951), p. 35.

10 James H. Cousins and Margaret E. Cousins, *We Two Together* (Madras: Ganesh, 1950), pp. 54-55.

11 Ibid., p. 108.

12 Francis Sheehy-Skeffington, "To Hanna," handwritten manuscript (14/2/3), Ms. 22,256ii, National Library of Ireland.

13 Francis Sheehy-Skeffington, handwritten fragment, Ms. 22,256ii, National Library of Ireland.

14 Stanislaus Joyce, p. 86.

15 Ibid.

16 Ibid.

17 Cousins, p. 105.

18 Margaret MacCurtain, "Women, the Vote and Revolution," in *Women in Irish Society,* p. 46. A similar connection is made between "ancient wis-

dom" and female leadership by Carolyn Heilbrun. See *Reinventing Womanhood* (New York: W.W. Norton, 1979), pp. 115-116.

19 See Shulamith Firestone, *The Dialectic of Sex* (New York: Bantam, 1971), p. 20, and Sheila D. Collins, "Socialism and Feminism: A Necessary Ground for Liberation," *Cross Currents*, 26, No. 1 (1976), p. 34. Dora Marsden also criticizes the narrowness of their goals, "Views and Comments," *The Egoist*, June 15, 1914, 223-226. Elizabeth Cady Stanton also held broader goals for the movement in America.

20 Francis Sheehy-Skeffington, typed extract from a letter (June 1, 1904), Ms. 21,641ii, National Library of Ireland.

21 Norman Atkinson, *Irish Education* (Dublin: Allen Figgis and Co., 1969), pp. 116-117. Additional information from telephone interview with Eileen Breathnacht, June 1977.

22 Ibid., pp. 116-117.

23 Stanislaus Joyce mentions in September 1904 that May is at Mt. Joy Convent and that Eileen is due to join her. *Diary*, p. 87. Sister Augustine O'Sullivan, who attended school with the girls, reports that they were in attendance there when their mother died in April 1904. Interview, Sion Hill Convent, September, 1981. On the Irish census of 1901, it is reported that all of the sons of the Joyce family are students; none of the daughters is designated as such.

24 Mary Colum and Padraic Colum, *Our Friend James Joyce* (Garden City, N. Y.: Doubleday, 1958), p. 14.

25 Margaret MacCurtain, "Women of Eccles Street," unpublished typescript, p. 4.

26 Ibid., p. 2.

27 Mary Colum, *Life and the Dream* (Garden City, N. Y.: Doubleday, 1974), pp. 91-92. In the world of *Stephen Hero*, male boarders had some, though probably lighter restrictions. Attendance at *Othello* was forbidden because of its "coarse expressions" (SH, 29).

28 Ibid., pp. 40-42. Father Tom Finlay had argued for a Catholic counterpart to English women's colleges that would be free from several disadvantages of convent school attachments. The disadvantages he detected included convent schools's lack of full commitment to higher studies, their limited financial status, and their limited faculty. "Women's Higher Education in Ireland," *Lyceum*, VI, no. 67 (April 1893), 143-147.

29 Brigid Vallely, "St. Mary's University College," unpublished paper in files of Eccles St. Convent, pp. 23-24. 30 See *St. Stephen's*, Feb. 1902, p. 75.

31 Francis J. C. Skeffington, "A Forgotten Aspect of the University Question," in *Two Essays*, by Skeffington and James Joyce (1901; rpt. Minneapolis: McCosh's Book Store, 1957), p. 6.

32 The memorial was signed, among others, by Sheehy-Skeffington, C. P. Curran, Hugh Kennedy, Thomas Kettle, R. J. Sheehy, George Siegerson, and Louis Walsh—all acquaintances of Joyce. It argues that since Trinity College admitted women as of March 1903, Irish Catholic women now had accentuated disabilities in respect of higher education. Its exclusion of women would injure UCD "in the eyes of the enlightened public." It urges that women be admitted to all lectures. Ms. 23,641i, National Library of Ireland.

33 Mary Hayden and Hanna Sheehy-Skeffington, "Women in Universities: A Reply," typescript, Ms. 22,262, National Library of Ireland. See also Hanna Sheehy, Radio Interview, p. 4.

34 A comparable section of Skeffington's original essay states:

> The two sexes, in equal and untramelled (sic) intercourse, exercise the strongest beneficial influence on each other; the predominant faults of each are restrained, the nobler qualities of both are fostered, and men and women of the best type are the result. . . . The life of school and college is brought more closely into accord with the natural order the more it approximates to the conditions of a large family circle of brothers and sisters. . . . It is not on behalf of women alone that the claim for coeducation is made; for men also, this system is the only wholesome and natural one. Mentally and morally, the unrestrained companionship, and intellectual and social comradeship between man and woman which is thus produced cannot fail to rebound to the advantage of both sexes and to the future well-being of the race. [F. J. C. Skeffington, pp. 9-10]

Skeffington with his "brothers and sisters" concept is as unconcerned with the physical attraction between male and female as Joyce is preoccupied with it. The polarities are preserved in McCann and Stephen.

36 Arthur Power, *Conversations with James Joyce*, ed. Clive Hart (New York: Barnes and Noble, 1974), pp. 33-36.

37 George Moore, *Muslin* (London: Heinemann, 1915), p. ix.

38 Ibid., pp. 68-69.

39 George Moore, *Evelyn Innes* (London: Unwin, 1898), pp. 254-255.

40 Albert J. Solomon, "The Backgrounds of Eveline," *Éire-Ireland*, 6, No. 3 (Fall 1971), 30-38.

41 George Moore, "John Norton," in *Celibates* (London: Walter Scott, 1895), pp. 418-422.

42 Portions of the observations on Moore were published in an earlier form in, "Joyce's Schooling in the Field of George Moore," *Éire-Ireland*, 9, No. 4 (1974), 137-138.

43 Colin MacCabe suggests that Joyce may have adopted Ibsen as a lost father figure. See *James Joyce and the Revolution of the Word* (New York: Barnes and Noble, 1979), p. 53.

44 Björn J. Tysdahl, *Joyce and Ibsen* (Oslo: Norwegian University Press; New York: Humanities Press, 1968), pp. 28-32.

45 Power, p. 35.

46 George Bernard Shaw, *The Quintessence of Ibsenism* (New York: Brentano's, 1913), p. 33.

47 Harold Pinter's 1971 production was well received. The dialogue made an impression of strength in the 1977 production by the Dublin Stage One Theatre, Trinity College, according to my observation.

48 James T. Farrell, "Exiles and Ibsen" in *James Joyce: Two Decades of Criticism*, ed. Seon Givens (New York: Vanguard, 1963), p. 115.

49 Jill Perkins, *Joyce and Hauptmann: Before Sunrise* (Chicago: Huntington Library, 1978), p. 40.

50 Elaine Rapp Unkeless, "Leopold Bloom as Womanly Man," *Modernist Studies*, 2, No. 1 (1976), 36-37.

51 See Suzette Henke, "Stephen Dedalus and Women," in *Women and Joyce* (Urbana, Ill.: University of Illinois Press, 1982), p. 83. Henke refers to Dorothy Dinnerstein's *The Mermaid and the Minotaur* (New York: Harper & Row, 1977), a sociological study which stresses the problems derived from the cultural norm of the female domination of early childhood.

52 Dora Marsden, "Views and Comments: The Chastity of Women," *The Egoist*, Feb. 2, 1914, pp. 45-46.

53 Perkins, p. 38.

4. The Female Family of Joyce

1 Edna O'Brien provides a frequently inaccurate and questionably selective rehashing of Joyce's relationships with Nora and (in less detail) May and Lucia Joyce in "Joyce and Nora: A Portrait of Joyce's Marriage," *Harper's Magazine*, September 1980, 60-73.

2 Mark Shechner, *Joyce in Nighttown* (Berkeley: University of California Press, 1974), p. 54.

3 Ibid., pp. 237, 209-211, 219-223.

4 See Tillie Olsen, *Silences* (New York: Delacorte Press, 1978).

5 Stanislaus Joyce, *The Complete Dublin Diary of Stanislaus Joyce*, ed. George H. Healey (Ithaca, N. Y. and London: Cornell University Press, 1971), pp. 8-10, 14, 17-18, 24, 44, 56, 58.

6 Bozena Berta Delimata, "Reminiscences of a Joyce Niece," ed. Virginia Moseley, *JJQ*, 19 (Fall 1981), 45-62.

7 Harriet Shaw Weaver, letter to Mrs. Cotten, n.d., Ms. 57,353, British Library.

8 Sheldon Brivic, Margot Norris, and Shechner all offer Oedipal interpretations. See Brivic, *Joyce between Freud and Jung* (Port Washington, N. Y., and London: Kennikat, 1980), pp. 17-83 (Part I of this book is titled "Stephen Oedipus"); Norris, *The Decentered Universe of Finnegans Wake* (Baltimore and London: Johns Hopkins University Press, 1976), pp. 28-30; Shechner sees most of Joyce's women characters and even his choosing Nora for his wife as Joyce's attempt to recreate a lost primal mother, first represented in May Joyce, pp. 247ff.

9 Robert Scholes and Richard M. Kain, *The Workshop of Daedalus* (Evanston, Ill.: Northwestern University Press, 1965), p. 31.

10 Stanislaus Joyce, *Complete Dublin Diary*, p. 8.

11 Ibid., pp. 17, 19, 98. Stanislaus seems to find "strength" at the piano beyond women's normal capacities. Eileen Joyce's singing is further described by her daughter, who suggests that Eileen had "a dramatic quality suited to opera," and notes that she continued to study in Trieste after her marriage. See Delimata, pp. 47, 53.

12 Eugene Sheehy, *May It Please the Court* (Dublin: J. C. Fallon, 1951), p. 28.

13 Stanislaus Joyce, *Complete Dublin Diary*, pp. 8-10.

14 Ibid., p. 8.

15 Maria Jolas describes the household of Joyce's youth as a "gynaeceum." See "The Joyce I Knew and the Women around Him," *The Crane Bag*, 4, no. 1 (1980), 82.

16 Jane Lidderdale reports a very bitter account of her father from May Joyce, the third sister. Interview with Jane Lidderdale, October 1981. John Joyce's granddaughter Bozena Delimata reports her aunts' hatred of "Pappie," but also suggests that in old age "he kept up with all their interests" and has the opinion that "some of his children were rather unfair . . . in their treatment of him." Eileen Joyce Schaurek was visiting her ailing father when her husband committed suicide in Trieste in 1926; her children regularly brought "Pappie" Jameson whiskey, once they settled in Dublin in

1928. This suggests that Eileen was not one of his bitter children. Delimata, pp. 49, 50, 53, 54.

17 S. Joyce, *Complete Dublin Diary*, p. 10. One of May Joyce's last letters to James in Paris, written in March 1903, shows concern for her daughters, though the limited comments on them follow a lengthy discussion of the problems of her son, Charlie.

> The others are at school and May and Mabel showing cleverness the former anxious to advance herself and do well for the future the *latter* the peacemaker in troublesome times and invaluable to us all in this way though we fear her heart may suffer *frights*. Florrie too does her part in this respect and your Pappie shows affection to both.
>
> Poppie is beginning to cry out about herself she would go to any business or give time to be taught I would like to put her to some thing by which she would learn and have something for herself. The girl cannot even get shoes or a pair of gloves. (L II, 33)

18 Ibid., pp. 19, 45. Sister Augustine O'Sullivan reports that May Joyce and a younger sister were boarders at St. Joseph's Orphanage at the time of their mother's death. They attended a national school there, and only their religious instruction came from the Sisters. Interview, Sion Hill Convent, Dublin, October 3, 1981.

19 Ibid., pp. 18, 44.

20 Ibid., pp. 17, 56. Richard Ellmann seems to have found May the most reliable biographical resource among the sisters.

21 Delimata, p. 62. She notes that Eva worked for a solicitor, Florence was in the law department of the Hibernian Bank, and Eileen worked for the Irish Sweepstakes. May also worked in a bank. Jane Lidderdale interview, 1981.

22 Robert Kiely studies the marriage plots in modern short stories, suggesting that there are really two authors in each situation, and that the crisis comes because of a clash between languages, only one of them under the control of the "obtuse" husband narrators. Joyce's "The Dead" is one of his three texts. Robert Kiely, *Beyond Egotism: The Fiction of James Joyce, Virginia Woolf, and D. H. Lawrence* (Cambridge: Harvard University Press, 1980), p. 89. Quoted by Carolyn Heilbrun, "Women, Men, Theories, and Literature," *Profession 81*, 1981, p. 26.

23 S. Joyce, *Complete Dublin Diary*, p. 35.

24 Ibid., pp. 10, 15.

25 Ibid., pp. 55, 57.

26 Ibid., p. 76.

27 Joyce later wants that hair kept in good condition for him. See L II, 251. Remarking the same selection of Nora's aspects, Mark Shechner quips that Nora was "cherished as something less than the sum of her parts." Shechner, p. 241.

28 Hélène Cixous, *The Exile of James Joyce* (New York: David Lewis, 1972), p. 65.

29 Frank Budgen, *Myselves when Young* (London: Oxford, 1970), p. 204.

30 Letter from Nora Joyce to Harriet Weaver, March 28, 1930, Ms. 57,350, British Library. This letter is paraphrased since permission to publish an extract was denied by the Joyce Estate.

31 See Mary T. Reynolds, "Joyce and Nora: The Indispensable Countersign," *The Sewanee Review*, 72 (Winter 1964), 53.

32 Delimata, p. 48.

33 Ibid., p. 47.

34 Unpublished essay by Stephen Joyce.

35 Cixous suggests, to the contrary, that "Nora's maternal feelings gradually atrophied as she became more and more Jim's companion." Cixous, p. 66.

36 Letter from Maria Jolas to Harriet Weaver, Ms. 57,353, British Library.

37 Ibid. 38 "Autobiography" (typescript), Sylvia Beach Papers, Box 117, Princeton University Library.

39 Letter from George Joyce to Harriet Weaver, Dec. 27, 1941, Ms. 57,353, British Library.

40 Letter from Maria Jolas to Harriet Weaver, Oct. 18, 1947, Ms. 57,353, British Library.

41 Interview with Lucia Joyce, June 25, 1977.

42 Letter from Jane Lidderdale to Bonnie Scott, July 19, 1977, and interview, June, 1977. For Miss Lidderdale's account of Lucia Joyce's death and her relationship with Miss Joyce, see "Lucia Joyce at St. Andrew's," *The James Joyce Broadsheet*, 10 (Feb. 1983), 3.

43 Letter from Lucia Joyce to Katherine Sargent, June 5, 1922, Houghton Library, Harvard University.

44 Interview, 1977.

45 Letter from Lucia Joyce to Sylvia Beach, Nov. 6, 1922, Lockwood Memorial Library, SUNY Buffalo.

46 Letter from Joyce to Harriet Weaver, Mar. 11, 1931, Ms. 57,350, British Library. This passage is omitted from L I, 302-303.

47 Beckett was still a friend and correspondent of Ms. Joyce in 1977, at the time of my interview with her. He was only one of a number of "boyfriends" recalled in the random autobiographical fragment which she wrote for Richard Ellmann in 1961. Box 117, Sylvia Beach Papers, Princeton University Library.

48 Mary and Padraic Colum, *Our Friend James Joyce* (New York: Doubleday, 1958), p. 214. Padraic Colum describes Lucia's outspoken resentment of the attention her father was getting and some of her "deracinated" behavior, pp. 208-213.

49 Interview, June 1977; the same costume is probably described by Bozena Delimata, p. 50. The dominant color seems to have been silver, not gold: "It was in silver sequins edged with green. One leg was covered to the heel and the other came right through the costume, so that when she put one foot behind the other she created the illusion of a fish tail." Ellmann describes it as a "shimmering silver fish" (JJ, 612).

50 See Frank Budgen, *James Joyce and the Making of Ulysses* (1934; rpt. Bloomington, Ind.: Indiana University Press, 1960), p. 190.

51 Louis Gillet, "Preface," *A Chaucer A. B. C.*, by James Joyce, illustrated by Lucia Joyce (Paris: Obelisk, 1935), p. 1.

52 Interview with Jane Lidderdale, Oct. 10, 1981. "Miss Kathleen Neel Kitten" is the first of several female friends from Paris, Zurich, and Trieste recalled by Miss Joyce in her autobiographical fragment. Box 117, Sylvia Beach Papers, Princeton University Library. That collection also contains a printed business card inscribed:

Kathleen Neel, Lucia Joyce
Physical Training
Private Lessons

53 Letter from Dominique Gillet Maroger to Bonnie Scott, Nov. 13, 1981. Ms. Maroger describes more about her acquaintnace with Lucia Joyce, and Ms. Joyce's dancing in a special numer of *Cahiers de l'Herne*, forthcoming.

54 Sylvia Beach writes to Harriet Weaver from Paris, ". . . also his family has begun to make friends here and dreaded the transplant to a new place after having moved so many times already." Letter from Sylvia Beach to Harriet Weaver, June 18, 1922, Ms. 57,353, British Museum.

55 Explanatory note on the collection, probably written by Sylvia Beach.

56 Helen Vanel, "La Danseuse Artiste et Educatrice, II," *Cahiers Rhythme et Couleur*, Nov. 1925, pp. 34-36.

57 Helen Vanel, "La Danseuse Artiste et Educatrice, III," *Cahiers Rhythme et Couleur*, May 1926, pp. 69-71.

58 Interview with Lucia Joyce, July 1977.

59 Ibid.

60 Jane Lidderdale interview, 1981.

61 Ibid.

62 Letter from Joyce to Harriet Weaver, March 11, 1931, Ms. 57,350, British Library. This passage is eliminated in L I, 302-303.

63 Lucia Joyce wrote Miss Weaver, "I have allready (*sic*) several orders and I hope to be able to stick to this as I may later be able to combine the initials with this work." Letter from Lucia Joyce to Harriet Weaver, Dec. 24, 1932, Ms. 57351, British Library.

64 Yeats's female family did flourish in this kind of environment; his sisters founded the Cuala Press, and his daughter Anne became a notable artist. Ironically, Joyce had satirized the Yeats sisters as "the weird sisters" (U, 13). The Yeats family had the tremendous advantage of an artistic tradition, inaugurated by John Butler Yeats, the poet's father; William Morris was in fact a family friend.

65 Ms. 57,351, British Library. This is probably a fragment that Lucia Joyce wrote to her nurse while resting at Feldkirch. Joyce says that he will forward such a piece to Miss Weaver in a letter of Aug. 6, 1932 (L III, 254).

66 Interview with Richard Ellmann, Oct. 15, 1981.

67 See Delimata, pp. 54-57, for an account of Lucia's exploits in Ireland, and Joyce's responses. Some may question the reliability of this memoir.

68 Miss Joyce's letters to Sylvia Beach from the 1950s are in Box 117, Sylvia Beach Papers, Princeton University Library.

69 Letter from Lucia Joyce to Harriet Weaver, Aug. 8, 1932, Ms. 57,351, British Library.

70 Typed copy of "A Flower Given to my Daughter," 1927, Ms. 57,349, British Library.

71 See Cixous, p. 66.

72 Robert Boyle reports that during a visit he made to Lucia Joyce in 1975, she recited this stanza of the poem in "her sweet youthful voice." He "seemed to hear the musical, confident, quick rhythms of her father as she had heard him speak it to her." Conversation with Robert Boyle, S.J., February 1982, and his notes of the interview, held June 28, 1975.

5. New Free Women in the Company of Joyce

1 Robert McAlmon, *Being Geniuses Together* (London: Secker and Warburg, 1938), p. 42.

2 Jane Lidderdale and Mary Nicholson, *Dear Miss Weaver* (New York: Viking, 1970), p. 46. Rebecca West, "Spinster to the Rescue" (review of *Dear Miss Weaver*), *The Sunday Telegraph*, Nov. 8, 1970, p. 12.

3 Dora Marsden, "Views and Comments: The Chastity of Women," *The Egoist*, Feb. 2, 1914, pp. 44-46.

4 Lidderdale and Nicholson, p. 46.

5 West, "Spinster to the Rescue," p. 12.

6 Lidderdale and Nicholson, pp. 118-121.

7 Harriet Shaw Weaver, "The Egoist" (typed essay), Ms. 57,355, British Library.

8 Interview with Dame Rebecca West, October 16, 1981.

9 Lidderdale and Nicholson, p. 453.

10 West, "Spinster to the Rescue", p. 12. West repeated this reaction in the 1981 interview, calling Marsden "brilliant and glamorous."

11 Interview with Jane Lidderdale, Oct. 13, 1981. Rebecca West felt that Weaver showed "intellectual deafness" in taking so long to realize that "the mainspring" of Marsden's mind had "broken." "Spinster to the Rescue," p. 12. West also recalled Marsden's strange crafting of embroidery in white thread on white cloth. Interview, 1981.

12 Letter from Dora Marsden to Harriet Weaver, Feb. 1917, Ms. 57,354, British Library.

13 Letter from Dora Marsden to Harriet Weaver, Apr. 6, 1918, Ms. 57,354, British Library.

14 Letter from James Joyce to Harriet Weaver, Oct. 2, 1928, Ms. 57,349, British Library.

15 Letter from James Joyce to Harriet Weaver, Dec. 2, 1928, Ms. 57,349, British Library.

16 Dora Marsden, *The Definition of a Godhead* (London: Egoist Press, 1928), p. i.

17 Lidderdale and Nicholson, p. 54.

18 Lidderdale interview, 1981.

19 Interview with Richard Ellmann, Oct. 15, 1981.

20 McAlmon, p. 42.

21 As his memoirs betray, McAlmon's obsession with alcoholic consumption rivals that of Ernest Hemingway. He unfortunately considered a glass of wine an indispensable part of Miss Weaver's Paris education. In a well-described scene, Ezra Pound arrives and mirthfully accuses Miss Weaver of being "drunk," to everyone's horror, and Miss Weaver's mortification. *Being Geniuses Together*, p. 55. McAlmon's memoirs are written for flair, not objectivity, and contain inaccuracies like the statement that Miss Weaver was a Quaker. She had not, in fact, sheltered herself from the world to the extent he suggests—her East End social work proving most world-revealing. McAlmon felt that Joyce received too much hero-worship from women in Paris, and disliked Paris literary gatherings and parties focused on Joyce. McAlmon, pp. 284, 324. Despite their biases, McAlmon's memoirs do offer brief sketches of many of the women writers and artists in Paris in the 1920s, including Sylvia Beach, Adrienne Monnier, Jane Heap, Emma Goldman, Mina Loy, and Djuna Barnes. McAlmon was at this time the husband of a wealthy Englishwoman, Bryher (Winnifred Ellermann). Theirs was a marriage of convenience, which Bryher seems to have entered to liberate herself from the conventional constraints upon young, single women, imposed by her family. Bryher was a friend of Harriet Weaver and subsidized Egoist Press publications. Weaver liked her ability to come "to terms with life in an independent way." Lidderdale and Nicholson, p. 177. Through this con-

nection, McAlmon had received Miss Weaver's introduction to Joyce. Bryher was also a very dear friend of Sylvia Beach and a companion of H. D.

22 Lidderdale and Nicholson, p. 87. See also p. 347 for a discussion of Weaver's interpretation of Marxism. She worked for the Labour Party in the 1930s and joined the Oxford City Branch of the Communist Party in the 1940s.

23 Ibid., p. 44.

24 Letter from Harriet Weaver to Sylvia Beach, March 15, 1931, Box 232, Sylvia Beach Papers, Princeton University Library.

25 Lidderdale and Nicholson, p. 83.

26 Lidderdale interview, 1981.

27 West, "Spinster to the Rescue," p. 12; Lidderdale and Nicholson, p. 40; and Lidderdale interview, 1981. Lidderdale and Nicholson consider this attitude "by no means uncommon among young women of her generation, class and interest. It was enough for them to be free to choose not to marry."

28 Harriet Shaw Weaver, *Symposium on Time* (typescript), Oxford Philosophy Library.

29 Lidderdale interview, 1981.

30 Lidderdale and Nicholson, p. 94.

31 Letter from Dora Marsden to Harriet Weaver, July 19, 1916, Ms. 57,354, British Library.

32 Letter from Dora Marsden to Harriet Weaver, 1916, Ms. 57,354, British Library.

33 *The Egoist*, Jan. 1, Feb. 1, Mar. 1, Apr. 1, 1916.

34 Ibid., Jan. 1, 1916, pp. 2-3.

35 Ibid., Mar. 1, 1916, p. 34.

36 Ibid.

37 Ibid., Mar. 2, 1914, pp. 98-99; Apr. 1, 1919, p. 139.

38 Ibid., Mar. 1, 1916, p. 35.

39 Ibid., Dec., 1919, p. 71.

40 See "Harriet Weaver's Letters to Joyce," ed. John Firth, *Studies in Bibliography: Papers of the Bibliographical Society of Virginia*, 20 (1967), 151-188. Though most of Joyce's letters to Weaver are now available, fewer of hers have been made public. Maria Jolas regretted this in a 1973 interview: "Giorgio has them and I think that he is not ready to publish them." "An Interview with Carola Giedion-Welcker and Maria Jolas," ed. Richard Kain, *James Joyce Quarterly*, 11 (1974), 113-114. This may only be a myth, akin to the persistent rumor that a trunkful of manuscripts waits to be found somewhere in Europe.

41 Kain, pp. 113-114.

42 Letter from Stuart Gilbert to Peter du Sautoy, Sept. 18, 1950. Quoted in Lidderdale and Nicholson, p. 420.

43 Lidderdale and Nicholson, pp. 161, 410-411.

44 Firth, p. 175 (July 18, 1917).

45 Ibid., p. 183 (Nov. 2, 1919).

46 Ibid., p. 184 (Dec. 10, 1919).

47 Ibid., p. 186 (Jan. 28, 1920). The same gradual cultivation of close friendship is visible in Weaver's letters to Sylvia Beach. They begin in 1920 with business exchanges, as Egoist Press supplied books to Shakespeare and Company. By 1924, Weaver was offering mild jokes and discussing vacation plans. In 1926, she began to sign herself "Josephine" and to use the first name "Sylvia" in her salutation. This became "Dearest Sylvia" by 1931.

Letters, Box 232, Sylvia Beach Papers, Princeton University Library. Weaver never used anything but "Mr. Joyce" in her salutations to Joyce.

48 Lidderdale and Nicholson, pp. 198-199.

50 Ibid., p. 190. See n. 11 for Rebecca West's reaction to this attitude.

50 Ibid., p. 190. "Miss" is used for both Weaver and Lucia Joyce because these were the terms they employed.

51 Rebecca West has her own witty variation: "She was more than a patron, she was a patron saint." "Spinster to the Rescue," p. 12. Weaver humorously resisted this kind of praise from Sylvia Beach: "I have been looking all round for the halo you spoke of but can't catch sight of such an uncomfortable thing anywhere." Letter from Harriet Weaver to Sylvia Beach, May 20, 1924, Box 232, Sylvia Beach Papers, Princeton University Library.

52 Ibid., pp. 168, 175, 176, 182.

53 Ibid., p. 171 (April 25, 1917).

54 Lidderdale and Nicholson, p. 191. Joyce was sufficiently amused by both her reaction to "Cyclops" and her "melancholy letter" on her age to report them in letters to Budgen (SL, 244, 245).

55 Ibid., p. 237.

56 Firth, p. 179 (Mar. 8, 1918).

57 Ibid., p. 180 (Jan. 19, 1918).

58 Lidderdale and Nicholson, p. 162.

59 Virginia Woolf, A Room of One's Own (New York: Harcourt, Brace and World, 1957), p. 70.

60 Lidderdale and Nicholson, p. 436.

61 Interview with Noel Riley Fitch, Dec. 28, 1981. See her Sylvia Beach and the Lost Generation (New York: Norton, 1983), which was in press when this book was completed. Adrienne Monnier and her endeavors with Sylvia Beach are well represented in The Very Rich Hours of Adrienne Monnier (New York: Scribner's, 1976), with introduction, commentaries, and translations of representative articles of Monnier's, by Richard Mc Dougall.

62 Kain, p. 112.

63 Maria Jolas, "The Joyce I Knew and the Women Around Him," The Crane Bag, 4 (1980), 85-86.

64 Sylvia Beach, Shakespeare and Company (1956; rpt. Lincoln, Neb.: University of Nebraska Press, 1980), photographs following p. 108, especially numbers 1, 17, 13.

65 Lidderdale interview, 1981. This is also displayed in a filmed interview, made when the Joyce Tower was opened in Dublin, parts of which appear in the RTE tape. "Is there anyone who understands me? The World of James Joyce" (1982).

66 Beach, p. 85.

67 Fitch interview, 1981.

68 Letter from Sylvia Beach to Cyprian Beach, Sept. 26, 1913, Box 19, Sylvia Beach Papers, Princeton University Library. Beach rather irreverently refers to Mrs. Pankhurst as "Mrs. Spankfirst" in this same letter—a typical example of her love of word play—a trait congenial to Joyce.

69 Letters from Sylvia Beach to Eleanor Beach, March 1916, and to Cyprian Beach, June 21, 1919, Box 19, Sylvia Beach Papers, Princeton. Sylvia also expresses her admiration for Shaw and Hauptmann to Cyprian. Letter, Jan. 30, 1914, Box 19, Beach Papers, Princeton.

70 Mc Dougall, p. 71. Translated from Rue de l'Odéon, first published 1920.

71 Letter to Eleanor Beach, August 3, 1919, Box 19, Beach Papers, Princeton. Beach's close relationship to her mother is shown in her usual salutation, "Dearest Little Mother." Her correspondence with her father is sparse and relatively formal.

72 Mc Dougall, pp. 3-5, 75.

73 Sylvia Beach describes details of an initial agreement with Monnier in a letter to her mother. She agreed not to open a French bookshop in competition with Monnier, and to give Monnier 5% of her profits. Beach favors these stipulations: "I should prefer not to be under *any* obligations to Monnier." Letter of August 20, 1919, Box 19, Beach Papers, Princeton.

74 Mc Dougall, p. 69.

75 Sylvia Beach reports going on a country outing with "Stein and her friend . . . in their undertaker car," and receiving news abourt a rival bookshop from her—suggesting some friendly contact between their circles. Letters from Sylvia Beach to Eleanor Beach, May 10 and July 20, 1920, Box 19, Beach Papers, Princeton. Louise Bernikow sees Beach, Monnier, Stein and others like Natalie Barney as the flourishing of a brief "literary culture" in which women were "full citizens," and where lesbianism was widely accepted. See *Among Women* (New York: Harper & Row, 1980), pp. 156-192.

76 Ibid., p. 48.

77 *Sylvia Beach (1887-1962)*, ed. Jackson Mathews and Maurice Suillet (Paris: Mercure du France, 1963), p. 48.

78 Ellmann interview, 1981.

79 Mc Dougall, p. 131.

80 Ibid., p. 118. Translated from *Les Gazettes d'Adrienne Monnier*, May 1940.

81 Ibid., p. 125.

82 Letters to Holly Beach, April 23, 1921, and Eleanor Beach, April 1, 1921, Box 19, Beach Papers, Princeton.

83 Beach, p. 205. Justifying Joyce's transfer of *Ulysses* to another publisher in 1930, Beach allows him the superior claim of "mother." Interestingly, her statement ends in a tag question, a typically female linguistic form, and one which defers to the audience, inviting dispute: "A baby belongs to its mother, not to the midwife, doesn't it?" In her RTE film interview, Beach repeats with implied approval a journalist's description of her as the "mother hen of the 20's."

84 *Sylvia Beach*, p. 47.

85 Simone de Beauvoir, Preface to *James Joyce in Paris: His Final Years*, by Gisèle Freund and V. B. Carleton (Cassell: London, 1965), p. viii.

86 Beach, pp. 196-205.

87 Ibid., p. 191. 88 Woolf, pp. 35-36.

89 Beach, p. 35, and RTE film interview.

90 Ibid., p. 40, and RTE film interview.

91 Ibid., p. 41.

92 Ibid., p. 42.

93 *Ibid.*, p. 43. "Paternal" might have been a better term. Beach is also very impressed by Ernest Hemingway's skill as a nursemaid (*Shakespeare and Company*, p. 82), making devotion to children seem an important criterion for her admiration. McAlmon also reports that in a conversation in the early twenties, while inebriated, Joyce expressed a hope for more chil-

dren. McAlmon, p. 15. This wish may have been as vague as that expressed by Molly Bloom in the "Penelope" chapter of *Ulysses*.

94 Lidderdale and Ellmann interviews, 1981. See also Lidderdale and Nicholson, pp. 437, 451.

95 Letter from Sylvia Beach to Harriet Weaver, June 6, 1922, Ms. 57,353, British Library.

96 Letter from Sylvia Beach to Harriet Weaver, June 18, 1922, Ms. 57,353, British Library.

97 Ibid.

98 Fitch interview, 1981.

99 See letters of Sylvia Beach to Harriet Weaver, May 25, 1950, June 1958, and Harriet Weaver to Sylvia Beach, May 25, 1950, June 28, 1958, Ms. 57,353, British Library; letters of Harriet Weaver to Sylvia Beach, Nov. 12, 1924, March 15, 1931, Box 232, Beach Papers, Princeton; and Lidderdale and Nicholson, pp. 450-451. "Josephine" was the first name that Harriet Shaw Weaver asked intimates like Dora Marsden and Sylvia Beach to use for her. She chose the name of a relative (Joseph Wright) who had died young to give him a new lease on life. Lidderdale interview, 1981. She first used it when writing to *The Egoist*. Letter from Harriet Weaver to Sylvia Beach, July 22, 1922, Box 232, Beach Papers, Princeton. Joyce retained the more formal "Miss Weaver" in all of his salutations. Even with male intimates like Frank Budgen, Joyce evaded the use of first names. He wrote always, "Dear Budgen."

100 Kain, p. 95.

101 Beach, p. 102.

102 Letters from Maria Jolas to Harriet Weaver, 1943, 1947, 1948, Ms. 57,353, British Library.

103 Jolas, p. 82.

104 Ibid., p. 86.

105 Ibid., p. 87.

106 Djuna Barnes, "Vagaries Malicieux," *The Double Dealer*, 3, no. 17 (May 1922), 253.

107 Ibid.

108 Ibid., pp. 252-253.

109 Djuna Barnes, "James Joyce," *Vanity Fair*, April 1922, 65.

110 Ibid.

111 Barnes, "Vagaries," p. 242.

112 Ibid.

113 Barnes, "Joyce," p. 65.

114 McAlmon, p. 88.

115 Barnes, "Joyce," pp. 65, 104.

116 Ibid., p. 65.

117 Ibid.

118 Ibid.

119 Burton Rascoe, *A Bookman's Diary*, ed. C. Hartley Grattan (New York: Horace Liverwright, 1929), p. 27. Quoted in Louis F. Kannenstine, *The Art of Djuna Barnes: Duality and Damnation* (New York: New York University Press, 1977), p. 48.

120 Barnes, "Joyce," p. 65.

121 Kannenstine, pp. 39, 48-50, 107, 128, and Jack A. Hirschmann, *The Orchestrated Novel: A Study of Poetic Devices in the Novels of Djuna Barnes*

and Herman Broch and the Influence of James Joyce upon Them. Ph.D. dissertation, Indiana University, 1962.

122 Freund, p. 72. The photograph is published in JJ, plate LIII.

123 See Patricia Meyer Spacks, *The Female Imagination* (New York: Knopf, 1976), pp. 167-168.

124 Arthur Power, *Conversations with James Joyce,* ed. Clive Hart (New York: Barnes and Noble, 1974), pp. 68-69.

125 Margaret Anderson, *My Thirty Years War* (1930; rpt. Westport, Conn.: Greenwood Press, 1971), pp. 244-245.

126 Ibid., pp. 219-220.

127 Carola Giedion-Welcker, "Meetings with Joyce," in *Portraits of the Artist in Exile: Recollections of James Joyce by Europeans,* ed. Willard Potts (Seattle and London: University of Washington Press, 1979), pp. 266, 274.

128 Carola Giedion-Welcker, "Carola Giedion-Welcker on *Ulysses*" in *James Joyce: The Critical Heritage,* Vol. 2, ed. Robert H. Deming (New York: Barnes and Noble, 1970), pp. 441-442.

129 Ibid., p. 438.

130 Ibid.

131 Ibid.

132 Carola Giedion-Welcker, " 'Work in Progress': A Linguistic Experiment by James Joyce," trans. Eugene Jolas for *Transition,* 1929, in *In Memoriam: James Joyce,* ed. Carola Giedion-Welcker (Zurich: Futz and Wasmuth,1940), p. 37.

133 Ibid., p. 40.

134 Giedion-Welcker, "Meetings with Joyce," pp. 264-265.

135 Ibid., p. 279.

136 Interview with Varena Clay, June 1979.

137 Giedion-Welcker, "Meetings with Joyce," p. 271.

6. Feminist Critics on Joyce

1 Mary Colum, "The Confessions of James Joyce," *Freeman,* 5, No. 123 (19 July 1922), 450-452, in *James Joyce: The Critical Heritage,* ed. Robert H. Deming (New York: Barnes & Noble, 1970), pp. 233-234.

2 Ibid., p. 373. See also Mary and Padraic Colum, *Our Friend James Joyce* (Garden City, N. Y.: Doubleday, 1958), p. 130.

3 M. Colum, p. 233.

4 Ibid., p. 232.

5 M. and P. Colum, p. 115.

6 Ibid., p. 132. See also JJ, 635.

7 Ibid., pp. 132-133.

8 Patricia Rimo, *Mary Colum: Woman of Letters,* unpublished doctoral dissertation, University of Delaware, 1982, p. 42.

9 Interview with Dame Rebecca West, October 16, 1981.

10 Ibid.

11 Nathan Halper, "James Joyce and Rebecca West," *Partisan Review,* 16 (July 1949), 761. Halper is repeating what Padraic Colum had told him. Colum later published his account. See M. and P. Colum, p. 125. See also Bernard Benstock, *Joyce-Again's Wake* (Seattle, Wash.: University of Washington Press, 1965), p. 229n for an extensive review of the references to West in the *Wake.* Benstock states on a somewhat more positive note that Joyce took Miss West "robecca or worse" (203.4-5) and married her into his involved framework for the *Wake.*

12 Rebecca West, *The Strange Necessity* (Garden City, N. Y.: Doubleday, Doran, 1928), p. 22. West's charge of sentimentality is not unique, though to appreciators of Joyce's ironic power, it may seem surprising. Clive Hart has noted, "Sentimentality was always the greatest hazard for Joyce." *Structure and Motif in Finnegans Wake* (Evanston, Ill.: Northwestern University Press, 1962), p. 29.

13 West, pp. 33-34. She still holds the opinion that "Leopold Bloom should have got on with it or forgotten it," a judgment that shows some lasting sympathy with the philosophy of H. G. Wells. Wells had once tried to describe his difference from West in his "drive," that "says everlastingly oh *Get on* with it." Quoted in Gordon N. Ray, *H. G. Wells and Rebecca West* (New Haven: Yale University Press, 1974), p. xviii.

14 Ibid., pp. 32-33.

15 See Sheldon Brivic, *Joyce between Freud and Jung* (Port Washington, N. Y.: Kennikat Press, 1980), pp. 30-32.

16 West, pp. 43-44.

17 Frank Budgen, *James Joyce and the Making of Ulysses*, ed. Clive Hart (1934; rpt. Bloomington, Ind.: Indiana University Press, 1960), pp. 318-319.

18 West, p. 14.

19 Ibid., p. 39. Dame Rebecca West recently hailed Molly as "a very living person," admirable because her "feelings are in accord with her emotions." West interview, 1981.

20 Ibid., p. 41.

21 Ibid., pp. 192, 203-205.

22 West interview, 1981.

23 Suzette Henke, "Woolf's *Ulysses* Notebook," paper delivered at the 8th International James Joyce Symposium, June 1982. Several of the following quotations were cited by Henke. "Modern Novels" contains both Woolf's first reactions to *Ulysses* and her notes toward the essay, "Modern Fiction." The notebook is in the Berg Collection, New York Public Library. It contains no page numbers.

24 Woolf, "Modern Novels."

25 Virginia Woolf, "Modern Fiction," in *The Common Reader*, first series (New York: Harcourt, Brace and World, 1953), pp. 154-155.

26 Ibid., p. 155.

27 Virginia Woolf, *A Writer's Diary* (New York: Harcourt Brace Jovanovich, 1954), p. 27 (Sept. 26, 1920).

28 Woolf, "Modern Fiction," p. 156. This remark is anticipated in the notebook, "Modern Novels": "The necessity of magnanimity and generosity—trying to see as much of other people as possible and not oneself—almost a love for character the bane of prejudice."

29 Woolf, *Diary*, p. 22 (Jan. 26, 1920).

30 Woolf, "Modern Fiction," p. 156. See Patrick Parrinder, "The Strange Necessity: James Joyce's Rejection in England (1914-30)," in *James Joyce: New Perspectives*, ed. Colin MacCabe (Bloomington, Indiana: Indiana University Press, 1982), pp. 151-167. Parrinder notes the common attack on "taste" by Woolf and West, and argues that both of these critics were exhibiting "Bloomsbury values," which he considers a "genteel" English "dilution" of pre-1914 international modernism (p. 162).

31 Woolf, "Modern Novels."

32 Woolf, *Diary*, p. 349. Maria Jolas has expressed shock at this description of Harriet Weaver: "You would have thought she was a total idiot." "An Interview with Carola Giedion-Welcker and Maria Jolas," ed. Richard Kain, *JJQ*, 11 (1974), 112-113. Coincidentally, Rebecca West also uses furniture to distance herself from Joyce. His mind is "furnished like a room in a Westland Row tenement in which there are a bedstead and broken chair." West, *The Strange Necessity*, p. 51. This and related quotations are cited by Parrinder, who links them to Wyndham Lewis' charge that Bloomsbury was hostile to "anything above *salon* scale." Parrinder, p. 163. The images and the denigration of the *salon* invite feminist scrutiny in a future study.

33 Quentin Bell, *Virginia Woolf: A Biography*, Vol. 2 (London: Hogarth, 1972-73), p. 54. See also Herbert Mitgang, "How Mrs. Woolf Felt About Mr. Joyce," *The New York Times*, January 25, 1982, p. C23. Mitgang portrays a begrudging Woolf and emphasizes her slurs on Joyce's breeding. His remarks are based upon manuscripts displayed for the Joyce-Woolf joint Centenary from the Berg Collection of the New York Public Library. Like many other critics, he tends to emphasize Woolf's most biting comments on Joyce.

34 Woolf, *Diary*, p. 49.

35 Ibid., p. 349.

36 Florence Howe, "Feminism and Literature," in *Images of Women in Fiction: Feminist Perspectives*, ed. Susan Koppelman Cornillon (Bowling Green, Ohio: Bowling Green University Popular Press, 1972), p. 260. 37 Ibid., pp. 263-264.

38 Carolyn Heilbrun, "Afterword," *Women in Joyce* (Urbana, Ill.: University of Illinois Press, 1982), pp. 215-216.

39 Patricia Meyer Spacks, *The Female Imagination* (New York: Knopf, 1975), p. 24, 27.

40 Mary Ellmann, *Thinking about Women* (New York: Harcourt Brace Jovanovich, 1968), p. 75.

41 Ibid., p. 77.

42 Ibid., p. xv.

43 Ibid., p. 107.

44 Ibid., p. 10.

45 Ibid., p. 16.

46 See Judith A. Spector, "On Defining a Sexual Aesthetic: A Portrait of the Artist as Sexual Antagonist," *The Mid-west Quarterly*, forthcoming. For an article discussing the same fallacy, Erica Jong uses a quotation from Joyce's letters to Nora: "sitting at the table thinking of a book I have written, the child which I have carried for years and years in the womb of the imagination as you carried in your womb the children you love . . . ." Jong, "Creativity vs. Generativity," *The New Republic*, Jan. 13, 1979, pp. 27-30.

47 M. Ellmann, pp. 196-197.

48 Ibid., p. 196. A related point is her comparison of Woolf's woman's sentence to Joyce's own experience with informal syntax and straight perception. M. Ellmann, p. 172.

49 Ibid., p. 202. She also attributes this capacity to Tolstoy and Sartre.

50 Ibid., pp. 76-77, 202.

51 Kate Millett, *Sexual Politics* (Garden City, N. Y.: Doubleday, 1970), p. 285. In her comparisons of these always-contrasted writers, Howe finds that, unlike Joyce, Lawrence never bored her.

52 Ibid., p. 296.

53 Shulamith Firestone, *The Dialectic of Sex* (New York: Morrow, 1970), p. 165.

54 Marilyn French, *The Women's Room* (New York: Summit Books, 1977), p. 8.

55 I cannot help wondering whether Stephen's "old sow" line didn't figure somewhere in the framing of this passage—a feminist retort to one of the stereotypes detected by Mary Ellmann.

56 Marilyn French, *The Book as World* (Cambridge, Mass. and London: Harvard University Press, 1975), pp. 258-259. At the James Joyce Symposium in June 1978, French offered a more restricted vision of Molly, proclaiming her a "cunt."

57 Carolyn G. Heilbrun, *Toward a Recognition of Androgyny* (New York: Harper & Row, 1974), p. 86.

58 Ibid., p. 259.

59 Adaline Glasheen, *Third Census of Finnegans Wake* (Berkeley: University of California Press, 1977), pp. xxvi, xlviii.

60 Ibid., p. 16.

61 Margot Norris, *The Decentered Universe of Finnegans Wake: A Structuralist Analysis* (Baltimore and London: Johns Hopkins University Press, 1976), pp. 41-72 passim (Chapter 3: "The Themes").

61 Ibid., p. 48.

63 Ibid., p. 53.

64 Ibid., p. 67.

65 Ibid., pp. 71, 68.

66 Margot Norris, "Anna Livia Plurabelle: The Dream Woman," in *Women in Joyce*, ed. Suzette Henke and Elaine Unkeless (Urbana, Ill.: University of Illinois Press, 1982), pp. 197, 212-213.

67 Colin MacCabe, *James Joyce and the Revolution of the Word* (New York: Barnes and Noble, 1979), pp. 107-110.

68 Ibid., pp. 53-55.

69 Ibid., p. 66.

70 Ibid., pp. 125-126.

71 Ibid., p. 131.

72 Julia Kristeva, whose studies in semiology and psychoanalysis (semanalysis) MacCabe cites, also writes about the importance of desire. Her discussion of the human mind as a split subject (semiotic and symbolic) and her association of the mother with the semiotic are similar to MacCabe's ideas. See Julia Kristeva, *Desire in Language: A Semiotic Approach to Literatuare and Art*, ed. Leon Roudiez (New York: Columbia University Press, 1980), pp. 5-7.

73 MacCabe, pp. 150-151.

74 Ibid., p. 151.

75 Kristeva, "From One Identity to Another," in *Desire in Language*, p. 137.

76 Kristeva, "The Father, Love and Banishment," in *Desire in Language*, p. 157.

77 Ibid., p. 151.

78 Kristeva, "How does One Speak to Literature?" in *Desire in Language*, p. 92.

79 Nor Hall, *The Moon and the Virgin* (New York: Harper and Row, 1980), pp. 1-2.

80 Ibid., pp. 47, 51.

81 Ibid., pp. 189, 205.
82 Ibid., p. 205.

7. Emma

1 Colin MacCabe, *James Joyce and the Revolution of the Word* (New York: Barnes and Noble, 1979), p. 55.

2 Ibid., pp. 53-54. The Stephen-Emma subplot of the novel does achieve an ending, contrary to MacCabe's analysis. It is precipitated by Emma's refusal of Stephen's amorous plan. Her decisive withdrawal has ideological feminist appeal.

3 Theodore Spencer, "Introduction," *Stephen Hero*, ed. John J. Slocum and Herbert Cahoon (New York: New Directions, 1959), p. 12.

4 Bernard Benstock, "James Joyce and the Women of the Western World," in *Litters from Aloft*, ed. Ronald Bates and Harry J. Pollock (Tulsa: University of Tulsa Press, 1971), p. 101. Expanded remarks are contained in Benstock's *James Joyce: The Undiscover'd Country* (Dublin: Gill and Macmillan; New York: Barnes and Noble, 1977), pp. 8-12.

5 See Charles Rossman, "Stephen Dedalus and the Spiritual-Heroic Refrigerating Apparatus: Art and Life in Joyce's Portrait," in *Forms of Modern British Fiction*, ed. Alan Warren Friedman (Austin: University of Texas Press, 1975), 101-131.

6 Charles Rossman, "Stephen Dedalus' Villanelle," *JJQ*, 12, No. 3 (Spring 1975), 284, 287-288.

7 Florence Howe, "Feminism and Literature," in *Images of Women in Fiction: Feminist Perspectives*, ed. Susan Koppelman Cornillon (Bowling Green, Ohio: Bowling Green University Popular Press, 1972), p. 260.

8 Mary Hayden, one of the outstanding early female graduates of the Royal University and Alexandria College, writes in retrospect that some women who "are actresses, scientists, doctors and so forth whose pursuits are really interesting and absorbing" and to whom marriage presents "serious obstacles to the concentration demanded for hight class work" may now decide against matrimony. Mary Hayden, "The New Woman: A Reply," Ms. 24,011, National Library of Ireland. This relatively rare group implicitly includes herself. Hayden denies that feminism is inimicable or opposed to marriage—a charge still made against feminism by reactionaries today.

9 Stanislaus Joyce, *The Complete Dublin Diary of Stanislaus Joyce*, ed. George H. Healey (Ithaca, N. Y.: Cornell University Press, 1971), p. 14.

10 Portions of this chapter were published, in an earlier form in "Emma Cle ry in *Stephen Hero*: A Young Woman Walking Proudly through the Decayed City," in *Women in Joyce* (Urbana, Ill.: University of Illinois Press, 1982), pp. 57-81.

11 It is notable that Joyce attributes his mother's death, in part, to his "cynical frankness of conduct" (L II, 48).

12 Throughout *Stephen Hero*, Stephen shows scorn for eunuch priests and tries to imagine the sex life of the priesthood and of Jesus.

13 The comparison to Synge and especially to *In the Shadow of the Glen* was suggested to me in conversation by Mary Reynolds, March 1982. The subject arose from her Yale lecture, "Yeats, Joyce, and the Irish Renaissance." Synge also had a character who is suggestive of the woman in the black straw hat and her supposed indifference to marriage—Mary Byrne, the old tinker woman of *The Tinker's Wedding*.

14 Stanislaus writes of Mary Sheehy, "She is romantic but clever and sensible and therefore dissatisfied. She wants Hero." *Diary*, p. 23. "Hero" is a quality he attributes to brother James, p. 22.

15 Mark Shechner, *Joyce in Nighttown: A Psychoanalytic Inquiry into Ulysses* (Berkeley: University of California Press, 1974), pp. 162, 179.

16 M. Esther Harding, *Woman's Mysteries Ancient and Modern* (New York: Harper, 1976), p. 117.

17 Interestingly, this poem was inspired by Nora Barnacle's early love of Sonny Bodkin in Galway—also the source of Gretta's memories of early love in "The Dead." For a discussion of the image clusters of moon and water, associated with woman as life, see Maurice Beebe, "Barnacle Goose and Lapwing," *PMLA*, LXXI (1956), 302-320.

18 Stanislaus had attributed "what the medieval schoolmen called pride of the flesh" to Katsy Murray, the young cousin who inspired first James's and later Stanislaus's admiration. *Diary*, p. 11.

19 Harding, p. 144.

20 The selection is particularly ironic in reference to Joyce's biography. Lynch's character is based upon Cosgrave, the "friend" who maliciously intimated to Joyce that he had been intimate with Nora before the Joyces' elopement.

21 Emma mentions MacCann's engagement and may imply by her amusement that he is an unlikely lover. This aspect of marriage may interest her too. Stephen fails to take up the subject.

22 For a convincing analysis of Bertha as the goddess Hertha, see Ruth Bauerle, "Bertha's Role in Exiles," in *Women in Joyce*, pp. 108-128.

23 Stanislaus Joyce, *Diary*, p. 27.

24 William Butler Yeats, "The Adoration of the Magi," in *The Tables of the Law and the Adoration of the Magi* (privately printed, 1897), p. 37.

25 Ibid., p. 36.

26 Ibid., p. 39.

27 Ibid., pp. 42-43.

28 Ernest Renan, *The Life of Jesus* (New York: Random House [1927]), p. 367.

29 See Bonnie Kime Scott, "The Woman in the Black Straw Hat: A Transitional Priestess in *Stephen Hero*," *JJQ*, 16 (Summer 1979), 407-416.

8. Molly

1 Stuart Gilbert, *James Joyce's Ulysses* (1930; rpt. New York: Vintage, 1952), p. 30. This is the entry supplied for "technic" in the celebrated chart that Joyce provided to Gilbert.

2 *Ibid.*

3 Mark Shechner, *Joyce in Nighttown* (Berkeley: University of California Press, 1974), p. 197.

4 See Robert Boyle, *James Joyce's Pauline Vision* (Carbondale: Southern Illinois University Press, 1978), pp. 28-30, and John Gordon, *Joyce's Metamorphoses* (Dublin: Gill and Macmillan; New York: Barnes & Noble, 1981), pp. 124-133, for two examples of this tour. Boyle's goal is spiritual; Gordon finds a narrative voyage of "reconvergence." Female critics tend to avoid this geography.

5 This idea of replacing the B.V.M. with Molly was pioneered by William York Tindall. See *James Joyce: His Way of Interpreting the Modern World* (New York: Scribners, 1950), p. 37.

6 Shechner cites these three, as Erwin Steinberg had in an earlier article; he adds Frank Budgen and R. P. Blackmur and offers extensive quotations from several. See Tindall, pp. 35-38; Edmund Wilson, *Axel's Castle: A Study of the Imaginative Literature of 1870-1930* (New York and London:, 1931), pp. 223-224; Harry Levin, *James Joyce: A Critical Introduction* (Norfolk, Conn.: New Directions, 1964), pp. 125-126. See also Erwin Steinberg, "A Book with a Molly in it," *The James Joyce Review*, 2 (Spring-Summer, 1958), 59.

7 Gilbert, p. 386.

8 Hugh Kenner, *Dublin's Joyce* (Bloomington, Indiana: Indiana University Press, 1956), p. 262.

9 He suggests this in his recent *Ulysses* (London: Allen and Unwin, 1980), p. 146, where he labels Molly's exchange with Poldy in "Ithaca" a "sharp questioning." This neglects Molly's thought in "Penelope," "I hate having a long wrangle in bed" (U, 739). Molly also notes you "were not to ask any questions but they want to know where were you where were you going" (U, 746). The conspiracy between Molly and Milly is also based upon observations in "Ithaca" (U, 736), and was articulated by Kenner in "The Look of a Queen: Women of the James Joyce Repertory Company," paper presented at the 14th International Seminar of the Canadian Association for Irish Studies, Peterboro, Ontario, March 1981. His article "Molly's Masterstroke," *JJQ*, 10 (Fall 1972) was a witty but condescending effort to make an honest woman of Molly. His suggestion that Molly tried to reduce the ardor of Blazes Boylan by first having him move her furniture was duly refuted by a critic with a more intimate knowledge of female strength and other pertinent qualities. See Margaret Honton, "Molly's Mistresstroke," *JJQ*, 14, No. 1 (Fall 1976), 25-30.

See Margaret McBride, "At Four She Said: II," *JJQ* 18, No.4 (Summer 1981), 417-431 for another view of the kind of questioning that goes on between husband and wife in *Ulysses*. McBride detects "verbal repression" on Bloom's part of the hour of Boylan's appointment, but infers considerable preparation for the event.

10 See especially Edwin R. Steinberg, "A Book with a Molly in It," and J. Mitchell Morse, "Molly Bloom Revisited," in *A James Joyce Miscellany*, 2nd series, ed. Marvin Magalaner (Carbondale: Southern Illinois University Press, 1959), pp. 139-149.

11 James Van Dyck Card, " 'Contradictory': The Word for Joyce's Penelope," *JJQ*, 11 (Fall 1973), 20-21. See also Card's *The Anatomy of Penelope*, forthcoming.

12 Steinberg, p. 58.

13 Morse, p. 142

14 Shechner, pp. 200-202 and Darcy O'Brien, *The Conscience of James Joyce* (Princeton: Princeton University Press, 1968), p. 211. In more recent work, O'Brien reiterates that "Joyce's conception of the sexually powerful woman" was "necessarily something of a whore." In establishing Molly's Irish "determinants," O'Brien constructs a tradition of male "contempt and fear" of women. He likens Molly to the Sheela-na-gig, which by his limited definition is "a whorish creature who seduced and emasculated her victims." While the patterns O'Brien detects do exist and the attitudes are even comparable with Kenner's view of women in Joyce, they are regrettably one-sided. Chapter 2 has attempted a counter-balance. See O'Brien's "Some Determinants of Molly Bloom," in *Approaches to Ulysses: Ten Essays*, ed.

Thomas F. Staley and Bernard Benstock (Pittsburgh: University of Pittsburgh Press, 1970), pp. 153, 139.

15 Ibid., p. 197n.

16 Ibid., pp. 209-211, 219-223. Erich Neumann assigns the phallic mother to a relatively early phase of imagination. See *The Great Mother* (New York: Pantheon, 1955), p. 13.

17 Ibid., pp. 224-226.

18 Ibid., p. 196.

19 See p. 117.

20 Suzette Henke, *Joyce's Moraculous Sindbook* (Columbus, Ohio: Ohio State University Press, 1978), p. 238.

21 See Colin MacCabe, *James Joyce and the Revolution of the Word* (New York: Barnes & Noble, 1979).

22 Shechner's depiction of Molly as a lost primal mother (Shechner, p. 251), can be fit to newer concepts of desire. Julia Kristeva's considerations of "infantile language," "maternal attentiveness," and the principle of "desire" also enrich our sense of female principles. See Kristeva, "Place Names," in *Desire in Language*, p. 277ff.

23 Henke, p. 234.

24 Marilyn French, *The Book as World* (Cambridge, Mass: Harvard University Press, 1976), p. 259.

25 Useful articles and studies include James Van Dyck Card, "A Gibraltar Sourcebook for 'Penelope,' " *JJQ*, 8 (Winter 1971), 163-175; Philip F. Herring, "Toward a Historical Molly Bloom," *ELH*, 45 (1978), 501-521; and Phillip F. Herring, *Joyce's Ulysses Notesheets in the British Museum* (Charlottesville: University Press of Virginia, 1972), pp. 64-73, 490-517.

26 Elaine Rapp Unkeless, "More on Molly's Conventionality," Paper presented at MLA Convention, New York, 1975 and "The Conventional Molly Bloom," in *Women in Joyce* (Urbana, Ill.: University of Illinois Press, 1982). pp. 150-168.

27 Frank Budgen, *James Joyce and the Making of Ulysses* (1934; rpt. Bloomington, Ind.: Indiana University Press, 1967), pp. 65, 263; Tindall, p. 36.

28 Mary Power, "Joyce and Popular Culture," paper presented at the 7th International James Joyce Symposium, Zurich, 1979. Power also relates Kathleen's career in *Dubliners* to Molly in *Ulysses*.

29 Unkeless, "More on Molly's Unconventionality."

30 Nora Barnacle apparently asked Joyce comparable questions. He tells Stanislaus Joyce of her interest in learning geography in a letter that generally depreciates her intellectual development (L II, 173). Joyce's notesheets for "Penelope" observe of Molly, "She asked LB questions and forgets answer" and "MB asks question and doesn't listen to answer." Herring, *Notesheets*, pp. 505, 510.

31 See Henke, p. 235.

32 Herring, "Toward a Historical Molly Bloom," p. 504.

33 Nora Joyce's noninsistent Catholicism resembled Molly's. She kept priests away from Joyce's funeral, but she herself received last rites (JJ, 743).

34 Herring, *Notesheets*, p. 496. The eternal feminine of the close of Goethe's *Faust II* is also associated with roses.

35 Bruce Williams suggests that in her description of the sexual act with Boylan, Molly displays what Masters and Johnson call the "longitudinal phallacy"—a male construct of the female experience apparently unduly em-

phasizing the length of the penis. See "Molly Bloom: Archetype or Stereotype," *Journal of Marriage and the Family*, 33 (August 1971), 545.

36 Sylvia Plath, *The Bell Jar* (Toronto, New York and London: Bantam,
1972), p. 55.

37 David Hayman attributes penis envy to Molly. See Haymann, "The
Empirical Molly," in *Approaches to Ulysses: Ten Essays*, ed. Thomas F. Staley
and Bernard Benstock (Pittsburgh: University of Pittsburgh Press, 1970), p.
121.

38 Molly does not use the words "prick" or "cunt," although she has the
desire to use such slang as "fuck" and "shit" (U, 754). Bloom (U, 61) and
Joyce (in letters to Budgen and the notesheets) do use the first two terms.
See SL and Herring, *Notesheets*, pp. 492, 494, 504.

39 Herring, *Notesheets*, p. 490. Ellmann's revised, 1982 edition of *James
Joyce* reveals Joyce's encounter with Gertrude Kaempffer in the 1916-1918
era. According to her, Joyce made sexual overtures to her and wrote her
erotic letters. "She was interested in his mind, he indifferent to hers." Ellmann finds in her name a source for Gerty. There is a peculiar resonance
with Emma Clery in this incident as well. JJ, 418-419.

40 Herring, "Toward a Historical Molly Bloom," 507-511.

41 See Elaine Rapp Unkeless, "Leopold Bloom as a Womanly Man," *Modernist Studies*, 2 (1976), pp. 35-44.

42 See Jane Ford, "Why is Milly in Mullingar?" *JJQ*, 14, No. 4 (Summer
1977),436-449, and Tillie Eggers, "Darling Millie Bloom," *JJQ*, 12, No. 4
(Summer 1975), 386-395 and McBride, "At Four She Said: II," p. 418.

43 Herring, *Notesheets*, p. 505.

44 McBride, p. 417ff.

45 See Robert Boyle, S.J., "Worshipper of the Word: James Joyce and
the Trinity," in *A Star-Chamber Quiry*, ed. E. L. Epstein (London: Methuen,
1982), pp. 133-135. Father Boyle offers evidence that the "spirit" or third
person of God has often been treated as "feminine," usually as a female
bird. He offers the book of Genesis and the works of Gerard Manley Hopkins
and Dante as examples. Though this is an exalted vision of Molly, it can also
be seen as her dismissal to a spiritual pedestal. Boyle also calls Molly the
"cosmic goddess of Eccles Street" and sees her operating as earth-goddess
on the allegorical level. See also Boyle's *James Joyce's Pauline Vision*, pp.
19, 20, 35.

46 For an appreciation of Molly as urinary heroine, see Shechner, pp.
211-219.

47 *The Táin*, trans. Thomas Kinsella (London: Oxford University Press,
1970), p. 53.

48 Herring, *Notesheets*, p. 515

49 Unkeless, "More on Molly's Conventionality." "Ithaca" also casts the
female in a passive linguistic role. But the reference to Greek grammar and
the overcomplication of Bloom's sleepy reflections create their own denial:

> the natural aorist peterite proposition (parsed as masculine subject, mon-
> osyllabic onomatopoeic transitive verb with direct feminine object) from
> active voice into its correlative aorist preterite proposition (parsed as fem-
> inine subject, auxiliary verb and quasimonosyllabic onomatopoeic past par-
> ticiple with complementary masculine agent) in the passive voice. (U, 734)

50 Julia Kristeva, "The Father, Love, and Banishment" in *Desire in Language* (New York: Columbia University Press, 1980), pp. 148-149. Kristeva

does attribute the positive sexual quality of enjoyment, "jouissance," to Molly. See p. 151.

51 Robert Graves, *The White Goddess* (New York: Creative Age Press, 1948).

52 MacCabe, pp. 131-132. 53 Scholars have argued this point the other way. Robert Boyle, for example, sees Molly as the central part of Joyce's trinity in his "Worshipper of the Word," discussed earlier.

9. Issy

1 Hélène Cixous, *The Exile of James Joyce*, trans. Sally A. J. Purcell (New York: David Lewis, 1972), p. 66. Shari Benstock finds it "inconceivable that Joyce—facing the inevitability of his daughter's madness during the years he was writing *Finnegans Wake*—would choose to make her the subject of this kind of literary psychoanalysis." See "The Genuine Christine: Psychodynamics of Issy," *Women in Joyce*, ed. Suzette Henke and Elaine Unkeless (Champaign-Urbana: University of Illinois Press, 1982), p. 192, n. 4.

2 Adaline Glasheen, *Third Census of Finnegans Wake* (Berkeley: University of California Press, 1977), p. 138.

3 See Margot Norris, *The Decentered Universe of Finnegans Wake* (Baltimore: Johns Hopkins, 1976), p. 53; and Margaret C. Solomon, *Eternal Geomater: The Sexual Universe of Finnegans Wake* (Carbondale: Southern Illinois University Press, 1969), p. 118. Norris feels that the narcissism of Issy and other women of Joyce's late texts diverts them from attitudes of "alienation and intrasubjective conflict" and costs them a price in "self-awareness."

4 Anthologies on the subject include *The Madwoman in the Attic: The Woman Writer and the Nineteenth Century Literary Imagination*, ed. Sandra M. Gilbert and Susan Gubar (New Haven and London: Yale University Press, 1979); and Phyllis Chesler, *Women and Madness* (Garden City, N. Y.: Doubleday, 1972).

5 Adaline Glasheen, "*Finnegans Wake* and the Girls from Boston Mass," *The Hudson Review*, VIII (1953), 90-96.

6 James Atherton, *The Books at the Wake* (Mamaroneck, N. Y.: Appel, 1974), p. 41.

7 S. Benstock, pp. 174, 177.

8 See M. J. C. Hodgart, "Music and the Mime of Mick, Nick, and the Maggies," in *A Conceptual Guide to Finnegans Wake*, ed. Michael H. Begnal and Fritz Senn (University Park, Pa. and London: Pennsylvania State University Press, 1974), pp. 84-86. Hodgart does not find the topic "congenial."

9 Fritz Senn, "Every Klitty of a Scolderymeid: Sexual- Political Analogies," in *A Wake Digest*, ed. pp.27-38. Fritz Senn has noted to me that Joyce was writing *Finnegans Wake* when Swiss women were trying to get the vote—a right which they finally achieved on the national level in 1971. Issy warns in one of her letters, "Hold hard till I've got my've got my latchkey vote and I'll teach him when to wear what woman callours" (FW, 146.15-16).

10 Bernard Benstock has identified this as Shaun's "soberly ecclesiastical voice." See "Concerning Lost Historeve: Book I, chapter V," in *A Conceptual Guide to Finnegans Wake*," p. 49.

11 Ronald E. Buckalew remarks that "Issy's racy, colloquial wordplay in the footnotes . . . contrasts most markedly with Shaun's solemn, Latinate paragraph headings in the right margins (to p. 293, when they move to the left). . . . See his "Night Lessons on Language: Book II, chapter ii," in *A Conceptual Guide to Finnegans Wake*, p. 93.

12 See Patrick A. McCarthy, *The Riddles of Finnegans Wake* (Cranbury, N. J.: Asssociated University Presses, 1980), p. 27, and Chapter 6: "Whose Hue: Izod's Heliotrope Riddle," pp. 136-156.

13 Clive Hart, *Structure and Motif in Finnegans Wake* (Evanston, Ill.: Northwestern University Press, 1962), p. 29.

14 Colin MacCabe, *James Joyce and the Revolution of the Word* (New York: Barnes and Noble, 1979), p. 149.

15 Ibid., p. 15.

16 Ibid.

17 Roland McHugh, *The Sigla of Finnegans Wake* (Austin, Texas: University of Texas Press, 1976), p. 62.

18 Hart, p. 188.

19 Roland McHugh, *Annotations to Finnegans Wake* (Baltimore and London: Johns Hopkins University Press, 1980), p. 265.

20 See Box 19, Sylvia Beach Papers, Princeton University Library.

21 Vladimir Nabokov, *Lolita* (New York: Berkeley Medallion, 1977), p. 202. In 1981, Feminists Against Pornography organized picketing against Edward Albee's dramatic version of *Lolita*, alleging that it had pornographic appeal.

22 Lorna Reynolds, "Women in Irish Legend, Life, and Literature," paper delivered at CAIS Fourteenth International Seminar, March 19, 1981. Margot Norris offers a rich interpretation of ALP as Arrah. See *The Decentered Universe of Finnegans Wake*, p. 71. Here ALP is interchangeable with Issy.

23 See Nor Hall, *The Moon and the Virgin: Reflections on the Archetypal Feminine* (New York: Harper and Row, 1980), p. 46.

24 Ibid., p. 81. It is interesting that as part of the rites to Demeter, gravid sows were buried in mystery pits to decay. Both the pig and the decay process were revered. Stephen's denigrated old sow that eats her farrow belongs to a later, patriarchal age.

25 M. Esther Harding, *Woman's Mysteries Ancient and Modern* (New York: Harper, 1976), pp. 103, 105. See also Hall, p. 11.

26 Glasheen, *Third Census*, p. 138.

27 Hall, 148-149, 151. Hall also identifies Deirdre, who is also associated with Issy, as a maiden of the same father-companion type.

28 See Harding, p. 135 ff.

29 Ibid., p. 161.

30 Hall, pp. 11-13.

31 See Grace Eckley, " 'Petween Peas like Ourselves': The Folklore of the Prankquean," *JJQ*, 9 (1971), 186.

32 Hall, p. 18.

33 Atherton, pp. 191-193.

34 Helena Petrovna Blavatsky, *Isis Unveiled*, II (Los Angeles: Theosophy Company, 1968), p. 50.

35 The Celtic moon goddess Anu or Annis would be a more local source for Anna Livia Plurabelle. See Harding, pp. 98-99, 219. Anu seems to be referred to repeatedly (FW, 511.31—"anulas"; 389.28—"Anumque"; 409.27—"anuncing"; 585.22 "Ananska").

36 Harding, pp. 171-172.

37 McHugh, *Sigla*, pp. 52-53.

38 Harding, pp. 181-183.

39 McHugh, *Sigla*, p. 64; Atherton, pp. 197-199; Harding, pp. 174-175.

40 Atherton, p. 237.

41 McHugh, *Sigla*, pp. 59, 67-71.
42 Hall, pp. 75-76.
43 Ibid., p. 84.

10. A Joycean Feminist Re-vision

1 Colin MacCabe, *James Joyce and the Revolution of the Word* (New York: Barnes & Noble, 1979), p. 151.

2 Sandra M. Gilbert, "Life Studies, or, Speech after Long Silence," *College English*, 40, No. 8 (1980), 862. Elaine Showalter, "Towards a Feminist Poetics," in *Women Writing and Writing about Women*, ed. Mary Jacobus (London: Croom Helm in association with Oxford University Women's Studies Committee; New York: Barnes & Noble, 1979), p. 39.

3 Its sensitivity to the customs of Galway is probably the best feature of the otherwise very derivative biography, *Nora Barnacle: A Portrait*, by Padraic O Laoi (Galway: Kennys Bookshops, 1982).

4 Fionnula Flanagan's one woman show, "Joyce's Women," which incorporates some of Nora's letters, is a first step in this direction.

5 Critical reception of Dominic Manganiello's *Joyce's Politics* (London: Routledge & Kegan Paul, 1980) suggests a willingness to detect a political consciousness in Joyce that transcends his own national experiences and age. Seamus Deane sees Joyce's "real disaffection with politics . . . translated into his creed of artistic freedom," a process whereby "political reality dissolved into fiction . . . realised . . . purely in terms of its own medium, language." See "Joyce and Nationalism," in *James Joyce: New Perspectives*, ed. Colin MacCabe (Sussex: Harvester; Bloomington, Indiana: Indiana University Press, 1982), p. 168.

6 The need for a critical methodology to discuss the various movements of this age is detected by Colin MacCabe, who notes that nationalism and feminism resist traditional Marxist analysis in terms of class struggle. In a footnote, he recognizes the feminist effort to "combat and analyze" the "forms of representation and identities" within which political demands are articulated—a line he pursues in nationalist analysis. *James Joyce and the Revolution of the Word*, p. 166.

7 An alternate form is visible in Susan Griffin's *Woman and Nature: The Roaring Inside Her* (New York: Harper & Row, 1980). The book first takes on a general male voice, based on texts cited in the notes at the back. It moves to separate male and female voices and toward a vision no longer dominantly male. The scholarly apparatus of notes identifies sources of voices without intruding upon the drama of the main discourse. A comparable combination of creative discourse and scholarly notes is provided by Louise Bernikow in *Among Women* (New York: Harper & Row, 1980).

Critics are showing renewed interest in multiply-voiced discourse as discussed by Mikhail Bakhtin. See "Discourse Typology in Prose," trans. Richard Balthazar and I. R. Titunik, in *Readings in Russian Poetics: Formalist and Structuralist Views*, ed. L. Matejku and K. Pomorska (Cambridge, Mass.: MIT Press, 1971), 176-218. First published in Bakhtin's *Problems of Dostoyevsky's Poetics*, 1929. Bakhtin's interest in the medieval carnival spirit, expressed in *Rabelais and his World*, trans. Helene Iswolsky (Cambridge, Mass.: MIT Press , 1965),is also a search for an alternate discourse. Elements of the carnival and the grotesque could be seen as more ancient than the medieval sources detected by Bakhtin. They suggest the pagan goddess, as discussed in Chapter 2.

8 Joyce can be contrasted with D. H. Lawrence for this. Joyce offers no Ursula. In *The Rainbow* and parts of *Women in Love*, Lawrence presents images of women who are strong, generative, and autonomous. It was a vision Lawrence did not sustain; instead he brought his women to kneel in homageto the phallus as part of his anti-modern, vitalist philosophy. Joyce's refusal to rest with such visions and his overall progression into bisexual language may be seen as more affirmative.

Index